05

Motorbooks International

WARBIRD HISTORY

F4U CORSAIR

Nicholas A. Veronico with John M. and Donna Campbell

So that everyone will remember the dedication and sacrifices made by those who built, flew, and fought in the Corsair.

First published in 1994 by Motorbooks International Publishers & Wholesalers, PO Box 2, 729 Prospect Avenue, Osceola, WI 54020 USA

Library of Congress Cataloging-in-Publication Data
Veronico, Nick.
F4U Corsair/Nick Veronico, John M. Campbell, Donna Campbell.
p. cm.—(Motorbooks International warbird history)
Includes bibliographical references.
ISBN 0-87938-854-4
1. Corsair (Fighterplanes)—History.
I. Campbell, John M. II. Campbell, Donna. III. Title. IV. Series.
UG1242.F5V47 1994
358.4'383—dc20 93-34451

On the front cover: An F4U-4 Corsair of VF-64 folds its wings after trapping aboard the USS *Valley Forge* (CV-45) during a combat cruise in 1951. This was *Happy Valley*'s second Korean War combat cruise, which lasted from December 6, 1950, to April 7, 1951. VF-64 was commanded by LCdr. B. M. Barrackman. *Bill Crouse via Robert F. Dorr*

On the back cover: Top, Ben McKillen flew this F2G-1 Corsair to a third place finish in the 1949 Thompson Trophy race. The F2G-1s flown by Cook Cleland and Ron Puckett took first and second, respectively. *H.G Martin, Robert J. Pickett Collection, Kansas Aeronautical Historical Society.* Center, F4U-4s of VF-64 prepare to launch for a combat mission over Korea in 1951. *Bill Crouse via Robert F. Dorr.* Bottom, an F4U-1. *Vought.*

On the frontispiece: Bruce Bagwell, a Vought F4U-4 Corsair pilot with VF-871, part of Air Task Group Two (ATG-2) on USS *Essex* (CV-9) on the carrier's Korean cruise which lasted from June 16, 1952, to February 6, 1953. An ATG was a carrier air group in everything but name, and enabled the Navy to get around a Congressional limit on the total number of carrier air groups. The pilot is attired in garb typical of the period. *Bruce Bagwell via Robert F. Dorr*

On the title page: The one and only F4U-4N nightfighter. *Vought Aircraft*

Printed and bound in Hong Kong

Contents

Acknowledgments

Dozens of people have given unselfishly of their time, knowledge, and experiences to help me gather information for this volume. I have received help from and made lasting friendships with many who share a love for the Corsair.

Special thanks are due to my partners John and Donna Campbell and to Kevin and Jackie Grantham, who opened their home to allow me to do the research that formed the foundation of this book. Ed Davies, W. T. Larkins, Robert Kropp, Milo Peltzer, Robert F. Dorr, Scott Thompson, Thomas Wm. McGarry, and James Nelson Bardin were always there with the right answer, document, photograph, and words of encouragement.

The following people provided me with their first-hand knowledge of the Corsair: Bill Horan, XF4U-3 project test pilot, Chance Vought Aircraft; Ralph O. Romaine, Brewster production and engineering test pilot; Don Armstrong, F2G project test pilot; C.D.S. "Dave" Millington, No. 1833 Squadron, Fleet Air Arm; W. K. Munnoch, lieutenant, No. 1833 Squadron, Fleet Air Arm; Robert A. Rice, plane captain, VC-3; Ens. Fred Blechman, VF-14; Francis X. Rozinski; Leo Horacek, VBF-88; Cy White, Fleet Air Arm; Bryan Cox, Royal New Zealand Air Force; Maj. Gen. Frank C. Lang; Lt. Col. Howard W. Bollman; Guy P. Bordelon Jr.; Cook Cleland, winner 1947, 1949 Thompson Trophy races; Dick Becker, F2G pilot Thompson Trophy races; Gene Akers, Reno race pilot; Steve Hinton, winner 1985 National Championship air races; Robert E. Guilford, owner/pilot N693M; Chuck Hall, owner/pilot N5812V; Gary Meermans, owner/pilot N97GM; and Jim Nettle, Mike Penketh, and Bob Ferguson, who shared their experiences recovering Corsairs from Honduras.

I also received valuable assistance from Jim Pera; Larry Smigla; Ron Strong; James Farmer; Jim and Lani Muche; Jerry Anderson; Simon Brown; Wayne Gomes; Ervan Hare; Dave Ostrowski; Harvey Donaldson; Karyn Dawes; Don Helgeson; John Harjo; Simon Brown; Marga Fritze; Geoff Jones; Jim Larsen; Roy Meyers; Tim Weinschenker; Steve Picatti; Taigh Ramey; Rick Ruhman; Sig Unander; Gary Copeland and Betty Anderson, Pacific Photo; El Ray; Ciro and Vickie Buonocore, *In Flight Aviation News*; the late Larry Smalley; David White; and *Mustang Ace* author Bob Goebel.

Thanks are due to Greg Field and the staff of Motorbooks International and to Jim Swett.

I received information, documents, and photos from Jerry Dalton and the public relations staff of the Vought Aircraft Company; Bill Byrd, Bill Byrd Aviation Books; Dan Hagedorn and Alex Spencer, National Air and Space Museum; Vickie Jensen, Pratt & Whitney; Ray Wagner and Liz Peck, San Diego Aerospace Museum; Doug Champlin, Linda Geiger, and Dave Goss of the Champlin Fighter Museum; Ward Boyce, American Fighter Aces Association; John Schackleton and Anne McMillin, Public Affairs, NAS Moffett Field; Dennis Parks and Susan A. Lurvey, Experimental Aircraft Association; Boeing Aeronautical Library, Oshkosh, Wisconsin; M.D. Dave Richardson, Fleet Air Arm Museum; Ken Ellis, *FlyPast Magazine*; Hersh and Dell Rourke, Jack Northart, and Larry Collins of the National Air Racing Museum; Rene Guilford, National Air Race Association; Peter Gutowski, Canadian Warplane Heritage; Barbara Donnelly, Naval War College, Newport, Rhode Island; and Dan Webb, Dan Webb Books. Barry Zerbe and Rebecca Livingston at the National Archives in Washington, D.C., helped locate hard-to-find documents.

I owe my family and a number of friends special thanks and a debt of gratitude. They include Pamela Veronico, Armand Veronico, Karen Haack, Tony and Kathleen Veronico, Ray and Caroline Bingham, Joan Delzangle, Mark and Lu Markowski, Mark Dentone, Kim Tamez, and the late Nicholas A. Veronico.

Nicholas A. Veronico
Castro Valley, California
July 1993

We wish to acknowledge the support and invaluable assistance provided by Jack Moses, Garry R. Pape, Gary James, Wayne Donnie Watts, Mike Conners, Mike Hill, Jim Sullivan, Jeff Ethell, A. Kevin Grantham, Jess and Jewell Easton, Bruce Smith, Paula Ussery, Gary Criswell, Guy Baird Jr., Raymond Christian, Guy Baird, Sr., Ron Piccianni, William T. Larkins, and Richard and Kathy Long. We also wish to acknowledge the staff of the Admiral Nimitz Pacific Theater Museum, and last and certainly not least Mr. F. D. Campbell and Ruth Campbell, John's parents, for their love and understanding during all these years of airplane madness. If not for their unyielding support this project might not have come to pass.

John M. Campbell
Donna Campbell
Oklahoma City, Oklahoma
July 1993

Foreword

The authors have certainly done their homework when writing this book about the marvelous Corsair. I have never seen such a complete assessment.

In June 1943 through 1945 I learned just what that bird would do in combat!

I consider the F4U to have been, by far, the best fighter that the United States offered. Yes, the P-51 was faster, as was the P-38, but both had liquid-cooled engines and one bullet would cause those planes to be lost.

My experience with the F4U was one of considerable love and respect—with a capital *R*.

Our transition from F4F to the F4U-1 was an experience where the Corsair flew us all over the sky until, with a lot of perseverance, we were able to master the aircraft.

Of the types we (VMF-221) flew, we started with the F4U-1, then the F4U-1A, followed by the F4U-1D, later the FG-1D, and finally we had one FG-1C with the 20mm cannons. I did not like the FG-1C or rather its armament due to the fact that above 15,000ft, you were lucky if you had more than one gun firing.

I stayed with VMF-221 from December 1942 until June 1945. We were based at Guadalcanal for the early part of 1943 until May when we received our first Corsairs. Our skipper insisted that we practice aerobatics—which was great sport, and gunnery practice came along as well.

My first kill in the Corsair came on June 30, 1943, when we intercepted a flight of thirty Betty bombers and their Zero escorts. We (VMF-221, 121, 123) attacked the Bettys first and Zeros second—none survived! The USS *McCawley* was hit in the stern but it survived and had to be towed. It was mistakenly sunk that night by one of our own PT boats!

After a stint in the Solomons, ending with the landing on Bougainville in November 1943 and where I accumulated 15.5 kills, we returned to NAS (Naval Air Station) Santa Barbara, California, to train a new squadron of youngsters.

Five of the original pilots remained, and we acquired thirty-five pilots who had zero time in a Corsair. By this time we were equipped with F3A-1 and FG-1 Corsairs. We were alerted to the fact that we were to be one of ten squadrons to go aboard a fast carrier —namely the *USS Bunker Hill* (CV-17)—and become a part of Carrier Air Group Eighty-four (CVG-84) along with VMF-451.

In January 1945, we went aboard the *Bunker Hill*, and we were equipped with FG-1Ds which offered improved vision and ease of landing aboard a carrier.

Col. James E. Swett, USMCR.

Alas! I didn't see a single Jap during the six months on the ship until the last day when I caught a lone Jill, obviously piloted by a young Kamikaze who had chickened out and was headed for Japan, but instead he went elsewhere—into the ocean!

When we were returning to the ship, we watched in horror as two Kamikazes slammed into the *Bunker Hill* and set her on fire! We dropped our dye marker, Mae Wests, and seat boats into the water for the poor people in the water, so that destroyers could locate them. We then landed on the *USS Enterprise* (CV-6), where sixteen of the twenty-two Corsairs that came aboard were pushed over the side because they had no room for us.

In closing allow me to say one more thing about my Corsair and particularly about that wonderful Pratt & Whitney R-2800 engine. My flight of eight Corsairs was on a fighter sweep of Kyushu and its lower islands. My wingman, Walter Goeggel, was hit by anti-aircraft fire and lost the entire lower third of his engine. We throttled way back to 1,350rpm, and Goeggel flew 150 to 200 miles without oil pressure and with his cylinder head temperatures through the roof before the engine seized. Walt made a water landing with a Kingfisher from the cruiser *USS Wilkes-Barre* alongside. He would have had dry feet if he hadn't slipped while boarding the Kingfisher.

Semper Fidelis.

—Jim E. Swett, Colonel, US Marine Corps, Retired, 16.5 confirmed kills, 9 probable, Medal of Honor

Chapter 1

Vought and the XF4U-1

Chauncey Milton Vought was born in New York City on February 20, 1888. Vought attended New York public schools and after graduation enrolled at the Pratt Institute in Brooklyn. He later entered New York University and then, searching to further his engineering studies, he transferred to the University of Pennsylvania.

Distracted from his studies, Vought decided not to finish school in order to join Harold F. McCormick as an engineer in Chicago. McCormick, treasurer of the International Harvester Corporation and a founding member of the Aero Club of Illinois, was backing the unconventional aviation designs of William S. Romme. Vought worked with Romme in developing Romme's Umbrella Plane—a craft with a circular wing around the fuselage. In 1912, Vought began flying lessons in a Wright B model biplane with Max Lillie. On August 14, 1912, Vought was granted Aero Club of America flying license number 156.

One year later, Vought began his association with *Aero and Hydro* magazine. At the end of one of his monthly columns in 1914, Vought signed his name "Chance M. Vought," and it stuck.

Vought left *Aero and Hydro* in late 1914 to work for the Mayo Radiator Works where he was the sole design engineer of the company's first aircraft, the Mayo Type A.

After a stint at Wright-Martin, Vought left to form his own aircraft company with Birdseye B. Lewis, known as the Lewis & Vought Company. Lewis & Vought's first product was the Vought VE-7 (Vought Experimental model 7). This advanced two-seat trainer was powered by an American-built 150hp Hispano-Suiza Model A engine. Seven different subtypes of the VE-7 were constructed and the 180hp Wright-Hispano E-3-powered VE-9 was derived from the basic VE-7. An advanced version of the VE-7, the VE-7SF, which was equipped with floatation devices, made its first takeoff from the aircraft carrier USS *Langley* on October 17, 1922.

Chance Vought is seated in the Wright B biplane in which he learned to fly. Vought Aircraft

That same year, Vought reorganized Lewis & Vought under the name Chance Vought Corporation. Improving on the VE-7 design, Vought delivered the UO-1 to the US Navy (USN). This two-seat observation biplane was fitted with fixed landing gear for shore-based operations and a float kit for battleship and cruiser deployment. A single-seat fighter version of the UO-1, the FU-1, was powered by a 220hp Wright J-5 engine.

The first Vought-built Corsair was the O2U delivered to the USN in 1927. Powered by a 450hp Pratt & Whitney R-1340-88 radial engine, the O2U-2 could reach speeds of 150mph at sea level and had a range of just over 600 miles.

Chance Vought merged to become a division of the United Aircraft Corporation in 1929 and shortly thereafter moved its production facilities from New York to East Hartford, Connecticut. The next aircraft it delivered to the USN was the Vought O3U observation biplane powered by the 550hp Pratt & Whitney R-1340-12 radial engine. The scout version of the O3U, the SU-1, sat a pilot and observer in tandem seats behind a 600hp Pratt & Whitney R-1690-42 engine. Both the O3U and SU series of biplanes were also called Corsairs.

Chance M. Vought died on July 25, 1930, at his home in New York. He left behind a magnificent and talented aeronautical engineering and aircraft production company. Two years after his death, Vought designers delivered their last biplane to the USN. The Vought SBU scout bomber was powered by a 700hp Pratt & Whitney R-1535-80 radial engine capable of a maximum speed of 205mph at 8,900ft.

Vought designers delivered the USN's first all-metal, low-wing carrier-based scout and dive bomber, the SB2U Vindicator, in January 1936. This plane would set the standard for all future USN aircraft until the jet age.

Because of Vought's years of experience in constructing scout and observation aircraft for the USN, the company was the logical choice for the next generation of scout aircraft. The USN contracted with Vought to build the prototype XOS2U-1 Kingfisher in March 1937. It was a two-seat, all-metal, low-wing monoplane powered by a Pratt & Whitney R-985-50 engine. Flown primarily as a float plane, the Kingfisher and its crews would be responsible for saving hundreds of Allied pilots in the coming world war.

The USN distributed the requirements for a new ship-based fighter in the early months of 1938. Vought received an invitation to submit a proposal on February 1, 1938. The Vought engineering department, headed by Rex B. Beisel, began work on the preliminary design proposal on February 21.

Two proposals were conceived in-house. The first, proposal V-166A, in-

Vought chief test pilot Lyman Bullard flies the prototype XF4U-1. Note the gun fairing in the engine cowling. In an effort to reduce all unnecessary aerodynamic drag, the air intakes for the oil cooler and the intercooler for the two-stage, two-speed supercharger were moved to the wing roots. The squirrel cage or bird cage canopy would become a trademark of the early model Corsairs. Vought Aircraft

corporated the Pratt & Whitney R-1340 radial engine. The second, proposal V-166B, was submitted to the Bureau of Aeronautics (BuAer) on April 8, 1938.[1] Designated XF4U-1 by the USN, it described an all-metal low-wing fighter capable of speeds over 400mph, designed around the new 1,800hp experimental Pratt & Whitney XR-2800-2 radial engine with a two-stage, two-speed supercharger. The aircraft was fitted with a three-blade 13ft 4in diameter propeller. Beisel and his design team fitted it with an inverted gull-wing, which allowed them to use shorter landing gear legs than would have been needed to gain propeller clearance had a straight wing been fitted.

The landing gear retracted rearward with the wheels rotating 90deg tucking flush into the wings. The retracted gear were completely removed from the slip stream with three gear doors; one on the forward gear strut, and two doors attached to the wing on either side of the wheel well.

The major benefit of the gull-wing design is the reduction in aerodynamic drag. The wings are joined to the fuselage at 90deg angles, which allows the air to flow smoothly over the wing/fuselage joint, eliminating the need for a wing fillet. In addition, the XF4U-1 featured spot-welded external skins, further reducing aerodynamic drag.

The "stub wings" were of all-metal construction and were built as an integral part of the fuselage center section. The carburetor air, supercharger intercooler, and oil cooler air inlets were at the leading edge of the stub wings thus eliminating a separate drag producing scoop for each.

The outer wings were metal forward of the spar and fabric-covered plywood to the trailing edges. They folded upward over the cockpit canopy, folding at the elbow of the gull wing. Fabric-covered-plywood flaps spanned the width of the stub wings and one-half the distance of the outer wing panels. Ailerons formed the balance of the outer wing panel's trailing edge.

The wings featured small bomb bays in the outer wing panels which, in theory, would be used to drop bombs on formations of enemy bombers. The pilot could sight the bomb drop through a glass panel in the cockpit floor. The XF4U-1 was armed with a single .50cal machine gun in each wing outward of the wing fold mechanism and a .30cal and a .50cal in the engine cowling firing through the upper propeller arc.

The BuAer awarded Vought contract number 61544 for a single prototype XF4U-1 on June 11, 1938.[2] The XF4U-1 was assigned Bureau Number (BuNo.) 1443.

Beginning in January 1939, United Aircraft Corporation shifted its subsidiaries, moving Chance Vought Aircraft into buildings shared with the Sikorsky Aircraft Division. Under this reorganization Chance Vought Aircraft was named the Vought-Sikorsky Aircraft Division, United Aircraft Corporation.[3]

By July 1, 1939, the basic design of the XF4U-1 was 95 percent complete. And on May 29, 1940, it made its first flight with Vought test pilot Lyman Bullard at the controls. "The airplane immediately exhibited a lot of problems and we knew we were in for a long tour," said Boone T. Guyton,[4] one of two test pilots employed by Vought at the time of the XF4U-1. According to Guyton, "It had a peculiar landing characteristic. Despite its huge size, nice wings, and the graceful look of the inverted gull [wings], the stalling of the airplane as you approached and finally began to touch down it had a tendency to [stall] its left wing. The left wing sag was caused, we found aerodynamically, by the big old 13 foot 4 inch propeller which at that time was the biggest propeller, I won't say in the world, but the biggest propeller around."

The XF4U-1 had sticky brakes, bouncy landing gear, and aileron, spin, and engine cooling problems. In addition, the 9,357lb fighter quickly reached compressibility in a dive. Guyton took over the XF4U-1 test program near the airplane's twelfth flight. On July 11, 1940, Guyton was performing the cabin pressure tests in the XF4U-1 when the weather closed in. Low on fuel, unable to return to Stratford or locate an alternate landing field, Guyton was forced to put the XF4U-1 down on a golf course fairway. The Corsair overturned in a ditch, and Guyton was lucky to walk away from the crash. The prototype Corsair was damaged, one wing torn away, and the empennage ripped from the fuselage, but it was rebuildable.

Workers at Vought set about reconstructing the Corsair. It was their top priority, and within two months the XF4U-1 was back in the air. Lyman Bullard demonstrated the XF4U-1 for USN officials on October 1, 1940. He flew from Stratford to Hartford, Connecticut, at a speed of 405mph, making the Corsair the first single-engine single-seat USN fighter to fly over 400mph.

The USN began evaluations of the XF4U-1 on October 24, 1940, when the aircraft arrived at the NAS Anacostia. Having witnessed this 400mph flight and other demonstrations of the XF4U-1's performance, the BuAer invited Vought to propose a production version of the XF4U-1.

The XF4U-1 was returned to Vought on November 19 for further testing, remaining at Stratford through April 19, 1941. A few weeks earlier, Vought had submitted Proposal V-317, which would become the F4U-1. The BuAer awarded Vought Contract 82811 for 624 F4U-1 aircraft.[5]

On June 14, 1941, the XF4U-1 returned to NAS Anacostia. It would spend a few months at Vought and then be transferred to the Naval flight test center then at Anacostia in an attempt to debug the prototype. The XF4U-1 was so sleek aerodynamically that it would accelerate to the edge of compressibility, making recovery from extremely steep dives almost impossible. One of the demonstrations for the USN was in the spinning attitude. At the time, spinning an almost 10,000lb aircraft was pushing the envelope. During a test flight at the factory, Guyton entered a spin and attempted to pull out. Guyton said, "The airplane wouldn't recover. It felt like a flat spin. I went thirteen turns and I was really trying to do two turns of the spin and then recover. Incidentally, on the spin requirements you are supposed to hold full controls with the spin until you start the recovery. That meant full aft stick and full rudder. After about twelve turns, I forgot about the anti-spin chute. I was busy trying to figure out whether to drop the landing gear, put power on, take it off, try the flaps, anything to stop the autorotation. I decided against that and was about to get out when this nice voice came over our scratchy little very low frequency radio and said, 'It's about time for that spin chute chum.' I finally came to my senses, reached over, pulled the red handle and it did its trick. It pulled the tail up enough so that I could get the stick now forward of neutral...So I finally got the controls on and got it down, after I stopped shaking. Everything was 'Jim Dandy' from then on."[6]

After this test flight the USN eliminated the two-turn spin requirement from the final acceptance tests and required that the Corsair be spun only once.

Almost two months later, on June 14, 1941, the XF4U-1 was flown to the National Advisory Committee for Aeronautics (NACA) facility at Langley Field, Virginia. Less than one month later, the XF4U-1 was back at Anacostia only to be transferred to the Naval Aircraft Factory (NAF) in Philadelphia on August 1, 1941. The XF4U-1 returned to Vought later in August where it remained with periodic postings to Anacostia and to the NAF.

In January 1942, the XF4U-1 was fitted with the XR-2800-4 engine rated at 1,850hp at takeoff.[7] Later that month the aircraft was flown to the Naval Aircraft Factory, Philadelphia, Pennsylvania, for field carrier landing tests on the base's runways. Here USN pilots got the opportunity to fly the XF4U-1 for five days before the aircraft was returned to the factory. May 12, 1942, saw the XF4U-1 depart for a 29-day test by the USN at NAS Anacostia. In the ensuing months the XF4U-1 was flown to test future modifications to the Corsair fleet. During early summer 1942, the prototype Corsair began to take a back seat to operations at the Stratford plant as new F4U-1s began to roll from the assembly line—with Guyton making the first flight of an F4U-1 on June 25, 1942.

The XF4U-1 left the Vought factory on December 3, 1942, as the production of the F4U-1 was getting off the ground. It was transferred to Anacostia for flight testing, and then, on June 30, 1943, it was moved to the new Flight Test Center at NAS Patuxent River, Maryland.

The XF4U-1 spent its final days at the technical training center at Norman, Oklahoma. The prototype Corsair, which was such a technological leap for Naval aviation, was stricken from the USN's inventory and presumably scrapped on December 22, 1943.

Underside of the XF4U-1 showing the main gear doors' shape. National Archives via Robert F. Dorr

CORSAIR   FIGHTER   1942   NAVY   H. P. F. 076-K

Chapter 2

F4U-1: Vought, Brewster, and Goodyear Team Up

Flight testing of the XF4U-1 was going extremely well when, on November 28, 1940, Vought received an invitation to submit a proposal for the production of F4U-1 Corsairs. A little over four months later Vought delivered its proposal to the USN. On April 18, 1941, Vought was given a second contract to build an additional 584 F4U-1s.

The production F4U-1, Vought model V317, differed from the XF4U-1 in a number of ways. First, the engine was changed to the uprated Pratt & Whitney R-2800-8 radial engine, which used a manual starter cartridge system. The cockpit was moved almost 3ft aft because the fuel tanks were moved from the XF4U-1's original placement in the wings to the F4U-1's large 237gal fuselage fuel tank, which was placed ahead of the cockpit and behind the engine accessory compartment. The armament was changed from the XF4U-1's .30cal and .50cal cowl-mounted guns and single .50cal gun in each wing to the F4U-1's six .50cal machine guns, three in each outer wing panel. The XF4U-1's wing bomb bays were also deleted. The F4U-1 featured armor plating in the cockpit and around the oil tank and a bulletproof windscreen. The F4U-1 had an increased aileron span for a higher roll rate and it had a jettisonable canopy. The F4U-1 was equipped with provisions to tow targets, and fittings had been installed in the outer wing panels for small bomb racks. Although some Corsairs did tow targets near the end of and shortly after the war, the wing bomb racks were never fitted to F4U-1s in combat.

F4U-1 at the final assembly point, Chance Vought Aircraft, Stratford, Connecticut. Note how the aircraft is pulled along a center rail on an individual cart and that the Corsair's wheels are not touching the ground. Vought Aircraft

Soon after the attack on Pearl Harbor, the USN ordered an increase in Corsair construction. The Brewster Aeronautical Corporation joined the F4U-1 production team on November 1, 1941. Brewster built a version of the F4U-1 with the designation F3A-1 that was identical to its predecessor and maintained a high degree of interchangeability. In all, Brewster would construct 735 Corsairs at its Johnsville, Pennsylvania, factory before being forced out of business by the USN. More than one-half of Brewster's production was delivered to the Royal Navy (RN) Fleet Air Arm.

One month later, Goodyear Aircraft Corporation, a division of the Goodyear Tire and Rubber Company, was brought to the Corsair team. During the war years, Goodyear would construct 35 percent of all Corsairs at their Akron, Ohio, facility. F4U-1s built by Goodyear were designated FG-1s. All future modifications would apply to all three manufacturers, that is, if a new engine was to be installed in production F4U-1s, Brewster's and Goodyear's -1 models would also be modified to meet that standard.

Test pilot Boone T. Guyton flew the first production F4U-1 on June 25, 1942. It produced a top speed of 415mph, a sea-level rate of climb of 3,120fpm, and a service ceiling of 37,000ft.[8] BuNo. 02156, the fourth production F4U-1, was the first production Corsair delivered to the USN—at NAS New York on August 15, 1942.[9]

BuNo. 02156 was flown aboard the USS *Sangamon* in Chesapeake Bay on September 25, 1942, for carrier qualifications. Four landings and four takeoffs were made to evaluate and establish the Corsair's shipboard compatibility. A number of problems came to light from this drill. First, the upper engine cowl flaps permitted a fine film of oil to coat the windscreen. The aircraft had poor visibility in the three-point landing attitude, and its stiff main gear caused the plane to bounce severely on landing. Also, its left wing had a tendency to stall before the right wing, especially during deceleration.

Vought's flight test and engineering departments quickly set out to remedy these problems. Vought instituted a record of service troubles and service bulletins to keep track of all identified problems with the aircraft. From the record of service troubles, the Vought engineers would solve the problems, instituting design changes. They entered and tracked the changes on the Master Change Record, allowing the three Corsair-producing factories to quickly incorporate problem-solving changes into aircraft proceeding down the assembly line.

Vought quickly sealed the top three cowl flaps to keep oil from fouling the windscreen and replaced the individual hydraulic cowl flap actuators with a single hydraulic cowl flap master actuator and mechanical linkage to the remaining cowl flaps. Before the USN approved this change, it requested that a test aircraft be flown at military power with both the top three cowl flaps opened and sealed to compile engine cooling data for comparisons.[10] As expected, sealing of the top three cowl flaps did not increase cylinder head temperatures significantly, but it did complicate engine maintenance be-

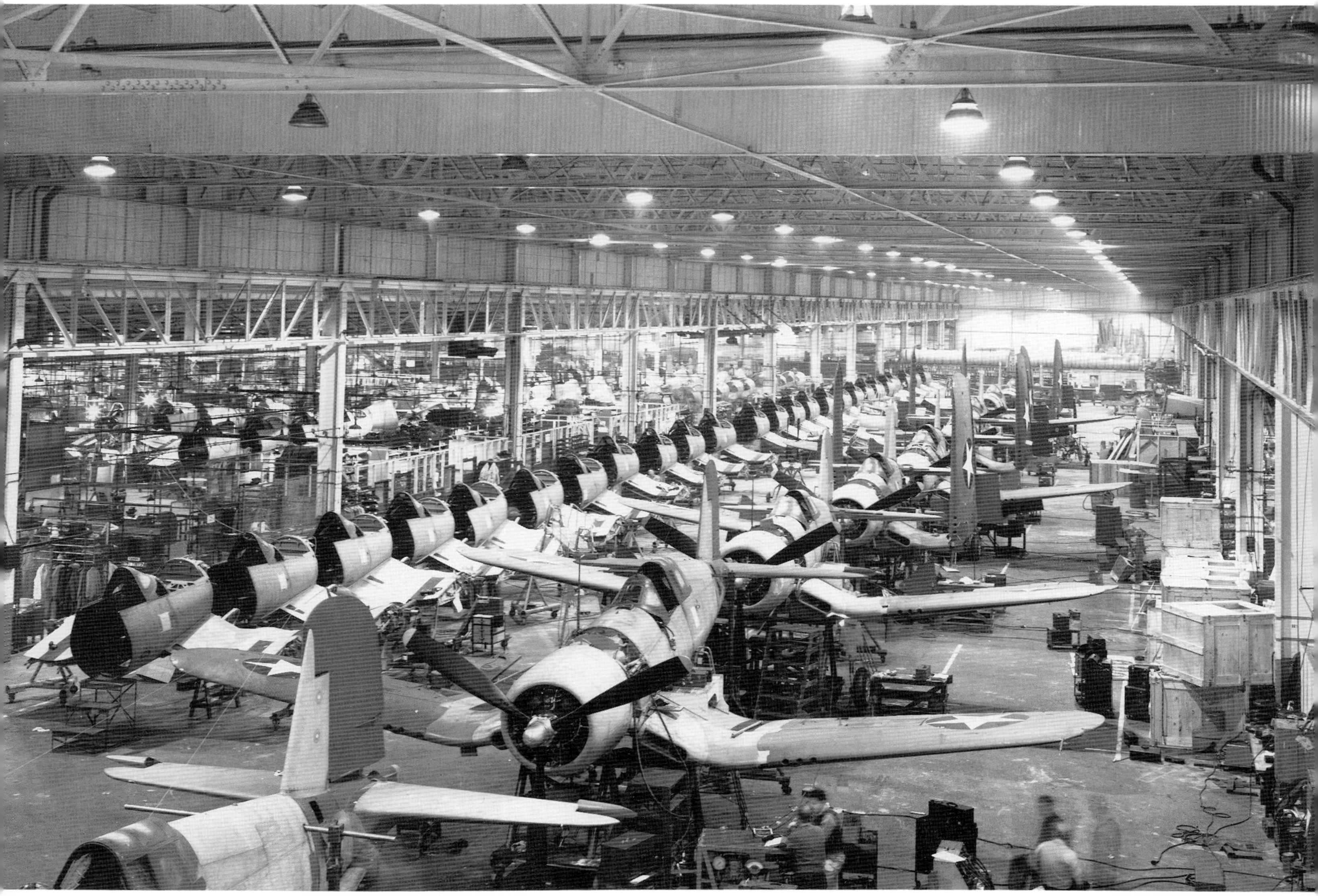

An overview of the Stratford assembly line. Corsair center sections are assembled in the background and then placed on the line twenty-five deep. As the planes make the turn at the far end of the plant, empennages are added along with outer wing panels, thus they become complete aircraft by the time they reach the foreground. Vought Aircraft

cause it made it necessary for mechanics to remove a pair of the mechanical cowl flap pulleys to gain access to the spark plugs of the top rear cylinder. This change was incorporated on BuNos 49759 and 56481 and all subsequent aircraft.[11]

Master Change 225 incorporated a small wooden spoiler on the right wing, causing both wings to stall at the same time. The first Corsair with a "stall improvement device" was BuNo. 02510, which was delivered to NAS Anacostia and then to the Naval Aircraft factory for testing.[12] The addition of the spoiler was incorporated continuously from the 943rd Corsair onward. The cost to fix this potentially dangerous flight characteristic came to only $3.67!

During flight testing, a number of Corsairs were also found to have a wing heaviness, which required aileron trim tab deflection of from 8–10deg out of the 15deg available to achieve level flight at cruising speed. Vought tried a number of corrective measures, coming to the conclusion that "the wing heaviness is caused by manufacturing irregularities in the ailerons which are too small to positively detect."[13] The problem could be corrected by replacing the ailerons, but a number of different pairs of ailerons had to be tried before the wing heaviness was corrected. Vought engineers solved the wing heaviness problem by gluing a 1/8in by 18in strip of wood to the bottom of the aileron on the wing that rode high. This modification was no longer required when all production aircraft, beginning with the F4U-4, were fitted with ailerons featuring balance tabs.

Changing the Corsair's landing characteristics was more of a challenge. During the slow speed approach to the carrier, when the pilot was given the cut over the deck, the aircraft descended almost stalling onto the deck in an

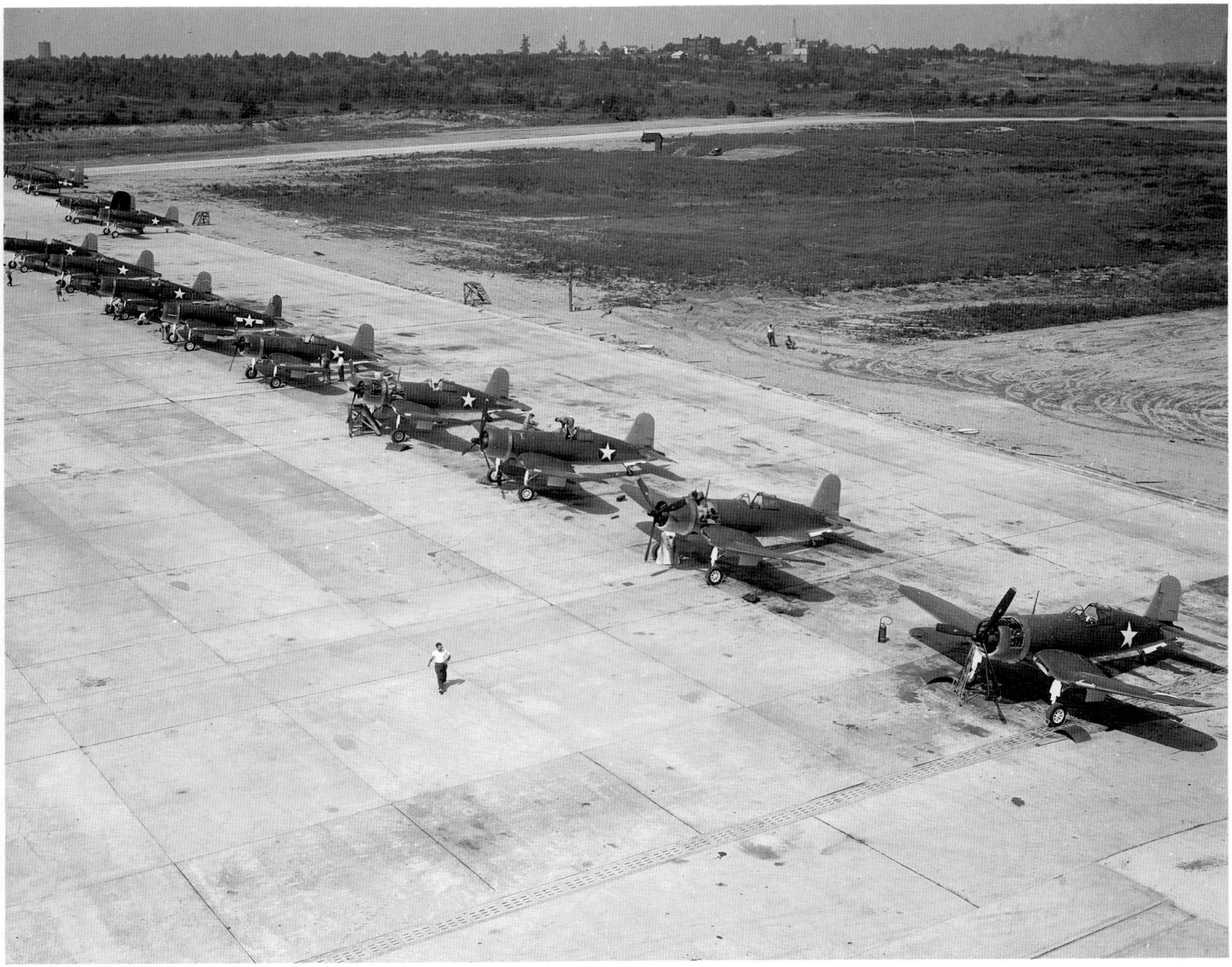

attempt to grab an arresting wire. But with the Corsair's stiff landing gear, the aircraft almost always bounced back into the air. The pilot would try to regain control, often touching down again with the brakes on, sending the airplane over on its back. Program Dog was instituted to get the landing gear modified quickly, and the Corsair carrier qualified. Program Dog reportedly resolved the landing gear problems in ten days. The landing gear oleo's Schrader valve was replaced by Chance Vought valve number 44213 and the strut's air pressure was increased. This change, Master Change Record 438, was incorporated on all production line aircraft and was performed on Corsairs in the fleet during major overhauls. Although it took a year to arrive at this solution, the final cost per aircraft to replace the Schrader valve was $3.47. Interestingly enough, this modification to the landing gear oleo reduced the F4U-1 series of Corsair's takeoff distance by 20ft in a 25kt head wind.

While the landing gear bounce was being investigated, Vought was asked to redesign the tail wheel yoke, raising the aircraft's tail by 6in and improving pilot visibility on the ground. At the same time, the arresting hook down angle was changed from 75 to 65 degrees to prevent airplanes from "sitting on the hooks in full stall landings."[14] The first aircraft with the extended tail wheel, BuNo. 02557, the 404th F4U-1, was delivered to the USN at NAS Patuxent River, Maryland, on September 8, 1944.

Corsairs undergoing predelivery flight checks at the Goodyear Aircraft airdock, Akron, Ohio, 1943. Goodyear Aircraft via A. Kevin Grantham

Test pilot Ralph Romaine taxis F3A-1 BuNo 04515, the tooling proof aircraft, a copy of the Vought F4U-1 Corsair. Note the low tail wheel strut. The tooling proof aircraft demonstrated the compatibility of the Brewster-built assemblies to mate with the subcontractor-built components. Ralph Romaine collection

The ninth Corsair constructed, BuNo. 02161, was delivered to the NACA full-scale wind tunnel at Langley, Virginia, and subjected to a number of tests. The results of the tests recommended a number of improvements to Vought's engineering department in an effort to reduce the aircraft's drag. NACA recommended the installation of smooth-surface wing walkways and smoother wing surfaces as well as smoother, tighter fitting wing access doors; the addition of aileron gap seals; and the addition of an arresting hook cut-out faring. The USN quickly incorporated NACA's recommendations except for the aileron gap seals. The tail hook was partially faired over with the extension of the tail wheel gear door, enclosing the hook up to the last 6in.

F4U-1A: Improvements Quickly Incorporated

The -1 model was fitted with a "squirrel cage" or "bird cage" canopy, so called for the number of reinforcing bars in the sliding cockpit canopy. What would become known as the F4U-1A featured a semibubble canopy with

only two reinforcing bars in the upper surface of the blown glass structure.

The BuAer wanted the pilot's seating position raised to increase the pilot's visibility. On February 27, 1943, Vought requested that a different model designation be given to airplanes with the raised-seating modification. One month later, on March 27, the BuAer Fighter Design Section requested the USN's Procurement Office to dispatch authorization for all three contractors to incorporate the raised-seating modification. The March 27 dispatch gave the contractors authorization to construct the -1A model with the raised seat and semibubble canopy, but due to pressures of wartime, the BuAer requested that the -1A modifications "be incorporated in the earliest airplanes in which it can be made without seriously affecting production." At the same time the BuAer stated that "a formal contract change will be initiated when information regarding the changes in cost, weight, and performance are received."[15] Thus, the -1A aircraft were constructed, delivered as F4U-1s, FG-1s, or F3A-1s, and then later labeled as F4U-1As, FG-1As, or F3A-1As when the change was approved and contracted for on May 16, 1944.[16] F4U-1 BuNo. 02557 would serve at the Vought plant as the prototype airplane with the raised-seating modification.[17]

Forty-two major changes were incorporated into the F4U-1A.[18] Some of the more notable changes included a new pilot's seat that could be raised and lowered approximately 9in, an armored pilot's headrest, lengthened control stick, revised rudder/brake pedals, new instrument panel, gun sight, and canopy; new turtle deck and cockpit armor plating; and reinforcement of the overturn structure.[19] The first raised cabin production F4U-1A was BuNo. 17647.

Beginning with BuNo. 17560, the water-injected R-2800-8W engine was installed. The water injection system mixes water with the fuel-air mixture feeding the engine. The water inhibits detonation in the engines cylinders, which allows higher manifold pressures for extra power during emergencies without detonating the engine to scrap. The F4U-1's water injection system had three tanks totaling 10.3gal. The system is activated when the throttle handle is pushed past the throttle stop into the War Emergency Power (WEP) position. On the F4U-1, the throttle stop was a piece of safety wire across the throttle handle's path. BuNo. 02625 was test flown at Vought as the prototype installation of the raised cabin modification and R-2800-8W engine combination.[20]

Results of carrier acceptability tests of the F4U-1A conducted at the Naval Auxiliary Air Station, Naval Air Materiel Center (NAMC) Philadelphia were reported on June 24, 1943. The report officially endorsed the raised cabin modification. "The raised cockpit installation in the F4U-1 airplane provides a definite improvement in pilot's visibility during catapulting, carrier approach and landing, and contributes to general

The regular production Brewster F3A-1A incorporated the extended tail wheel strut, raised seating position, and canopy. Ralph Romaine collection

Ralph Romaine was forced to belly-land the second Brewster-built F3A-1A Corsair, which was to be delivered to the RN. The landing gear hinge pins seized so the gear would not extend, making necessary the gear-up landing. The February 16, 1943, incident is thought to be the first belly landing of a Corsair. Hal Andrews collection via Dave Ostrowski

pilot comfort during all phases of flying."[21]

F4U-1C Cannon-Equipped Corsair

The F4U-1C was the first Corsair model to incorporate four 20mm cannons in place of the six machine guns. The BuAer requested that Vought provide 200 cannon-equipped Corsairs; Brewster and Goodyear did not participate in this modification. Vought then instructed Briggs Manufacturing, who subcontracted the outer wing panels, to provide 200 sets of cannon wings, with the first deliveries slated for June 15, 1944. These cannon wings also incorporated removable wing tips.[22] The second F4U-1, BuNo. 02154, was first tested with cannon-equipped wings in August 1943.[23]

From the outside, the F4U-1C appeared to differ from earlier Corsairs by only the wing cannon installation. But Vought took the opportunity to incorporate a number of major internal changes. To reduce the weight of the F4U-1C, Vought requested the BuAer' permission to delete the wing bomb racks and all provisions for towing aerial targets.[24] These changes would be incorporated into the first F4U-1C and all subsequent Corsairs coming down the assembly line. Also incorporated into the first F4U-1C was the installation of a Jack and Heintz electric starter in place of the starter cartridge system. Vought also used the F4U-1C model to streamline the installation of the hydraulic system in the fuselage and center section. The F4U-1C first saw combat over Okinawa in the last days of the war.

F4U-1D Fighter-Bomber

Allied air superiority in the Pacific changed the role the Corsair would play in the closing days of the war against Japan. Although the Corsair was still needed to intercept Japanese Kamikaze and high-flying fighter aircraft, the early days of roving squadrons of Japanese fighters looking to tangle with Allied fighters was over. The US Navy needed to add more versatility to the Corsair. Because it was an excellent fighter, the Navy intended for the Corsair to perform the dual role of fighter-bomber.

The raised-cockpit R-2800-8W powered F4U-1A design was adapted to create the fighter-bomber F4U-1D. Retaining the F4U-1A's six .50cal machine guns, the F4U-1D's offensive armament was supplemented with four rocket rails under each wing; a droppable centerline fuel tank; and pylons were fitted to the stub wings, just inboard of the wing fold mechanism, capable of carrying either two drop tanks, two napalm bombs, or two 1,000lb bombs. The -1A's unarmored leading edge wing fuel tanks were deleted from the -1D models built by Vought, Brew-

ster (F3A-1D), and Goodyear (FG-1D). BuNo. 50350 was the first F4U-1D to roll off the Vought assembly line.

In 1945, the normal procedure in the Pacific was to catapult a -1D Corsair loaded with one 1,000lb bomb and a drop tank on the two wing stub pylons. The -1D would fly to the target and while en route transfer the fuel from the drop tank to the fuselage tank. When empty it would retain the tank on the aircraft without dropping it, make its bombing or rocket runs with the empty tank still attached, and then return to the carrier with the empty tank, which could be used again. The stall characteristics became critical when flying with the drop tank because the Corsair would stall without warning if the plane's approach speed dropped below 85kt.[25]

The first F4U-1D was accepted by the Navy on April 22, 1944, and it participated in its first combat operations in the advance through the Marshall Islands that summer.

The Navy shut down the Brewster production line at the end of June 1944 because Brewster was continually behind schedule in delivering Corsairs

The F4U-1C was the first Corsair to incorporate the 20mm cannon. Two cannons were fitted in each wing, replacing the three .50cal machine guns in each wing. Only the wing panels were changed at the subcontractor level. The aircraft remained the same as the F4U-1 with the exception of a clear bubble canopy. Vought Aircraft

badly needed for the war effort. The final Corsairs built by Brewster were F3A-1D models. Ralph O. Romaine was a production and engineering test pilot at Brewster from November 1942 through June 20, 1944. Romaine said of

On March 25, 1943, Vought transferred one Corsair to Pratt & Whitney for installation and testing of the new XR-4360 Wasp Major engine. BuNo 02460, left, was selected to become the F4U-1WM. Compare the Wasp Major engine installation to the F4U-1 at right; the F4U-1WM required a cowling almost twice the length, employed a four-blade propeller, and the most obvious change was the air scoop over the engine accessory area. Vought Aircraft

Brewster and the Brewster-built Corsairs: "From the feedback we received from the Aircraft Delivery Units (ADUs) of the US Navy, the Brewster units were considered of very high quality and trouble-free. History was never very kind to Brewster, for some reason. At the time of contract termination, for the convenience of the government, it was stated in the media at the time that the unit cost [per Corsair] at Brewster was excessive to either Chance Vought or Goodyear. I have always found this hard to believe. The total employment at Brewster during peak production in 1944 was a bit less than 4,000 and they were producing about 100 Corsairs a month. I later learned that Goodyear in Akron had in excess of 12,000 workers and a production rate in the like period of around 150 Corsairs a month."[26]

F4U-1WM

The war in the Pacific showed the USN that they needed a point defense aircraft: one that had firepower and the ability to launch, climb to 38,000ft, and destroy high flying Japanese reconnaissance aircraft or, as realized later, high-speed Kamikaze aircraft.

Looking to the future, Pratt & Whitney design engineers had developed the Wasp Major TSB1-G experimental twenty-eight-cylinder radial engine capable of 3,000hp. This series of engines became known as the R-4360 engine.

Pratt & Whitney was loaned an F4U-1 for the project. Designated F4U-1WM, this Corsair became the proof-of-concept ship to determine if the airframe and engine combination were compatible.

The BuAer instructed, on March 24, 1943, that one F4U-1, either BuNo. 02447, 03456, 02457, 02460, or 02464 be delivered to Pratt & Whitney for the F4U-1WM program.[27] On March 25, 1943, the Inspector of Naval Aircraft Stratford replied that BuNo. 02460 would be allocated from deliveries to Jacksonville.[28]

Pratt & Whitney engineered the engine installation and flew the F4U-1WM from its plant at Hartford, Connecticut. The limited amount of testing completed by Pratt & Whitney quickly proved the feasibility of the Corsair/R-4360 match-up. The USN, unwilling to upset the Vought production line with the introduction of a new model, shifted the project to Goodyear Aircraft where the aircraft's designation became F2G. (See Chapter 8.)

Vought converted one F4U-1 into this tandem, two-seat trainer. Only one aircraft was so modified, and the program was dropped when the Navy showed no interest. Vought Aircraft

FG-1E

The FG-1E was a designation that was to be applied to a number of Goodyear-built radar-equipped Corsairs. The FG-1E was to incorporate the cannon wings of the F4U-1C and to carry an advanced APS-4 radar unit on the starboard wing outboard of the guns. No evidence that any aircraft were converted or designated as such has been found.

FG-1K

The designation FG-1K was supplied to aircraft used in the unmanned drone programs after the war. Thus, if an FG-1A had been converted to serve as an aerial target, its designation would have been changed to FG-1K. No aircraft ever rolled off the assembly lines bearing this designation.

F4U-1P

On October 30, 1941, while Vought was working to complete the first production F4U-1, the BuAer requested that the company submit a proposal to convert sixty F4U-1s to photo-recon-

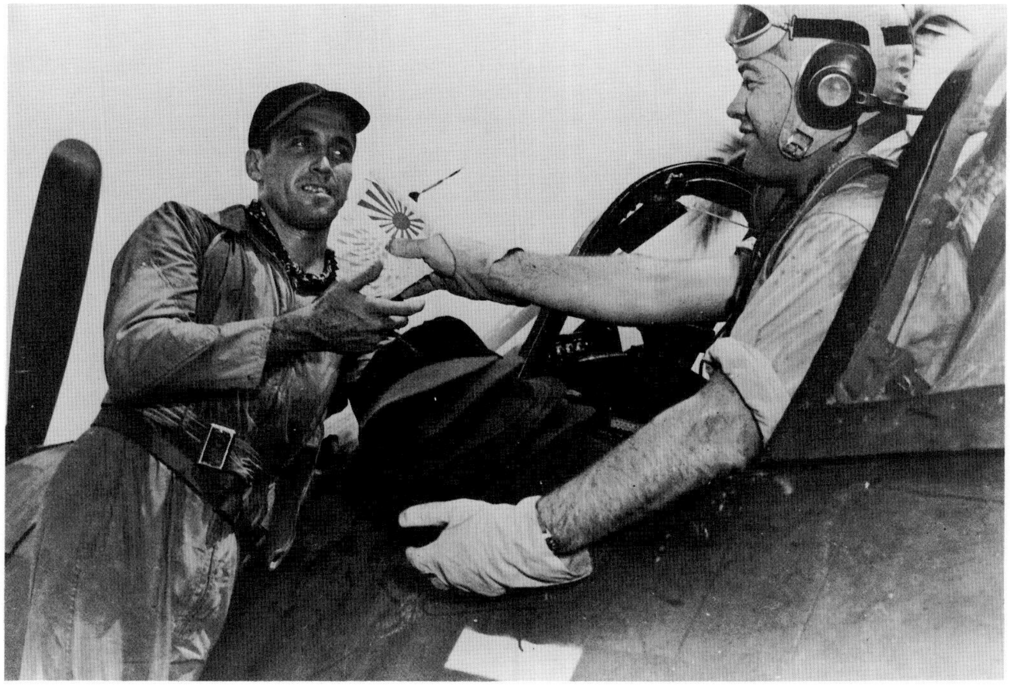

Maj. Gregory Boyington, seated in cockpit holding victory flags, is probably the Corsair's most famous ace. As commanding officer of VMF-214 Black Sheep squadron he downed twenty-two Japanese aircraft before being shot down himself in January 1944 and interned for the remainder of the war. Vought Aircraft

Aces and Corsair pioneers of VF-17 Jolly Rogers, from left to right: LCdr Roger E. Hedrick, 12 kills; LCdr John T. "Tommy" Blackburn, commanding officer VF-17, 11 kills; Lt. Ira C. Kepford, 16 kills. American Fighter Aces Association

naissance aircraft by mounting a K-18 camera in each plane's midsection. The cameras would be mounted through the lower fuselage in a specially designed Robinson Mount. Vought completed a wooden mock-up of the installation.

Vought forwarded preliminary design drawings to the BuAer on April 21, 1942. These drawings provided the installation requirements for the K-17, K-18, and F-56 aerial mapping cameras. Vought was asked by the BuAer to

A factory fresh F4U-1D displaying the twin center-wing pylons capable of carrying droppable fuel tanks, napalm, or bombs. The F4U-1D was the first factory built Corsair capable of both the fighter and fighter-bomber roles. The -1D also featured the water injected R-2800-8W engine adding extra boost available on demand. Vought Aircraft

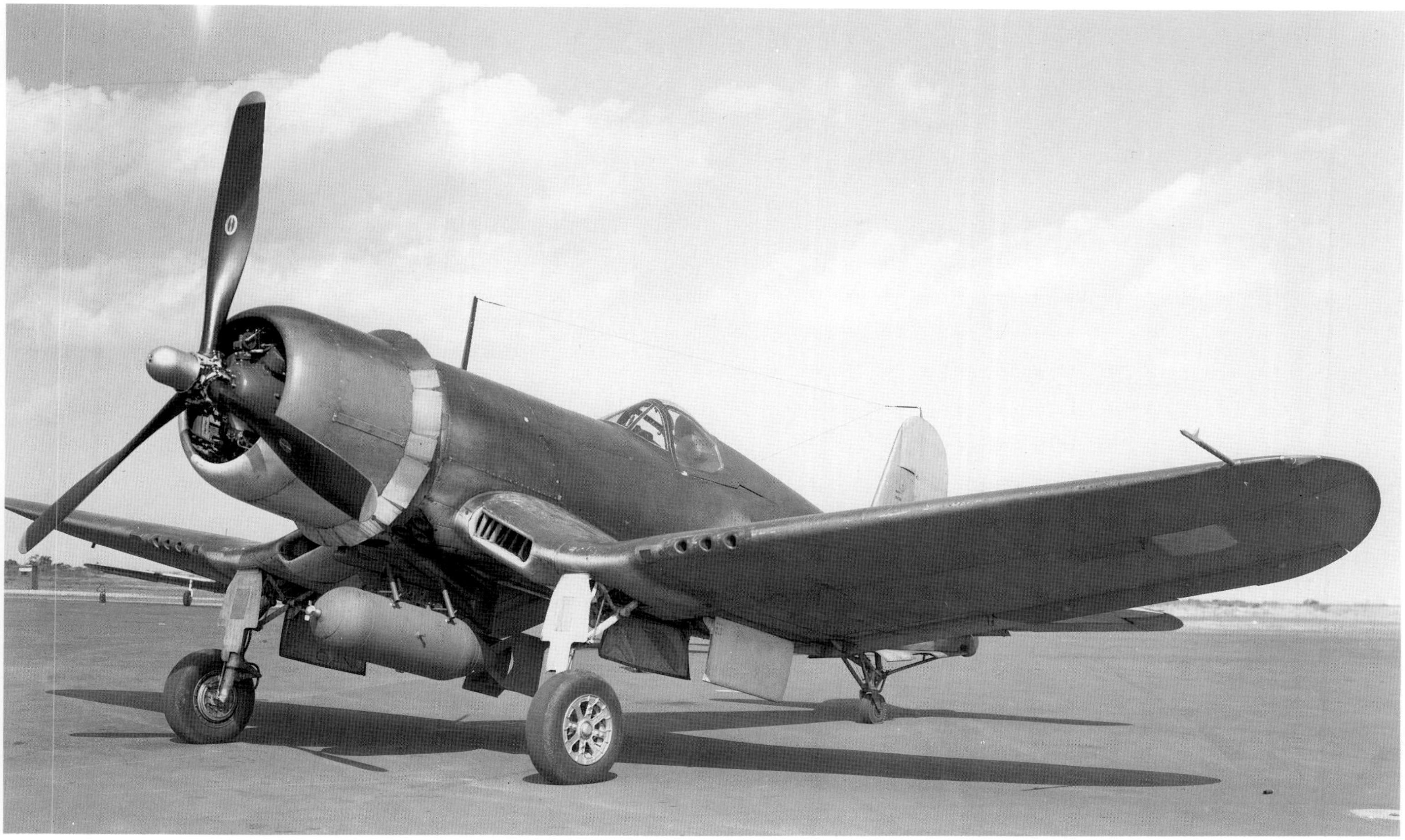

complete the F4U-1P camera installation engineering and provide the needed information to NAS North Island, San Diego, California, where the conversions would take place.

Because it was already operating at capacity, Vought requested that the BuAer forward its preliminary drawings to another engineering facility to complete the work. In a February 20, 1943, letter, Vought was informed that the F4U-1P engineering would be completed at NAS Norfolk, Virginia. Vought immediately transferred the wooden mock-up of the F4U-1P camera installations to Norfolk.[29] In all, only four aircraft are thought to have been converted to F4U-1P configuration and used by the USN and US Marine Corps (USMC) in the later stages of the war in the Pacific.

N-FG-1D and TR-FG-1D

During the late 1940s, Naval Reserve fighter aircraft used for training were given the N or TR designation.

In an attempt to make additional aircraft sales, Vought converted one F4U-1 into a two-seat trainer. Both seats were in tandem with bubble canopies. The USN showed no interest in this one-of-a-kind conversion. The program was quickly dropped and it is presumed that this aircraft was scrapped shortly thereafter.

Odd Mods

A single FG-1 was flown with a Westinghouse I-19A jet engine slung on the aircraft centerline. Flown under the Corsair for test purposes, the I-19A engine developed 1,200lb of thrust.

In the early, dark days of World War II, a number of different and what some may consider desperate aircraft designs were contemplated. One was BuAer Project Number 4293—the conversion of the F4U-1 to seaplane configuration. It was not such a bad idea when you consider the success of the Japanese float-equipped fighters such as the Kawanishi N1K Rex. When the project was considered in December 1942, the USN lacked sufficient aircraft carriers and advanced land-based fighters to do battle with the Japanese. The seaplane conversion progressed as far as the wind tunnel model stage. It was to be equipped with Edo Aircraft Corporation floats constructed from plans EX-1039, 52-A-002.[30] A ventral fin was located beneath the fuselage under the vertical stabilizer. The rapid American advance and defeat of the Japanese carrier forces negated the need for a float-equipped Corsair.

The F4U-1D was capable of carrying one 1,000lb bomb on the centerline hardpoint. This centerline bomb rack was designed by Brewster Aircraft. Vought Aircraft

Bellanca Alleges Patent Infringement

The Corsair's inverted gull wing design was extremely innovative. The fact that the airplane achieved a speed in

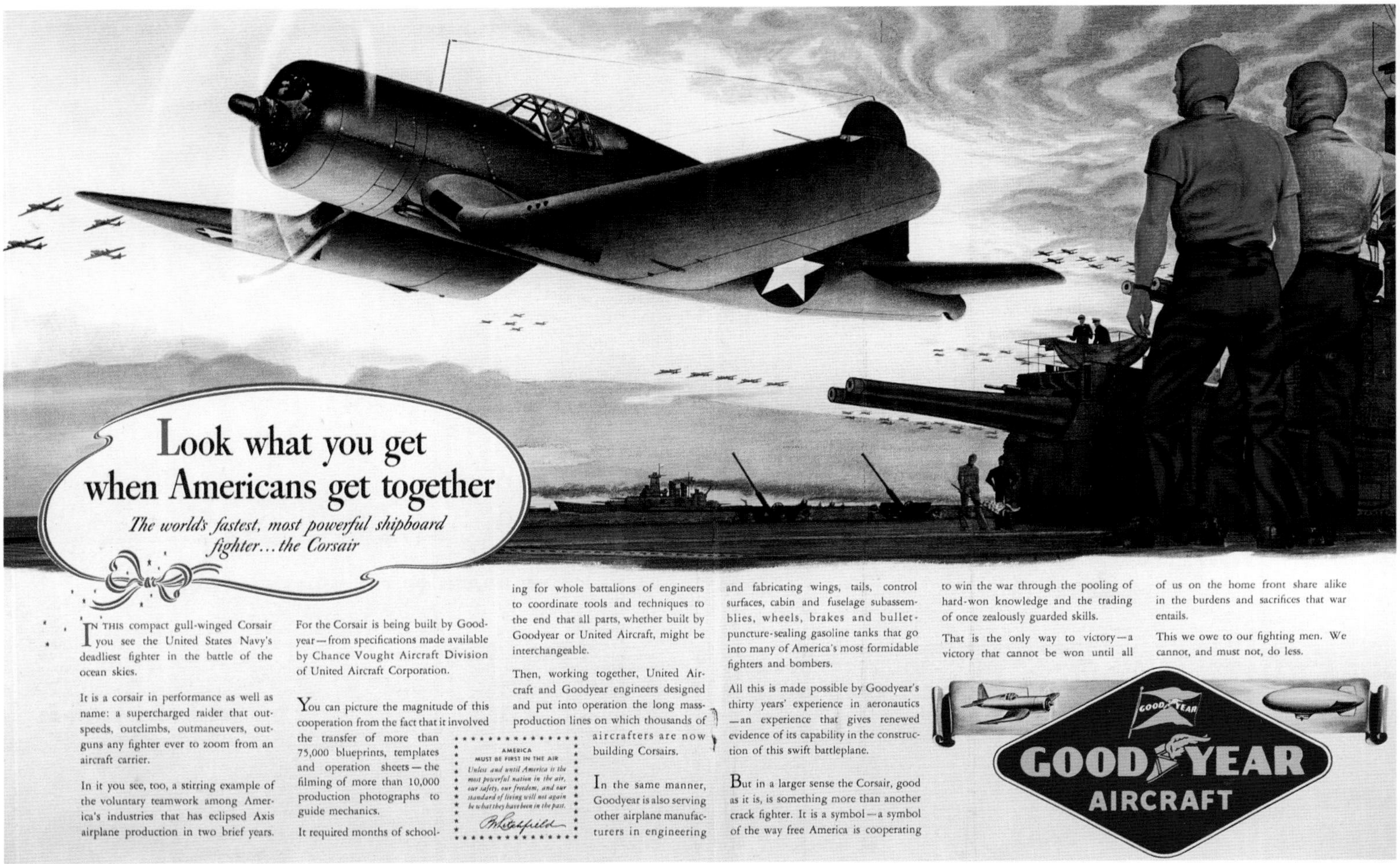

Look what you get
when Americans get together
The world's fastest, most powerful shipboard
fighter...the Corsair
IN THIS compact gull-winged Corsair you see the United States Navy's deadliest fighter in the battle of the ocean skies.
It is a corsair in performance as well as name: a supercharged raider that out-speeds, outclimbs, outmaneuvers, out-guns any fighter ever to zoom from an aircraft carrier.
In it you see, too, a stirring example of the voluntary teamwork among America's industries that has eclipsed Axis airplane production in two brief years.
For the Corsair is being built by Goodyear—from specifications made available by Chance Vought Aircraft Division of United Aircraft Corporation.
You can picture the magnitude of this cooperation from the fact that it involved the transfer of more than 75,000 blueprints, templates and operation sheets—the filming of more than 10,000 production photographs to guide mechanics.
It required months of schooling for whole battalions of engineers to coordinate tools and techniques to the end that all parts, whether built by Goodyear or United Aircraft, might be interchangeable.
AMERICA
MUST BE FIRST IN THE AIR
Unless and until America is the most powerful nation in the air, our safety, our freedom, and our standard of living will not again be what they have been in the past.
Then, working together, United Aircraft and Goodyear engineers designed and put into operation the long mass-production lines on which thousands of aircrafters are now building Corsairs.
In the same manner, Goodyear is also serving other airplane manufacturers in engineering and fabricating wings, tails, control surfaces, cabin and fuselage subassemblies, wheels, brakes and bullet-puncture-sealing gasoline tanks that go into many of America's most formidable fighters and bombers.
All this is made possible by Goodyear's thirty years' experience in aeronautics—an experience that gives renewed evidence of its capability in the construction of this swift battleplane.
But in a larger sense the Corsair, good as it is, is something more than another crack fighter. It is a symbol—a symbol of the way free America is cooperating to win the war through the pooling of hard-won knowledge and the trading of once zealously guarded skills.
That is the only way to victory—a victory that cannot be won until all of us on the home front share alike in the burdens and sacrifices that war entails.
This we owe to our fighting men. We cannot, and must not, do less.
GOODYEAR
GOODYEAR
AIRCRAFT

Two-page magazine advertisement showing Goodyear's ability to produce the Vought-designed Corsair. No mention of Brewster's involvement in Corsair production is made. Note early squirrel cage canopy in drawing and the aircraft carrier deck in the foreground. US Navy Corsairs would not operate from the decks of carriers for another two years. Nick Veronico collection

excess of 400mph early in its flying days is a testament to its superior design. The entire aviation community took notice of the Corsair.

Giuseppe M. Bellanca, chairman of the board of directors of the Bellanca Aircraft Corporation, New Castle, Delaware, read reports of the gull-winged Corsair, noticing the large orders placed for the aircraft. On September 17, 1935, Bellanca was issued US Patent number 2,014,366 for an inverted gull wing.

If Vought had infringed on Bellanca's patent, Bellanca would be able to seek compensation on a per-unit-constructed basis. On January 9, 1941, Bellanca wrote Igor Sikorsky, president of Sikorsky Aircraft, seeking a meeting to discuss the similarities of the Corsair and his patent: "This is a time of pulling together and cooperating for the common cause of Defense, and it is with that thought in mind that I would like to have an amicable talk with you."

On April 24, 1942, after reviewing the matter, Charles H. Chatfield, secretary of United Aircraft Corporation, informed Bellanca that there existed art and nonpatented aircraft designs that predated Patent 2,014,366.

Almost eight months later on December 17, 1942, Bellanca replied to Chatfield asking where such art could be found, saying, "Our own attorneys and the Patent Office Staff doubtless made a thorough search without locating it." Returning to the underlying current of the original letter, money, Bellanca closed his letter by stating, "I also wish to advise that the fact that we are not pressing this matter at the present time will not mean that we are in any way relinquishing any of the rights which might be derived from Patent 2,014,366."[31]

United Aircraft Corporation's attorneys Cooper, Kerr & Dunham responded to Bellanca's letter citing the following previously published examples of inverted gull wing aircraft: British patent to Short No. 190,576, accepted December 28, 1922; *Jane's All The World's Aircraft*, 1928, page 19C describing the Blackburn Ripon; *Flight*, March 1, 1928, page 124 describing the Gloster IV; *The Aeroplane,* August 21, 1929, description of the Gloster VI; and *Flight*, August 22, 1929, also describing the Gloster VI.

United Aircraft's attorneys concluded, "In our opinion, no claims capable of being asserted against the F4U-1 planes would have been allowed by the Patent Office, had it been aware of this

A flight of four F4U-1s on patrol in the Southwest Pacific area. Note that although the Corsairs retain the squirrel-cage canopies, a small blister has been incorporated in the top of the canopy allowing better rear vision with the pilot's mirror. Vought Aircraft

prior art. We believe that it would constitute a good defense to any action brought on that patent on account of the F4U-1 airplane."[32]

Vought sought the opinion of the BuAer, which went on to complete its own investigation, exonerating Vought from any patent infringements.

Lindbergh Flies the Corsair

Plans were set into motion on March 31, 1943, for Charles A. Lindbergh to fly a Corsair cross-country prior to departing for the Pacific.[33] Lindbergh was employed by United Aircraft as a civilian engineering consultant. He was to fly the Corsair from the factory, with stops at NAS Norfolk, Virginia; Jacksonville, Florida; and Eglin Field before continuing on to NAS North Island, San Diego.

During the spring and summer of 1944, Lindbergh spent four months in the South Pacific as technical representative of United Aircraft in support of the Corsair. Lindbergh's mission was to observe the Corsair in combat and to recommend changes in flying techniques to the squadrons in combat. On May 22 Lindbergh accompanied a flight of Corsairs on a patrol mission to Rabaul.

The F4U-1D fighter-bomber was just reaching squadron service while Lindbergh was in the South Pacific. Typical F4U-1D missions departed carrying a bomb load of 1,500lb. Lindbergh demonstrated to the combat pilots and crews that the Corsair could carry more than twice its 1,500 bomb load. On September 2, 1944, while departing for an attack on Wotje Atoll, Lindbergh took off in a 14kt crosswind with a 3,000lb bomb load, the heaviest load carried by a single-engine fighter at that point in the war. The next day, with only a 9kt crosswind, Lindbergh took off for another strike at Wotje Atoll, this time carrying a 4,000lb bomb load. Lindbergh scored near direct hits on these two missions. From these missions he developed dive-bombing tactics (dive angles) and mission profiles for the Corsair fighter-bombers.

Dash Ones at War

Marine squadron VMF-124, commanded by Maj. William Gise, received its Corsairs during the last week of October 1942. Among the squadron's complement were a number of pilots destined to become aces. At the same time, VF-12, the first USN squadron to receive Corsairs, commanded by LCdr Joe Clifton, was forming at NAS North Island, California. One month later, a Corsair modification center was formed at San Diego as Air Base Group Two, Fleet Marine Force West Coast commanded by Col. Stanley Ridderhoff. Chance Vought representative Jack Hospers supervised the incorporation of 159 changes to make the Corsair combat ready.

VMF-124 departed for the South Pacific campaign front in the early days of January 1943. Arriving on Guadalcanal early in the day of February 12,

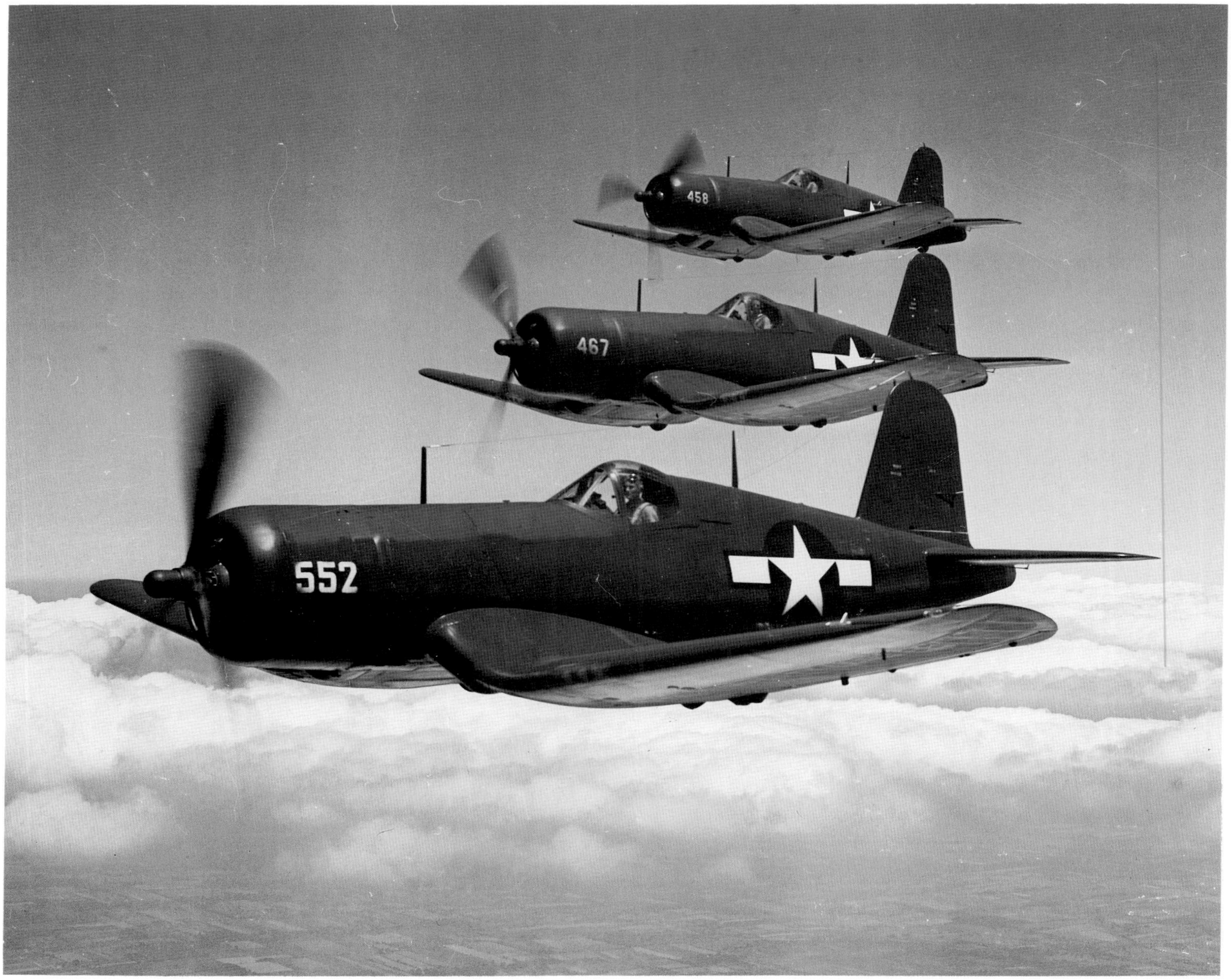

A formation of FG-1Ds from the USS Yorktown. *Then Lt. Leo Horacek flew from the USS* Yorktown *primarily attacking Japanese shipping and secondary military targets.* Robert F. Dorr Collection

the squadron spent the day flying combat air patrol (CAP) over the island. The next day, the Corsairs of VMF-124 escorted USN PB4Y-1s on a bombing mission to Bougainville Island, a 300-mile distance that prevented the shorter-legged F4F Wildcats from escorting the bombers all the way to the target.

During the third day of combat, the Japanese drew first blood on the Corsairs. While VMF-124 Corsairs were escorting a bombing mission to Kahili Airfield, the Corsairs were attacked by more than fifty Zeros. The Zeros downed two PB4Y-1s, two P-40s flying low cover, two Corsairs in the middle level escort cover, and two P-38s flying top cover. The American fighter shot down only four Zeros in return.[34]

In combat with the Zero, "We found out our advantages and disadvantages," said Lt. Col. Kenneth A. Walsh. "Anytime we were at equal altitude or had the altitude advantage, we could take the Zero on anytime and beat 'em. Particularly if it was in our ballpark. Because they couldn't out turn us, they couldn't out dive us, and they couldn't even out climb us at fast speed."[35] Walsh and others employed the famous "Thach Weave" fighter offense/defense against the Japanese Zeros. Conceived by then LCdr. John S. Thach, the "Thach Weave" changed Naval aviation tactics from three-ship formations to a two plane element which could "weave" providing both offensive fire while the second aircraft, or

F4U-1A BuNo 17884, which last flew with VMF-214, rests in the boneyard at Torokina, 1944. National Archives via Sullivan

wingman, could shift from side to side providing defensive cover to the leader.

Walsh downed two Zeros and a Val on April 1, 1943, when the Japanese sent a force of Val dive bombers escorted by Zeros to attack Guadalcanal. On May 13, Walsh downed three more Zeros and earned the distinction of being the first pilot of VMF-124 to become an ace, as well as becoming the first Corsair ace. Walsh eventually downed twenty-one Japanese aircraft with VMF-124, and had an additional kill with VMF-222. For his actions, Walsh was awarded the Medal of Honor.

During its tour, VMF-124 destroyed sixty-eight enemy aircraft in the air while losing eleven Corsairs and three pilots. By August 1943, all Marine fighter squadrons were equipped with the Corsair.

VMF-215 pilot 1st Lt. Robert M. Hanson was awarded the Medal of Honor for his actions during his third tour in the South Pacific. He downed five Japanese aircraft during his first two tours. During his third tour, he destroyed twenty aircraft in the air over a thirteen-day period.

The Corsair's most famous ace is Maj. Gregory Boyington. Prior to entering the war in the Pacific, Boyington had fought in China with the American Volunteer Group where he was credited with the destruction of six Japanese aircraft. Returning to the Marine Corps, Boyington was given command of the VMF-214 Black Sheep squadron. The squadron received its nickname, as the story goes, because Boyington asked the group commander on Espiritu Santo to form a squadron of pilots awaiting permanent placement, and many of these pilots were undisciplined, nonconformist troublemakers. Boyington destroyed twenty-two aircraft in the South Pacific, bringing his total to twenty-eight confirmed kills before being shot down into St. George's

F4U-1Ds line the Iwo Jima runway. Aircraft in the background include a PB4Y-2 Privateer, a B-29 Superfortress, and six P-51D Mustangs. Vought Aircraft

Channel on January 3, 1944. He was captured and held prisoner by the Japanese for the remainder of the war. After the war Boyington authored his autobiography, *Baa Baa Black Sheep,* which was the subject of a movie and television series of the same name.

VF-12's Corsairs began to emerge from modification at Air Base Group Two and on January 14, 1943, ten of the squadron's aircraft were combat ready. During the same month, VF-12 was able to practice combat maneuvers with a captured Japanese Zero. The Zero had been recovered intact from the Aleutian Islands and had been shipped to NAS North Island for repairs. From the evaluation of the captured Zero, the USN learned that the Zero had a better rate of climb until the Corsair got to altitude, above 20,000ft; never to attempt to turn inside of the Zero; or to combat the nimble Japanese fighter under speeds of 300mph. The Corsair had a better roll rate, could out climb the Zero above 20,000ft, and was also able to run away from the Zero at altitude.

VF-12 flew their first night practice mission on February 26 and began field carrier landing practice on March 3. LCdr Clifton and Lt. (j.g.) John Magda qualified the first VF-12 Corsairs aboard the USS *Core* on March 4. Each pilot made four landings but suffered tail-wheel blowouts. The pneumatic wheels could not handle the forces sustained during the arrested landings. Tail wheel blow-outs plagued the early Corsairs until hard rubber units were supplied. The remainder of the squadron was carrier qualified in April.

Arriving in the Pacific during the summer of 1943, VF-12 was ordered to turn its Corsairs over to Marine squadrons. This in part due to the USN's lack of spare parts while the Marines had ample F4U spares in their logistics pipeline. VF-12 was transitioned into Grumman F6F Hellcats and assigned to the USS *Saratoga*.

On the East Coast, LCdr J. T. "Tommy" Blackburn was forming the VF-17 Jolly Rogers, flying the new F4U-1A. "The flight test section for Fleet Evaluation was in Norfolk," said Blackburn, "and that was a branch of Flight Test at Anacostia. It was their mission to take the X model and do the preliminary carrier work with it and evaluate it, recommending techniques for use of production aircraft when the squadrons got them. Well, the Corsair had an extremely bad reputation with the Anacostia people and, to be blunt about it—they were scared to death of the airplane and didn't like it at all. It had a nasty stall characteristic and the forward visibility on the ground was horrible. It was a quantum jump from anything we'd had before. They did a couple of cat shots off an escort carrier and a couple of landings, period. That was all they did.

"We got no data from that whatsoever when we came to get the aircraft, some six months or nine months later. So essentially we started from scratch as far as developing carrier landing techniques, take-off techniques, and finding out what the limitations of the airplane were.

"We began working with our own private LSO, his name was 'Catwalk' Cummings. His formal name was Shailer. 'Catwalk' was really an appropriate name. A superb LSO. We went out aboard the escort carrier USS *Charger* in Chesapeake Bay and I have a very vivid recollection of my first approach to the *Charger*. All I could see in the last 100 yards in the grove was Catwalk Cummings out there holding a 'Roger' [both paddles at shoulder level] on me and to his right was a lot of Chesapeake Bay. And to my right side of the nose of the airplane was a lot of Chesapeake Bay. There wasn't any sign of the USS *Charger!* So he gives me a cut, and like an idiot—I knew better from field carrier work we had done—I shoved forward on the stick to get a look at the flight deck and immediately honked it back in my lap and by that time I had a rate of descent of about 30fps. The Corsair was stressed for 12fps. Anyway, I hit the deck on three points and fortunately caught the No. 1 wire."[36]

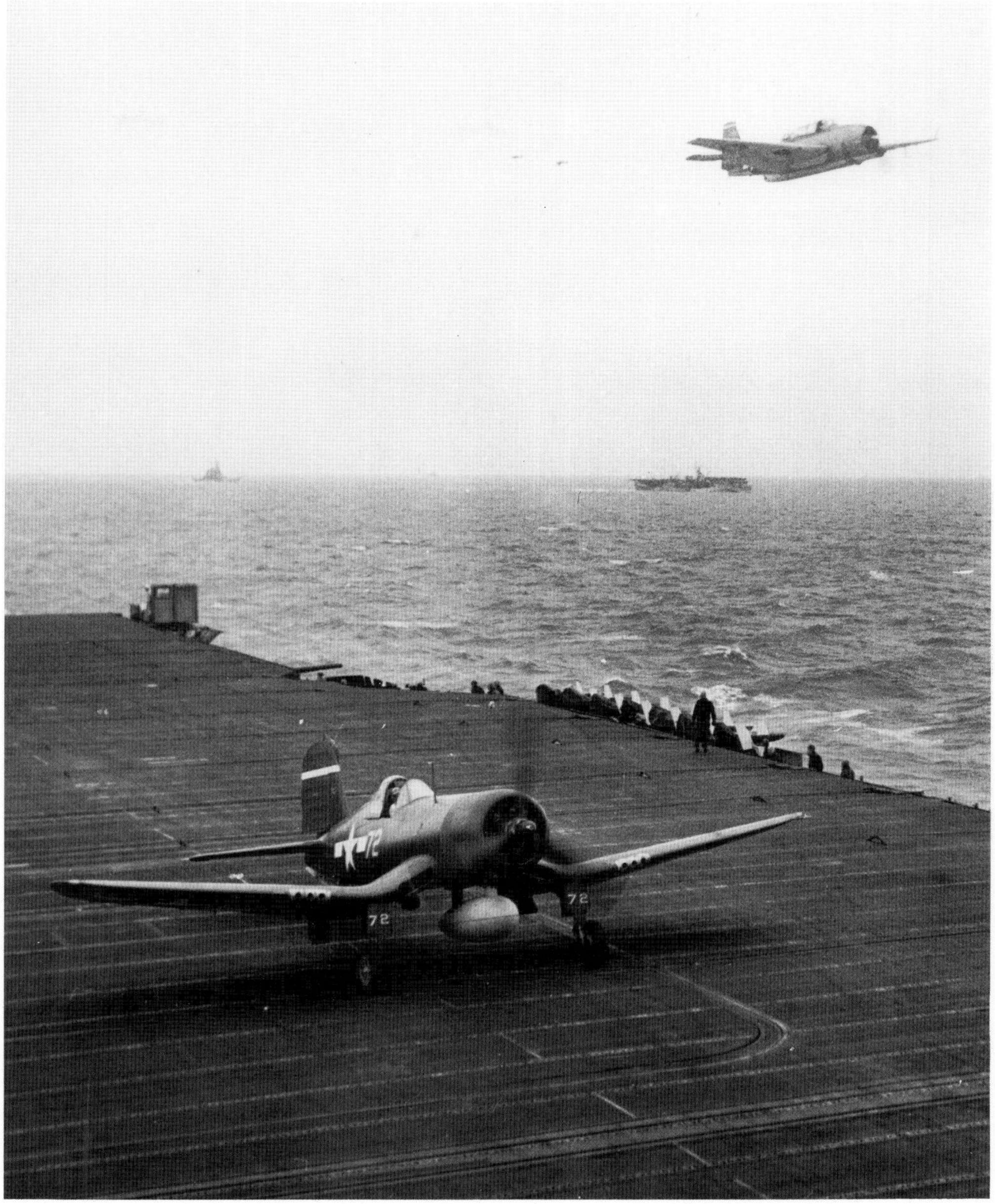

An F4U-1D of VMF-124 taxis forward after landing aboard USS Essex *on February 27, 1945.* National Archives via Sullivan

The Corsair, still attached to the wire, bounced, and decelerating, came back down to the deck. "Both main mounts blew, busted the wheels and everything else," continued Blackburn. "So, we decided that wasn't exactly the way to do it. They put a couple of new wheels and tires on it. I took off, came around and made some more landings. I didn't do quite the same thing again. We decided the basic technique was OK."[37]

Blackburn then set about qualifying his squadron. "We banged up a few airplanes. Some were wrinkled beyond repair. But nobody got hurt which was a really remarkable performance in qualifying on this postage stamp where the maximum speed of the thing was 16kt and the wind over the deck wasn't exactly up to 30kt where it was supposed to be. It was a terrific performance by the landing signal officer who was responsible in a large measure for it, but it was also a terrific performance by these young guys that had come out of flight training to the squadron and the most advanced thing they'd been in was an SNJ with an all up weight of maybe 5,000lb. They were taking this fancy fighter aboard a little bitty escort carrier and getting away with it. I'm still astounded that they were that able and that courageous to go ahead and do it."[38] Blackburn and VF-17 accomplished most of the preliminary field evaluation with the Corsair for carrier landings.

Blackburn's VF-17 departed San Diego aboard the USS *Bunker Hill.* Upon arriving at Pearl Harbor, VF-17

Lt. Ira C. Kepford leads a formation of VF-17 F4U-1Ds. Fuselage fuel-tank leaks in early F4Us required that the joints between the panels covering the tank be taped. Vought Aircraft

was immediately dispatched to Espiritu Santo, New Hebrides, aboard the escort carrier USS *Prince William*. Flying from Ondongo, New Georgia, VF-17 destroyed 154 Japanese aircraft in the air during seventy-nine days of combat, producing twelve aces.

VMF-124—now on its second combat tour, commanded by Lt. Col. Bill Millington—had been the first Marine squadron to fly the Corsair in combat and now became the first US squadron to operate Corsairs in combat from a carrier. VMF-124 and VMF-123, commanded by Maj. David Marshall, boarded the USS *Essex* on December 28, 1944, at Ulithi Harbor. Operating as one squadron commanded by Millington, their first attack was on Okinawa, January 3, 1945.

Carrier-based Corsairs would fly in every naval operation in the Pacific until war's end. Preparatory strikes against Iwo Jima, raids and ground support missions over Okinawa, and strafing missions against the Japanese home islands would become the operational theater for the Corsair. While attacking Japanese positions, the Corsair earned the name "Whistling Death" because of the whistling sound made by the oil cooler vanes in the wing's gull area.

"I flew FG-1D Corsairs from the USS *Yorktown* as a member of VBF-88, part of CVG-88 which was on the ship from June 17, 1945, to the end of the war," said LCdr Leo Horacek. "We ranged over Japan, mostly trying to eliminate aircraft on the ground that might be used as Kamikazes. They were generally in revetments and so well camouflaged that they were hard to find even when we had seen photos showing exactly where they were. I recall flying over airfields that seemed completely devoid of planes, and then after the end of hostilities visiting the same field, seeing rows of planes set out with their props off and on the ground in front of them according to the terms of the cease-fire.

"We also attacked ships, mostly in harbor, and other targets of military importance. Most of us never saw enemy planes in the air, but the squadron did shoot down a few and had some losses from enemy planes.

"On one of the flights, my wingman had failed to throw a switch that would permit him to drop his bomb. So on the way back as we went over a village, he dropped it. I scolded him for that, saying there were women and children down there, and that I didn't think he should have done that. So I told him the next time it happened, to tell me and I'd find him a target. The next flight, on August 10, 1945, he did it again. He told me about it on the radio. I saw an airfield off to one side as we were headed back to the fleet. I headed over toward it in a shallow glide. It looked totally abandoned. That was dumb because there could still be a lot of antiaircraft around any field. It was dumb for me to go into a shallow glide because that's where they could hit you easiest. So antiaircraft hit the plane and knocked out the oil pressure. I looked at the oil pressure just as it went down to zero. So I headed out to sea. We knew then how long they would fly, a couple minutes I think before the engine froze up, and fortunately there was a submarine sitting out there just to pick up flyers. So I put it down in the water without any problem and got into my life raft, and in a few

F4U-1Ds prepare to strike. South Pacific, March 28, 1944. Gary Pape collection

minutes the submarine came and picked me up. The sub had picked up one other flyer who was a good friend of mine. He was picked up that same morning from an attack on the same airfield."[39] Horacek was transferred to another submarine with fourteen American and British flyers, taken to Guam and returned to the fleet.

The -1D Corsairs flew the final Corsair missions of the war. During the surrender signing ceremonies aboard the USS *Missouri* on September 2,

An F4U-1A of VMF-115 damaged by fire from crashing Japanese aircraft on Leyte Island, December 6, 1944. USMC via Sullivan

An F4U-1A, BuNo 17911, of VMF-212 in a revetment on Vella La Vella Island, Solomon Islands, January 13, 1944. National Archives via Sullivan

1945, in Tokyo Bay, a massive flight of carrier aircraft passed in review. "It seemed to me that every ship in the fleet put most of their planes up," said Horacek. "We knew what was going on and what we were there for, so we just flew over to make a demonstration I guess. At the close of hostilities we dropped supplies to POW camps. They had the names written on the tops of the camps, and we knew where they were anyhow. All in all it was a great experience for those of us who survived it."[40]

The only aircraft of World War II to receive an official citation for flying 400 hours of combat with VMF-111 without turning back due to mechanical problems or other reasons. Vought Aircraft

'JSMC Capt. Philip C. DeLong of VMF-212 ormates his F4U-1D showing 11.5 kills. De-Long also flew the Corsair in combat during he Korean War and shot down two more en-emy fighters. Vought Aircraft

The -1 Corsairs were phased out of :he USN's inventory before the end of :he war, and most were consumed dur-ng the postwar scrap drives. The -1D Corsairs soldiered on with the US Naval Reserve into the late 1940s and early 1950s.

US Air Force weather forecaster Pfc. E. J. 'Mac" McGill (today an author of mystery novels) stands on the wing of a Goodyear FG-1D Corsair of the Naval Air Reserve's Denver, Colorado, unit during a protracted deployment to Hill Air Force Base near Og-den, Utah, in mid-1948. In the postwar iden-tifier system, the PF tail code (P for Denver, F for fighter) tells us where the FG-1D was stationed, while the red-orange fuselage band is typical of Reserve units of the period. E. J. McGill via Robert F. Dorr

349
340
PHOTO BY
GOOD YEAR
NEWS SERVICE

Chapter 3

F4U-1B: Britain Takes the Corsair to War

The F4U-1B was the first of a long line of Corsairs to be operated by the RN. The F4U-1B was an F4U-1 featuring a fuselage centerline hard point and modified wing tips. The British RN, and later the Royal New Zealand Air Force (RNZAF), would also acquire the -1 and -1D Corsairs from all three manufacturers.

The United States Congress passed the Lend-Lease Act on March 11, 1941, paving the way for Britain and other Allied countries to acquire American-made armament.

The British Air Commission selected American designs, assigned them a name, mark number, and serial number. The Corsair name was retained and mark numbers assigned, i.e., the F4U-1 in RN service became the Corsair I; the F3A-1, F4U-1A, and F4U-1D became the Corsair II; some F3A-1s and all F3A-1Ds became the Corsair III; and the FG-1 and FG-1D became Corsair IVs. Interestingly enough, Brewster was the first to deliver a "clipped wing" Corsair to the RN, and more than one-half of its entire production was delivered to the British.

The RN would equip forty-seven squadrons and eventually acquired 1,972 Corsairs of various models.[41] The first seventy aircraft, RN serials JT100–JT169, were F4U-1Bs. These aircraft were assigned Chance Vought constructor's numbers, but not US Navy BuNos. JT100–JT119 were constructor's numbers 3336–3355; JT120–JT144 were constructor's numbers 3492–3516; and JT145–JT169 were constructor's numbers of 3577–3601.[42] The first British Corsairs were delivered between May 20 and May 24, 1943.[43]

Corsairs were delivered to the RN's Fleet Air Arm and to the Royal New Zealand Air Force (RNZAF) under the Lend-Lease program. Here, two Goodyear FG-1Ds are test-flown prior to delivery to the Fleet Air Arm. Goodyear Aircraft via Robert F. Dorr

RN maintenance and air crews underwent stateside conversion training on the Corsair at NAS Quonset Point, Rhode Island, and at this time it was realized that the Corsairs would not fit into the hangar decks of the British aircraft carriers. Only 16ft of vertical clearance was available on the hangar deck while the F4U-1, with its wings folded, had a height of 16ft, 2 3/10in.

After discussions with the RN, the BuAer sent a letter January 23, 1943, asking Chance Vought to investigate ways to reduce the Corsair's overall height with the wings folded.

Rex B. Beisel, then engineering manager, responded on February 9, 1943, with ten possible ways to reduce the height of the Corsair to fit on board the British carriers:

One: Retract the tail wheel while the aircraft rested on a movable dolly. This would reduce the aircraft's height by 3 7/10in. (This left unresolved the problem of where the auxiliary hydraulic power needed to raise and lower the tail wheel would come from.)

Two: Fully deflate the tail-wheel oleo. Just over 750psi would be required to reinflate the oleo before each flight.

Three: Compress the main landing gear oleos with a specially designed oleo jack, or fully deflate them. (Beisel stated that this idea would not be practical because of the danger involved in compressing the high-pressure oleos, nor would it be practical due to storage space required for the jacks—two per aircraft.)

Four: Deflate the main tires to 11in rolling radius (flat tire radius is 10in); 90psi required to reinflate.

Number five called for two and four to be used together, while the sixth involved two and three.

The seventh proposal involved using numbers two, three, and four. This would reduce the aircraft's overall height by 6 2/10in to 15ft, 8 1/10in—almost 4in below the hangar deck's maximum vertical height.

The eighth suggestion called for number three and four to be used in combination thus reducing the height by 3 9/10in.

Number nine called for retracting the tail wheel (number one) and compressing the main gear oleos with the jacking devices (number three); and the tenth suggestion called for the tail wheel to be retracted (number one), and the main tires deflated (number four).

While offering these ten suggestions, Beisel discussed the reasons why redesigning the F4U-1's wing tips seemed out of the question. "No further studies have been made to refair the wing tips due to the great amount of engineering redesign involved. In the previous studies of this item it was estimated that 56 drawings would necessarily be revised and approximately 15 new drawings required. Several hundred drawings would be involved in connection with the next assembly numbers, and the problem of interchangeability would be difficult." [44] The pressures of time and money appear to be the underlying theme for Beisel's resistance.

Vought-built F4U-1B showing the aircraft's clipped wing tips to clear the low ceilings of the British aircraft carrier's hangar decks. The F4U-1B's other main modification that differentiates it from the F4U-1 is the centerline hard point. The RN Fleet Air Arm would eventually acquire 1,972 Corsairs of different models. Note the flat finish, a British standard, while US Navy Corsairs received gloss paint. Vought Aircraft

Beisel recommended the fifth solution. This could be used on aircraft already delivered to the fleet and those yet to be built. Number five called for the full deflation of the tail wheel and deflating the main tires to 11in rolling radius. This recommendation would reduce the overall height of the Corsair with folded wings to 15ft 9 97/100in, just under the 16ft needed to clear the British carrier's hangar decks.

H. J. Brow, Inspector of Naval Aircraft, Stratford, rubber stamped the solutions put forth by Beisel and Chance Vought. Of the ten suggestions in the Chance Vought memo, Brow recommended number six, which called for the deflation of the tail wheel oleo and the use of the cumbersome jacking device. Brow then sent the Chance Vought memo with his recommendations as a cover letter to the Chief of the BuAer.[45]

The British, upon seeing this memorandum filled with ideas impractical under combat conditions, responded eighteen days later. LCdr R. M. Smeeton, RN, of the British Liaison Office recommended that the wing tip of the Corsair be completely removed at Station 149 and "filled in with a wooden fillet" and that "no attempt be made to reproduce the contour of the existing wing tip."[46]

Smeeton took the idea up with Paul Baker, Chance Vought's chief of aerodynamics, who stated "that he had no objection to the suggested scheme from an engineering standpoint and that he would be prepared to authorize flight trials."[47]

This change would not affect assembly line work at Chance Vought because construction of the wing panels had been subcontracted to the Briggs Company. When consulted, Bert Taliaferro, production manager of Chance Vought, stated that "the Briggs Company was well up on their production tool-

All the Corsairs for the US Navy, Britain, and New Zealand were built on the same assembly lines. The clipped-wing panels were delivered to the three manufacturers from the subcontractor, Briggs, with the modification already completed. Goodyear Aircraft via Robert F. Dorr

ng and could easily handle the job as nad been outlined" in Smeeton's recommendations.[48]

The BuAer approved Smeeton's ecommendations in a letter to Chance Vought on July 16, 1943. The wing-tip changes were to be incorporated on BuNo 17952 (British serial JT270). Aircraft prior to JT270 were modified after delivery to the RN by Blackburn Aircraft of England[49] and by Andover Kent Aviation Corporation of New Brunswick, New Jersey.[50]

The removal of the tips at Station 149 was approved on the Master Change Record as Change Record 296. This modification would shorten each wing panel by 8in, would have a negligible change in the aircraft's performance, would increase the cost of each aircraft by $235.54, and decrease the aircraft's empty weight by 2.7lb.[51]

Changing the wing panels slightly improved the Corsair's stall characteristics by increasing the stall speed from 1–3mph, giving the pilot more of a warning buffet before stalling and less roll after the stall. The shortened wing tips increased the aircraft's takeoff distance in a 25kt head wind by 15ft.[52]

British Carrier-Landing Technique

In 1943, the standard way to land a fighter aircraft aboard an aircraft carrier was to fly the downwind leg abeam the length of the ship opposite to the ship's course, turn base leg perpendicular to the ship's course, turn again to set up the final approach, and then go straight onto the deck. When this method was used with the Corsair, however, a number of pilots were killed and many aircraft were written off due to the Corsair's uneven wing stalling and landing bounce.

W. K. Munnoch, then a lieutenant and senior pilot of No. 1833 Squadron said, "You couldn't do the standard carrier approach in the Corsair. We landed them on in a stalling turn all the way on to the deck."[53]

Munnoch said that during training on the River Clyde in Scotland, pilots of 1830 and 1833 Squadrons "devised a way of flying just above stalling speed, which meant that you were falling out

An elephant is used to move a Fleet Air Arm Corsair at Ceylon. Vought Aircraft

of the sky, and you had to judge the rate of fall exactly, so that when you got down to about ship height, the ship was underneath you. Then you cut the throttle and the Corsair fell onto the deck."[54]

British Corsairs Go to War

The F4U-1B was now ready to go aboard ship and begin her carrier-based combat career. F4U-1B and F3A-1s of the Fleet Air Arm went into action aboard HMS *Illustrious*, nine months before the US Navy would begin operating Corsairs from the decks of its aircraft carriers.

No. 1830 Squadron was the first Fleet Air Arm unit to travel to NAS Quonset Point for a five month conversion training course on the Corsair in May 1943. It was joined in July by 1831, 1833, and 1834 Squadrons, and these units would form the nucleus of the British Corsair force. Near the end of conversion training, the Corsair I was traded in for the updated Corsair II (F4U-1A), which featured the frameless canopy, extended tail wheel oleo, and right wing stall improvement device.

In October 1943, No. 1830 Squadron embarked aboard HMS *Slinger* while 1831 and 1833 Squadrons rode back to the United Kingdom aboard HMS *Trumpeter*. Upon returning home, No. 1831 Squadron was disbanded and its aircraft and crews divided between 1830 and 1833 Squadrons.

British Eastern Fleet

Nos. 1830 and 1833 Squadrons flew aboard the fleet carrier HMS *Illustrious* on December 25, 1943, as it headed to join the Far East Fleet tasked with driving the Japanese out of the Indian Ocean. "We flew every day that was possible on the long trip to Ceylon to get up to operational standards," said C.D.S. "Dave" Millington,[55] an airframe fitter first class with No. 1833 Squadron. Millington was W. K. Munnoch's plane captain.

Millington's position as an airframe fitter carried the same duties as a US Navy plane captain. He had overall responsibility for "his" aircraft to ensure that it was ready for the next day's combat sortie as well as its security any time it was moved on or between decks. Describing work aboard the HMS *Illustrious* with the British Pacific Fleet, he said, "Our work was totally different on board ship. We worked until the aircraft were repaired and serviceable again, replacing wings, etc., from an auxiliary carrier, HMS *Unicorn,* whose sole job was to carry spares and pilots. My aircraft, 6K, had a painting of Superman on the engine cowling 3ft high. My relief aircraft was lettered 6L for when we were on the other watch.

"In the main, Corsairs were a good aircraft to work on. The inverted gull wings made it a little difficult to climb on the fuselage especially when hot. The only real complaint I would make was with regards to the parking brake system, or lack of it. It meant as soon as a pilot landed I had to jump in the cockpit and keep my feet on the pedals, as my pilot was usually the first or second one on, it meant being right up front, on the edge, and hoping that nothing was going to jump the barrier. Occasionally they did. I then had to move very fast."[56]

In March 1944, 1830 and 1833 Squadrons became the first units to operate the Corsair in combat from an aircraft carrier when they carried out three days of raids against targets in the Bay of Bengal. HMS *Illustrious* attacked Sabang harbor in Sumatra with the USS *Saratoga*, on April 19. Harbor facilities, radar stations, and military installations were attacked by SBDs and Barracudas with Hellcats and Corsairs strafing targets of opportunity.

While the strike aircraft were recovering aboard HMS *Illustrious*, W. K. Munnoch was leading four No. 1833 Squadron Corsairs flying CAP when they spotted a Ki-21 reconnaissance bomber, Allied code name Sally, that had followed the strike aircraft back to locate and report on the Allied fleet. Munnoch led his flight to positions 4,000–5,000ft above and behind the Sally, with two Corsairs on each side and attacked. "We made a run on the Sally, one man from each side, then the other," said Munnoch. "I could see the orange flames out of the tail-turret guns, but they didn't shoot at me for long. I aimed for the tail and then pulled forward to hit the cockpit and the engines. I fired until I got quite close and then broke away. When I passed the Japanese plane, I must have been going 400mph, and I went past quite close to it. By the time I'd come down for a second pass, it was on fire and just about in the water."[57]

Corsairs of HMS *Illustrious* were in battle again on May 17, 1944, when British Avengers, Barracudas, and SBDs attacked the oil refineries at Soerabaya, Java. "Java was pretty bad," said Munnoch, "although we had a stroke of luck there. There were a lot of fighters based there, and we were horribly outnumbered. As we returned from attacking Soerabaya, we flew right over this Japanese airfield, and because they hadn't expected us they were just on the point of getting the aircraft in the air when we arrived. It was much easier to destroy them when they were still on the ground or just taking off. The antiaircraft fire there was very bad, and so it was at Palembang, but there the Japanese had barrage balloons and wires that caught one or two people."[58]

After attacking targets at Soerabaya, Port Blair, Sumatra and a second strike on Sabang during late May, June, and July 1944, *HMS Illustrious* departed on July 26 for Durban, South Africa. Here the ship was refitted for her next war patrol.

No. 1833 Squadron crew at rest, Koggala Airstrip, Ceylon, 1944. Airframe Fitter First Class C.D.S. "Dave" Millington is standing in the cockpit, center, of "his" airplane 6-K. Millington collection

British Pacific Fleet

The British Pacific Fleet's most unusual training squadron was No. 723 based at Bankstown, flying from Nowra, Australia. This squadron was equipped with eight Corsair IIs, which flew "throw off" flights. A throw off flight was an antiaircraft practice for ships' gunners who fired live ammunition at "attacking" Corsairs. Reportedly the ships' gun sights were offset 15deg to port so that the gunners could aim at the Corsairs with reduced chance of hitting them.[59]

After its refitting in South Africa, the HMS *Illustrious* sailed to Sydney,

Lieutenant Aiken veered to the left after landing and ended up on top of one of the 40mm gun mounts. This crash landing caused quite a panic as the ship's magazine is located directly underneath. Abandon ship stations were taken as a precaution in case the Corsair had caught fire. Millington collection

Australia, where it became the fourth fleet carrier of the British Pacific Fleet, which included HMS *Victorious*, HMS *Indefatigable*, and HMS *Indomitable*.

After departing Sydney around January 20, the British Pacific Fleet began a series of attacks on the oil refineries of Sumatra. Operation Meridian began with attacks on the oil refinery at Pladjoe on January 24, and the same targets at Soengei Gerong on the twenty-ninth.

During the Meridian attacks, the Fleet Air Arm employed a tactic known as "Ramrod." Prior to a strike mission, four four-plane elements of fighters would be launched to attack enemy airfields in an attempt to gain air superiority during the raid.

The British Pacific Fleet returned to Sydney on February 10, 1945, and seventeen days later they departed to join the Allied strike force destined for Okinawa.

After stopping at Manus Island in the Admiralties Islands, the fleet sailed with the US Navy's Task Force 57 for Ulithi Atoll and then on to attack Okinawa. The British Pacific Fleet was dispatched to soften up the Sakishima Gunto Island group east of Formosa, and southwest of Okinawa. Raids commenced on March 26, and were repeated on March 27, 31, April 1, 6, and 7. When not flying CAP, the Corsairs were tasked with strafing the aerodromes in the island group and maintaining complete air superiority. This kept the Japanese, who were intent on returning to defend the home islands, on the ground and unable to launch Kamikaze attacks. "Our duty was to create havoc over the little airfields to stop the Japanese fighters from hopping across to Okinawa," said Munnoch. "It was a monotonous duty. Day in and day out, going over the same place, we got to know it well. It was never really an enjoyable experience to go strafing over airfields because you were low level, subject to flak, but the Corsair could take punishment and was very rugged. I was always ever grateful that I flew it."[60]

During the attacks on the Sakishima Islands, the British Pacific Fleet flew 2,444 sorties, dropped 412 tons of bombs, and fired 325 rockets, with the loss of forty-seven aircraft and twenty-nine aircrew.[61]

Other Corsair squadrons that served with the British Pacific Fleet were Nos. 885, 1837, 1838, and 1843 Squadrons. All four squadrons arrived too late to see combat.

Escorting the Tirpitz Attacks

Nazi Germany began construction of the battleship *Tirpitz* in 1936. Completed in 1941, the 42,000-ton battleship boasted a main battery of eight 15in guns firing 1,750lb projectiles; twelve 5.9in guns in its secondary batteries; and sixteen 4.1in heavy antiaircraft guns. *Tirpitz* had a top speed of 29kt and 12 1/2in thick side armor plating. Operating from the fjords of Norway, *Tirpitz* posed a threat to convoys operating in the Atlantic or en route to Russia through the Arctic.

The RN had its first shot at *Tirpitz* on March 9, 1942, when the German battleship was reported in the Norwegian Sea northwest of Tromso, Norway. *Tirpitz* evaded all of the torpedoes launched by Albacores from HMS *Victorious* and quickly sailed into the protective cover of the Norwegian fjords.

Corsairs were fully operational in England by January 1944, and the major role of the Corsair in the Atlantic battles would be to provide top cover for the ensuing attacks on the battleship *Tirpitz*.

Operation Tungsten in the spring of 1944 would begin the Fleet Air Arm's campaign against *Tirpitz*. The carriers HMS *Furious* and HMS *Victorious* met at sea on April 2, 1944, for an attack on *Tirpitz* early the next morning. The attack was made in two waves, each consisting of Corsairs of 1834 and 1836 Squadrons escorting Barracuda dive bombers, Hellcats, Wildcats, and Seafires. Fourteen direct hits were made during the two-wave attack inflicting heavy damage to *Tirpitz*.

Three subsequent attacks were attempted on *Tirpitz* in as many months, but each was called back or canceled due to poor weather.

Operation Mascot involved the carriers HMS *Formidable*, HMS *Furious*, and HMS *Indefatigable* in a July 17, 1944, attack. Forty-four Barracuda dive bombers were escorted to the target by forty-eight fighters including the Corsairs of No. 1841 Squadron. The attack was sighted early and the Germans were able to fill Kaa Fjord with smoke, obscuring the *Tirpitz*. None of the Barracuda's bombs hit the battleship.

The Fleet Air Arm was to make four more attacks on *Tirpitz* in August under the code name Operation Goodwood. Corsairs of 1841 and 1842 Squadrons aboard HMS *Formidable* launched on the August 22 Operation Goodwood I and Goodwood II, which were recalled. Two days later another attack was launched, this one inflicting minor damage to *Tirpitz* with one No. 1842 Squadron Corsair lost to flak.

A fourth attempt, Operation Goodwood IV, was launched on August 29 without success.

Corsairs never met any Luftwaffe opposition during the *Tirpitz* attacks.

The RN, having completed its series of attacks on *Tirpitz*, sent HMS *Victorious* and HMS *Formidable* to join the Eastern and later, the British Pacific Fleet.

Tirpitz, at anchor in Kaa Fjord, succumbed to bombs from Royal Air Force bombers on November 12, 1944. Avro Lancaster bombers of Nos. 9 and 617 Squadrons, which had staged out of Russia, scored two direct hits and four near misses with 12,000lb bombs that capsized the battleship.

The End of the British Corsairs

War in Europe came to a close on May 7, 1945, when Nazi Germany unconditionally surrendered. The British Pacific Fleet was still occupied in combat with the Japanese and Goodyear continued to deliver Corsair IVs (FG-1Ds) to the Fleet Air Arm through August 9, 1945.[62]

According to the terms of the Lend-Lease agreement, the RN began returning to US Navy depots the Corsairs it operated stateside, as well as aircraft that had been accepted and not yet shipped to England. FG-1D KE104, BuNo 92181, was the first of the Corsairs to be returned when it arrived at NAS Norfolk, Virginia, in August 1945.[63]

On August 14, the Japanese accepted unconditional surrender terms. Lt. Cyril White, a Canadian pilot on loan to the Fleet Air Arm's No. 1846 Squadron aboard HMS *Colossus*, flew a Corsair into Formosa shortly after the surrender agreement. "We were on Formosa before it was actually secured," said White. "I had to land at Matsuyama. The Royal Marines took a medical party ashore to rescue a bunch of prisoners of war—British, American, French, Belgian soldiers. We provided air cover for the operation. At one point they needed more penicillin or something, and so I took it ashore at Matsuyama. The Royal Marines were supposed to meet me there. When I landed, my wingman stayed above me in the air. There was a huge bomb crater half way down the runway, but I was able to pull up in time and taxi back. So I sat there and the next thing I knew I was surrounded by Japanese. They all came out to look at me! Which was a little discomforting because I didn't know what they were going to do, and I'm not sure they knew what I was going to do. The war was basically over, but I wasn't sure they had gotten the word. They kind of gathered around the tail of the plane so I decided I'd make a big show of this thing and get out. The Japanese being what they are sort of respond to authority immediately, so I just waved at them and said, 'Get away,' hoping like hell they would. They did and it kind of surprised me. I must have sat there 20 minutes with the prop tickin' over, and finally the Marines arrived with a couple of doctors. They picked up the penicillin, and I got out of there, which I was thankful for."[64]

The Japanese signed the surrender documents aboard the USS *Missouri* on September 2, 1945, in Tokyo Bay, Japan. Less than one year later the Corsair was phased out of RN service when No. 1851 Squadron disbanded on August 13, 1946.[65]

New Zealand Corsair NZ5469 was flown from Jacquinot Bay to the RNZAF storage area at Rukuhia by Bryan Cox at the end of the war. Bryan Cox

Chapter 4

Kiwi Corsairs

Under the Lend-Lease program, the RNZAF received 424 Corsairs, beginning in May 1944. Transitioning from the Curtiss P-40 Kittyhawk and later P-40K Warhawks, thirteen RNZAF squadrons would fly the Corsair: Nos. 14 through 26 fighter Squadrons.

Operating from land bases in the Bismarck/Solomons area, the RNZAF was tasked with attacking the islands bypassed during the Allied advance. Operating from Espiritu Santo, Guadalcanal; Green Island; Emirair in the New Ireland group; and Los Negros on Manus, in the Admiralty Islands, the Kiwi Corsairs attacked targets on New Ireland, New Britain, and Bougainville.

On December 21, 1944, No. 16 Fighter Squadron moved forward from Guadalcanal to Ocean Strip, Green Island. From Green Island, No. 16 squadron flew patrols, strikes against Rabaul, and strafing runs on any Japanese vehicle or vessel brave enough to venture out in the daylight.

Although bypassed by the Allies, Rabaul was heavily defended by numerous antiaircraft batteries making life miserable for the RNZAF Corsairs and Lockheed PV-1 Venturas that were tasked with harassing the enemy garrison there.

Corsairs of No. 16 Squadron departed for an early morning strike on January 9, 1945. Flt. Sgt. Brian Cox and eleven of his squadron mates made dive bombing attacks on New Ireland's Namatanai Airfield. The Corsairs made a diving attack from 7,500ft dropping 500lb bombs while a squadron of RNZAF Lockheed Venturas made low-level strafing and bombing runs shortly after the Corsairs dropped their bombs on what was thought to be camouflaged Japanese aircraft parked in revetments. Flt. Sgt. Cox reported that Japanese antiaircraft fire was light and all bombs struck in the target area.[66]

Earlier in the war, RNZAF pilots flying P-40s had achieved ninety-nine confirmed kills against Japanese aircraft. On January 12, 1945, while they were on a bombing mission to Rabaul with 500lb bombs, the New Zealand Corsair pilots sighted a Val in the Rabaul area. Before any of the Corsairs could close on the Val, it ducked into a cloud layer, never to be seen again. This was the last opportunity the Kiwi Corsair pilots had to score their one hundredth victory.[67]

Moving to Bougainville's Piva North fighter strip in late April 1945, the New Zealand Corsairs supported the Royal Australian Army's battle to crush the enemy on Bougainville.

The RNZAF transitioned from the Curtiss P-40 to the Vought Corsair beginning in May 1944. Vought Aircraft

Flying from Piva North, the New Zealand Corsairs no longer were forced to patrol the skies above Rabaul. The Allied offensive on Bougainville Island, at the top of the Solomons chain, was attempting to force the beleaguered Japanese garrison into the sea. RNZAF Corsairs were now regularly flying with single 1,000lb bombs and attacking huts, trenches, roads, and gun emplacements. On May 9, 1945, No. 16 Squadron flew a forty-aircraft strike against Japanese positions on the banks of the Hongorai River. A twenty-eight-Corsair strike was flown against targets at Koya River using 1,000lb bombs. The last strike mission of the month flown

An RNZAF Corsair traps aboard a carrier operating in the South Pacific in late 1944. Vought Aircraft

by No. 16 Squadron pilots was a ten-plane bombing and strafing run on the headquarters of the Japanese 6th Division near Bougainville's Buin Road.

RNZAF Corsair pilots scored 99 confirmed air-to-air kills plus 19 probables. The highest scoring RNZAF pilot was No. 17 Squadron's Flt. Ldr. P.G.H. Newton. His confirmed kills included one Zero on October 11, 1943, while on an escort mission to Kangu; two Zeros, and one probable, on a December 24, 1943, sweep over Rabaul; and two more Zeros while escorting TBFs on January 9, 1944.

After the conclusion of hostilities, one squadron of Kiwi Corsairs, No. 14 Occupational Fighter Squadron, was transported by HMS *Glory* for occupation duties in Japan. They left Ardmore, New Zealand, on March 8, 1946, with the squadron's twenty-four new FG-1 Corsairs, and HMS *Glory* offloaded the FG-1s onto barges for the trip to shore at Iwakuni, Japan, on March 25.

No. 14 Occupational Squadron was charged with patrolling the western end of Honshu Island, Japan. The squadron also flew hours of formation practice flights, dive bombing missions, as well as rocket firing. In January 1947, No. 14 also flew observation missions over the earthquake and tidal wave damaged areas of Nakamura and Kochi, both on the island of Shikoku.

No. 14 Occupational Squadron was relieved of duty in Japan in October 1948. Their FG-1s were towed into a circle, piled with lumber, and burned at Bofu, Japan, in 1948 thus ending the RNZAF's relationship with the Corsair.

Although a few of the early Kiwi F4Us were returned to the US Navy as required under the Lend-Lease agreement, the majority of the Kiwi Corsairs were gathered at New Zealand's Rukuhia aircraft graveyard and subsequently scrapped. Of the 424 Corsairs delivered to the RNZAF, 154 were lost in combat and training missions with fifty-six of the pilots being killed.

End of the line for many of the RNZAF's Corsairs: Rukuhia. Within two years, these aircraft would be reduced to aluminum ingots. Only one former RNZAF Corsair survived, NZ5612, which is on display at the Museum of Transportation and Technology, Auckland, New Zealand. Bryan Cox

10

Chapter 5

F4U-2: Navy's First Nightfighter

The Naval Research Laboratory, NAS Anacostia, Maryland, began radar experiments after an unusual coincidence on September 27, 1922. Cdr. A. Hoyt Taylor and Leo C. Young of the Aircraft Radio Laboratory were conducting high-frequency radio wave experiments when a river steamer passed through the radio wave beam between NAS Anacostia and the receiver over the river at Hains Point.[68] The steamer interrupted the beam, signaling the ships presence to the operators. Known as the "Beat" method of detection, this early form of radar launched the Navy's slow and underfunded radar experiments.

Dr. Taylor authorized research into what would later become "pulse radar" on March 14, 1934.[69] Pulse radar was far more promising than the beat method. In pulse radar, bursts of radio energy are sent from the transmitting unit, each separated by a short period of time. If an object passes through the radio energy, it is reflected back to the antenna. This reflection not only reveals the presence of an object or target in the beam's path, but range and distance information on the target can be gained by computing the time it took for the echo return.

F4U-2 Corsairs of VF(N)-101 prepare to launch for the early evening CAP from the deck of the USS Intrepid. *Originally an F4U-1, the F4U-2s featured an 18in parabolic antenna mounted in a domed pod on the starboard wing and a radar display screen in the cockpit. The F4U Corsair and airborne radar combination, operating exclusively in the Pacific theater, produced a number of kills beginning in the fall of 1943.* Vought Aircraft

Two years later, in April 1936, R. C. Guthrie and R. M. Page of the Naval Research Laboratory, NAS Anacostia, tested a proof-of-concept pulse radar set.[70] This unit was able to detect aircraft up to 25 miles away.

President Roosevelt established the National Defense Research Committee on June 27, 1940. This committee set up Division 14, also known as the National Defense Research Committee Radar Division, which was tasked with obtaining "the most effective military application of microwaves in minimum time."[71] Two of the main products the committee supported were airborne intercept and airborne early warning radar.

Shortly thereafter, on August 29, 1940, the Navy met with the British Technical and Scientific Mission to the United States to exchange information on weapons and radar development. Sir Henry Tizard headed up the mission, later known as the "Tizard Mission," which discussed shipborne and airborne radar developments as well as the long-range detection and identification of friendly and enemy aircraft. From this meeting it was determined that Britain's development of centimeter wavelength radar far outpaced US radar-development efforts. The BuAer was able to arrange the loan of a number of different British radar sets that were studied and later improved upon.[72]

The National Defense Research Committee's Division 14 assisted in forming the Radiation Laboratory at the Massachusetts Institute of Technology. The Radiation Laboratory began work on November 11, 1940.[73]

Under the code name "Project Roger," the Radiation Laboratory contracted with the NAF in Philadelphia on May 3, 1941, for the installation and testing of radar sets in Naval aircraft.[74] The Chief of the BuAer released a preliminary plan on August 7, 1941, calling for the installation of radar in a number of aircraft in the fleet including the F4U Corsair.[75] This was followed by a formal request from the BuAer to the National Defense Research Committee and the Naval Research Laboratory on September 9, 1941, to develop an airborne intercept radar for single-seat fighters, specifically the F4U.[76]

Vought submitted Company Proposal VS-325 to the BuAer on January 6, 1942, for the radar-equipped nightfighter version of the Corsair, the XF4U-2.[77]

While Vought completed the mock-up of the XF4U-2, the Navy established Project Argus (which was shortly thereafter renamed Project Affirm) at NAS Quonset Point, Rhode Island, to test night-fighter aircraft and equipment, develop night-fighter tactics, and to train officers, enlisted personnel, and night-fighter directors.[78]

The XF4U-2 mock-up was complete and inspected by the Navy on January 28, 1942, at Stratford. The BuAer decided to have Vought deliver completed F4U-1s to the NAF where the radar sets and cockpit scopes would be installed. This would allow Vought to build the Corsair without interrupting the production line.[79]

BuNo 02153, the first production F4U-1, became the XF4U-2. After completing Navy flight tests at NAS Anacostia, 02153 was transferred to the NAF for modification and installation of the Radiation Laboratory's experimental 3cm-wavelength XAIA radar sets. The Navy's specification for

F4U-2 Corsairs of VMF(N)-532 prepare to launch from USS Windham Bay *on July 12, 1944. VMF(N)-532 was redeploying to Saipan for CAP and radar-guided night-bombing missions.* Vought Aircraft

the XAIA and production model AIA radar set required that the unit weigh not more than 250lb, have an antenna with minimum drag, an accuracy sufficient for blind gun aiming, a useful search range of 2 miles at altitudes of 2,000ft and higher, and a minimum dependable range of 500ft.[80] The 18in paraboloid antenna was mounted in an aerodynamically streamlined pod on the starboard wing panel, outboard of the guns. This domed antenna did not affect the Corsair's flying characteristics and only reduced the top speed by 2mph. A 3in scope was mounted on the pilot's instrument panel.

Exhaust flame dampeners were added when the aircraft were converted at the NAF.[81] Also the starboard outboard .50cal machine gun was deleted during the radar's installation—which provided for better weight distribution balancing out the radome's added weight.

Production AIA radar would be installed on subsequent aircraft and a total of thirty-four F4U-2s were converted, thirty-two at the factory and two field modifications completed by VMF(N)-532.[82] Thirty-two of the aircraft had the bird cage canopy while the two field-modified F4U-2s had the clear bubble canopy.

BuNo 02153 was flown from the NAF to Quonset Point on January 7, 1943, for the formation of the first Navy night-fighter squadron, VF(N)-75.[83] LCdr W. J. Widhelm was the commanding officer of VF(N)-75 and the squadron was commissioned on April 1, 1943.[84] The squadron was split into two units in August, the second unit becoming VF(N)-101. The two squadrons were equipped with three aircraft each. In September VF(N)-75 began its deployment to the Pacific theater with six aircraft. On October 2, 1943, VF(N)-75 arrived at Munda, New Georgia, becoming the "first and only Naval night-fighter squadron to be land-based; but was also the nucleus of the first carrier-based nightfighter squad-ron."[85]

The pilots and squadron personnel who remained behind at NAS Quonset Point formed the Navy's second night-fighter squadron, VF(N)-101, which was commissioned aboard the USS *Enterprise* on January 16, 1944, with LCdr R. E. Harmer as commanding officer. VF(N)-101 consisted of four F4U-2s crewed by seven night qualified pilots. VF(N)-101 flew missions during the Truk, Hollandia, and Palau raids as well as in support of the occupation of the Marshall Islands. From January through July, 1944, pilots of VF(N)-101 scored 5 confirmed, 4 damaged, and 1 probable kill. The squadron was disbanded at Pearl Harbor in July 1944.

Commissioned on the same day as VF(N)-75, Marine night-fighter squadron VMF(N)-532 with Capt. Ross S. Mickey as commanding officer began training at MCAS Cherry Point, North Carolina. Under new commanding officer Maj. Everett H. Vaughan, VMF(N)-532 arrived at Tarawa on January 13, 1944, and immediately began night CAPs.

VF(N)-75 drew first blood with a Navy radar-equipped nightfighter. During the night of October 31–November 1, 1943, Lt. H. D. O'Neill was vectored toward an enemy aircraft, and he was able to find it on his radar scope at a distance of 12 miles at an altitude of 10,000ft. O'Neill destroyed the Japanese G4M Betty bomber off Vella Lavella Island.[86]

The USMC's first three night-fighter kills occurred on the night of April 13-14, 1944, when aircraft from VMF(N)-532 based on Engebi, Eniwetok Atoll, Marshall Islands, intercepted a group of Japanese night raiders. Lt. Joel E. "Pete" Bonner made the first interception of the night when he was vectored toward a Betty at 20,000ft. Bonner fired from point blank range into the bomber's starboard wing. The Betty went down in flames, but not before its gunners had hit Bonner's Corsair with return fire. Bonner attempted to return to Engebi but was forced to bail out of his F4U-2 at 6,000ft. He was rescued later the following day by a destroyer escort after being spotted in his raft by a B-25 crew.[87]

Also on April 13–14, Lt. Edward A. Sovik made the climb from the Engebi runway to 20,000ft in 10 minutes and was able to acquire, track, and destroy the enemy aircraft within 4 minutes. Finally, Capt. Howard W. Bollmann destroyed a Betty on the same night.[88]

In his postmission debriefing, Bollmann said, "I had just returned to my tent after flying CAP from 2100 to 2400 and was getting ready to hit the sack when the command car driver came to pick up Lieutenant Frank C. Lang. He (the driver) told me that there was to be an alert so I rode to the line with Lieutenant Lang, not intending to fly but to help out on the ground. As we arrived at the line, Lieutenant Edward Spatz took off (April 14, 0025 hours) and Lang took off shortly afterward. I stood by the phone as Lieutenant Edward A. Sovik, the Duty Officer, was busy elsewhere. About this time the sirens sounded and at 0038 hours the phone rang, requesting another fighter.

I ran out and scrambled in F4U-2 212 at about 0045 hours, just in time to hear Lieutenant Bonner announce that he was ready to jump. I tested my guns immediately after takeoff; all were okay so I kept on all switches but master gun.

"I was vectored 270 degrees to Angels 20. When I had reached 20 miles from base, I orbited once in my climb and reached Angels 20 immediately. As soon as I reported 'level' I was given a customer, 'vector 260'; approximately a minute later I picked up a contact at 3 1/2 miles ahead. It soon became obvious that we were on opposite courses and at about 2 miles I commenced a hard starboard 180 degree turn, informing controllers of my actions. I turned a bit past 180 to 100 degrees to get back on my original track and immediately picked up the bogey at 2 1/2 miles, azimuth 30 left above; turned astern of target on course 080 degrees.

"I informed controllers I still had contact and they left me as they had two more fighters to watch. I closed rapidly to 1/2 mile while climbing to target's Angels 22. At a half mile, I slowed to speed of target to plan my attack; there was a white cloud base below and I had no desire to be seen against it. The moon was between one and two o'clock and 15 to 20 degrees elevation. I played with the idea of getting above the target so as to see him against the clouds but was afraid he might be lost under a wing or nose of my plane, so I decided to come in at his altitude and five or ten degrees on the down-moon side of the target. After checking my gun switches, I added speed and crept up on target—as I was about ten degrees off, the sight position was inoperative and I used search all the way—and at 300 yards I looked up and saw target exactly where he should have been. I immediately speeded up and closed very rapidly; opened fire at 150ft dead astern and 15ft below, aiming at his right wing root.

"I was startled by the lack of tracers—had the feeling that my bullets were going astray—and fired less than two seconds, but the starboard engine was smoking. I then transferred aim to port and after another two-second burst, I observed flame and smoke on the port engine. At first I mistook white flashes from my incendiaries to be return fire and instinctively ducked behind my engine; however, at no time did I receive return fire."[89]

Recalling the engagement, Bollmann said, "I think that was the first time I ever fired the guns at night. I was used to tracers from day fighters and I thought the guns weren't working. Later on we put tracers in, but the idea was then that tracers would hurt your night vision.

"By this time the target was in a 15deg nose-down attitude and I nearly rammed him. Employing what might be termed an outside snap roll to avoid him, I pulled around to one side and above to observe the plane; from this position it appeared that the flame had blown out so I gave him another short burst from 20deg above and astern 100 yards. Fifteen seconds later, he broke into two pieces and dropped to earth in flames."[90]

Beginning June 30, VMF(N)-532 began using the F4U-2's radar in the mapping mode for night-bombing missions, the first target being Wotje Atoll. The nightfighters would follow the radar fix to the island, pick out a surface feature, and then head for the target. VMF(N)-532 pilot Frank Lang said, "We would pick a night where we had some light available to make out the island itself when we got close enough. We had targets that were marked for us that we would go in after: night harassment tactics."[91]

The mapping mode also enabled the Corsair to take off in the dark of night and arrive over a target at daybreak. "There was an Air Force pilot down off Pagan Island [half-way up the Marianas chain 100 miles north of Saipan]," said Bollman. "The weather was poor and they were sending a rescue destroyer up there. I took another guy, I think it was H. E. 'Carl' Withey, we went up to the islands to cover for them at dawn. In fact we flew up there at about 3:00 in the morning. We were in clouds the whole way, and we were able to use our mapping gear on the radar to find the island, 150 or so miles away, and find the coordinate where we were told the destroyer would be. We came on down through the clouds at about an 800ft ceiling and we were right on top of the destroyer. I thought it was a pretty good thing. It was the first time to my knowledge that we used mapping for anything."[92]

VMF(N)-532 Corsairs on Saipan. Lt. Howard W. Bollman scored a kill in Number 212, left, on the evening of April 14, 1944. Bollman downed a Mitsubishi Betty bomber in the engagement. Maita via Garry R. Pape

After pioneering night-fighter tactics and proving the ability of single-seat, single-engine nightfighters, the F4U-2 was phased out of service by January 1945. Replacing the F4U-2 would be Grumman's F6F-3 and -5N Hellcats equipped with newer generation APS-4 and APS-6 airborne radar. The lessons learned by the pioneering Corsair nightfighters paid off handsomely during the Battle of Okinawa when Marine nightfighter squadrons VMF(N)-542, -543, and -533, flying F6F Hellcats, destroyed sixty-eight Japanese aircraft.

The radar-equipped F4U-2 led the way for the Navy's World War II nightfighter program and also proved that the Corsair and airborne intercept radar a compatible match, paving the way for the successful F4U-5 and F4U-5NL, which were flown in the Korean War.

516

Chapter 6

XF4U-3: Proposed High-Altitude Interceptor

Increased top speed and high-altitude performance was the goal of the XF4U-3, Vought Sikorsky proposal VS-331. Under the direction of contract Number 198, Lot One, Item Four, two F4U-1As were to be modified with larger, more powerful engines, turbochargers, four-blade Hamilton Standard Hydromatic propellers, torque-meters, and redesignated XF4U-3s. Each F4U-1A cost $98,385.96 and Chance Vought was awarded another $98,884.93 to complete the conversions to XF4U-3 configuration.

The most visible external difference of the XF4U-3 was its four-blade Hamilton Standard propeller and the turbocharger's large air-intake scoop located on the aircraft centerline just ahead of the lower cowl flaps. The -3 was the only Corsair model equipped with a turbocharger, but all subsequent model Corsairs delivered were equip-ped with the four-blade propeller.

Plans called for the installation of Pratt & Whitney XR-2800-16 engines and Birmann-type turbochargers in both aircraft. At military power, the turbo-supercharged XR-2800-16 could develop 2,000 continuous horsepower from sea level all the way to 25,000ft, whereas the F4U-1's water-injected R-2800-8W which, at military power, could only deliver 1,650hp at 22,500ft.[93]

The first of the two Corsairs to be converted, BuNo 17516, would receive the XR-2800-16. This aircraft, designated XF4U-3A, made its first flight on March 26, 1944, with Bill Horan at the controls.[94]

The XF4U-3's XR-2800-16 and Birmann-type turbo-supercharger required the large air scoop below the engine cowling and modifications to the engine accessory compartment and lower fuselage. Although successful, the F4U-3 did not enter full-scale production. Vought Aircraft

Due to delivery delays of the XR-2800-16, Chance Vought suggested to the BuAer that the R-2800-14W turbo-supercharged engine be substituted for the XR-2800-16 and installed in the second XF4U-3, BuNo 49664, which was designated XF4U-3B.[95] The BuAer responded affirmatively on March 18, 1944, and committed two R-2800-14W engines and one XTT13-14 turbocharger to the second XF4U-3 conversion program. Chance Vought also installed a water injection system that used the outer wing panel tank for a water reservoir, and it planned to complete the conversion by August 1, 1944. XF4U-3B 49664 made its first flight on September 20, 1944. Engineering and labor costs for installing the government-furnished R-2800-14W engine and XTT13-14 turbocharger in 49664 came to an additional $39,401.03.[96] The water-injected R-2800-14W could develop 2,100hp, continuous, and 2,800hp, maximum, at 28,500ft at military power settings.[97]

Chance Vought notified the BuAer that the above quote contained more than 9,000 additional engineering man-hours that would be required for the preparation of reports on flight test, weight and balance, structural analyses, and other studies. This duplication of effort would not have been necessary had both XF4U-3s been flown with the same engine installations. New sets of installation drawings, roughly 80 hours of flight testing (included in the 9,000 hours), plus reports and analysis of those flights would also be required. The additional costs of the modifications and the XF4U-3's eventual flight characteristics would not affect the performance guarantees in Chance Vought's fixed-price plus fee contract.

In December 1942, the BuAer called for the addition of a third aircraft to the XF4U-3 program.[98] Authorization was granted on December 26, 1942, when an additional $18,776.08 was authorized for the work. Word of the approval was delivered to Chance Vought under Change Order O.

The third aircraft slated for conversion was F4U-1 BuNo 02157. The aircraft record card for 02157 bears the notation, "Will become XF4U-3." Less than four months later, before 02157 could be removed from the test program, it was converted to XF4U-3 configuration and crashed at the Chance Vought plant at Stratford.[99]

The BuAer canceled Change Order "O" on February 4, 1944, citing the fact that Contract 198 already had provisions for two XF4U-3s. Had the XF4U-3 program continued to be funded under the change order, the company would have been paid for the same work twice.[100]

Bill Horan said that turbo-supercharging "didn't affect the flying qualities of the aircraft any, except the performance was better at altitude. It was the same old airplane, but it could get you up there pretty high. I had it to 40,000ft and it still had plenty of climb left in it. At rated power at 39,000 or 40,000ft it came up to about 480mph. However, if you banked the airplane above 15deg, she would start to buffet. As the wings loaded up, it came to the edge of compressibility."[101]

When the F4U-1 and -1A were converted to XF4U-3s, the turbocharger

From the left three-quarter view, the XF4U-3 looks the same as a standard F4U-1 with the exception of the four-blade propeller. While the speeds of non-turbo Corsairs decreased at altitude, the turbo-supercharger enabled the XF4U-3 to attain speeds of 480mph at 40,000ft. Vought Aircraft

and intercoolers were located on the bottom of the auxiliary section on the aircraft's centerline, which created a bulge in the airframe. Horan thinks this might have upset the airflow, adding to the compressibility factor.[102] "Should compressibility have occurred, no matter what speed you traveled, you could always put the landing gear down. It wouldn't hurt the airplane a bit," Horan said. Deploying the landing gear would double the drag, quickly slowing the aircraft.

Horan was basically alone on the project, logging eighty-three flights between both aircraft. Chance Vought test pilots Charlie Sharp and Bob Blain also flew the XF4U-3s. Although he put the XF4U-3 through its paces, which resulted in mountains of flight test reports, Bill Horan characterized their flights as "more out of curiosity than anything else."[103]

XF4U-3A made its last flight at Chance Vought on March 29, 1945, and was subsequently turned over to the Navy for evaluation. The XF4U-3B followed three months later on June, 29, 1945.[104]

Goodyear delivered twenty-six turbo-supercharged versions of the FG-1D, designated FG-3, to the Navy at Johnsville between July 3 and 7, 1945.[105] Here the aircraft were test flown and maintained, presumably engaged in high-altitude test work. Two FG-3s, BuNos 92382 and 92383, were assigned to Patuxent River for electronics testing in July 1947. The last FG-3 was stricken from the Navy's inventory on July 31, 1949.[106]

Horan summed up the XF4U-3 program by saying, "It was a good project, but a back-burner project. . . . Even though it did improve the performance, I can understand why they did not build them because they would upset a line of aircraft that they needed badly for the war effort. And, at the time, considering all, you just could not beat the F4U-4." [107]

Two aircraft supported the turbo-supercharged Corsair program. Vought test pilot Bill Horan logged eighty-three flights in both proto-types. XF4U-3B BuNo 49664 was powered by a turbo-supercharged R-2800-14W radial engine. Vought Aircraft

414
NAV
81913

Chapter 7

F4U-4: The Ultimate Corsair

XF4U-4 BuNo 80759 was the first of what many pilots would call the "Ultimate Corsair." The F4U-4 benefited from all of the lessons learned early in World War II. The F4U-4 featured a four-blade propeller turned by the 2,100hp R-2800-18W water-injected engine capable of a maximum speed of 451mph. Vought Aircraft

Suggestions from the battle front in the South Pacific as well as engineering improvements at the factory, were constantly being incorporated into the basic F4U-1 airframe. More than 600 major changes had been made to the F4U-1 design by the time the F4U-1D began rolling down the assembly line. Vought engineers realized that if the Corsair design was to evolve further, it needed a complete overhaul. The opportunity for a redesign came in the spring of 1943.

While Vought was constructing the F4U-1D with the Pratt & Whitney R-2800-8W water-injected engine, the Navy was making plans to mate the F4U to the new water-injected 2,100hp R-2800-18W. The Navy figured this new engine-airframe combination, when mated to a four-blade propeller, would deliver the required performance needed to fight the changing war in the Pacific.

While awaiting the official permission to begin design changes, Vought engineers gathered their ideas for the new Corsair. On April 5, 1943, Vought requested that if the Navy planned to go ahead with this change, it order engines with down-draft carburetors due to the necessity of using a larger supercharger intercooler used on the more powerful new engine. At the same time, Vought requested that a new designation be given to the R-2800-18W-powered Corsairs.[108] Thus the F4U-4 was born. (Postwar F4U-4Bs were upgraded with the installation of the Pratt & Whitney R-2800-42W. This water-injected radial was capable of 2,300hp on takeoff.)

Initial F4U-4 engineering work began on May 20, 1943, as Vought proposal V-354. The Navy modified Vought's contract to build the F4U-1, Contract Number 198, under Amendment Number 58 to include the conversion of two F4U-1As into F4U-4 prototypes. Cost of the conversions was estimated to be $219,623.01, plus a 6 percent fixed fee of $13,177.38, for a total cost of $232,800.39.[109] The actual price of the conversions escalated to $370,441.23 plus the original fixed fee.[110]

Two F4U-1As, BuNos 49763 and 50301, were selected to become the pro-

L-414 is an F4U-4 Corsair (BuNo 81913) belonging to VF-74, commanded by Cdr. C. D. Fonvielle, Jr., and embarked on USS Bon Homme Richard *(CVA-31) on the carrier's Korean combat cruise which lasted from May 10, 1951, to December 17, 1951. The aircraft is being hoisted with a full load of bombs, a somewhat inconvenient way of moving the gull-wing bird around the deck. VF-74 was part of CVG-7, commanded by Cdr. G. B. Brown.* Gene Conrad via Robert F. Dorr

The F4U-4X was a modified F4U-1A BuNo 49763 that was used to prove the feasibility of the F4U-4 powerplant-airframe match-up. The F4U-4X, two aircraft, were converted F4U-1As, while the XF4U-4, five aircraft, were prototypes constructed to F4U-4 standard from the outset. The air-intake scoop was moved to the cowling chin on the F4U-4. Vought Aircraft

totype F4U-4s. Both aircraft were given the nonstandard designations of F4U-4X (sometimes referred to as F4U-4XA and F4U-4XB respectively), denoting the fact that they were to be used to prove the F4U-4 powerplant concept. These proof of concept aircraft incorporated fifteen major modifications that would make up the nucleus of the F4U-4: a new engine mount for the R-2800-18W, which would retain the original firewall attach points; a four-blade propeller; redesigned engine exhaust outlets; a new ducting arrangement for the down-draft carburetor and enlarged intercooler intakes; completely new firewall forward engine accessory compartment; a Jack and Heintz JH4-NER electric starter system and additional battery capacity plus an external power receptacle replaced the Breeze Type III starter cartridge system; a new 21.5gal oil tank capable of sustained inverted flight under negative G loads; new fuel system with rerouted and enlarged fuel lines; a single tank for water injection; hydraulic system modifications; new electrical system from the firewall forward; redesigned cowl assemblies to accommodate the R-2800-18W; revised upper and lower air duct panels, intercooler support ribs; a fire extinguisher system; and additional flight test instruments requiring the installation of a new instrument panel.[111]

Vought test pilot Boone Guyton made the first flight in F4U-4X BuNo 49763 on April 19, 1944.

In an effort to increase the fuel capacity of the F4U-4X, experimental non-droppable wing-tip tanks were fitted to F4U-4X 50301 for a short series of flights. "I flew it with the wing tanks on," Vought test pilot Bill Horan said of the installation. "You couldn't tell the difference [in comparison with the standard F4U-4]." The tanks were deemed unnecessary, so the project was soon halted.

Aeromatic Aircraft Propellers, a subsidiary of the Koppers Company's Bartlett Hayward Division, was asked by the BuAer to make a preliminary design study of mating a six-blade contra-rotating propeller to the Corsair. Aeromatic asked Vought to provide it with the general outline of the cowling and fore and aft location of the cowling in relation to the propeller shaft; the maximum permissible propeller diameter; the requirements for a propeller spinner; altitude performance; and the specifications for a propeller deicing system.[112] This system was installed and successfully tested on one of the F4U-4Xs. The propeller gear boxes were a constant problem and were

thought to be unreliable for air-to-air combat. Any gain in performance was offset by the maintenance problems of such a complicated system. Like many other wartime attempts to increase the aircraft's performance, this was not adopted.

Preproduction tests of the F4U-4X aircraft showed that the R-2800-18W and the Corsair airframe were compatible. The R-2800-18W engine mated to the Corsair airframe produced a maximum speed in the 445mph range at higher altitudes than the F4U-1/R-2800-8W combination. These test aircraft produced the results the Navy was looking for.

F4U-4 Production Begins

Based on the Navy's future needs, and before the first flight of the preproduction prototype F4U-4Xs, Vought was awarded Contract Number 2720 for production F4U-4s on January 25, 1944. Five production prototypes were constructed, BuNos 80759–80763.

The first production F4U-4 made its first flight on September 20 and was accepted by the Navy on October 31, 1944. The combination of the R-2800-18W radial engine driving a 13ft, 1in Hamilton Standard four-blade propeller brought the F4U-4's maximum speed to 451mph.[113] The F4U-4's new propeller delivered increased thrust, which the F4U-4 a faster rate of climb and a shorter takeoff roll. The F4U-4's propeller was actually 2in shorter in diameter than those used on the F4U-1s.

Installation of the F4U-4's new R-2800-18W engine required significant changes to the aircraft. The intercooler area was increased from 2,090ci in the F4U-1 to 2,688ci. This change is significant because a larger volume of air was now being channeled in through the wing scoops to cool the compressed fuel-air mixture before it was fed into the auxiliary stage blower (the high-altitude or second stage of the supercharger), which makes the mixture more dense, allowing the engine to maintain its rated horsepower at higher altitudes. New cockpit engine controls were installed, which included automatic oil cooler and engine cowl flaps. The air-intake scoop was relocated to the lower engine cowl. The engine cowl was redesigned to allow easier access for repairs and maintenance as well as improved aerodynamic efficiency. The F4U-4 was also equipped with the Jack and Heintz electric starter, which allowed for quick starts without an external power source.

The F4U-4's fuel system was also changed. In place of the early F4U-1's 237gal fuselage tank plus one 57gal tank in each outer wing panel, the F4U-4 carried a 230gal fuselage tank supplemented by drop tanks on the stub wing pylons of either 100, 150, 154, or 170gal capacity.

The water injection system contained a single 13.5gal tank in the F4U-4. In the F4U-4, the WEP safety is bypassed by moving a switch accessible with the thumb on the throttle handle.

F4U-4X BuNo 50301 was fitted with tip tanks to increase the fuel load and range. This modification never made it into production. Vought Aircraft

Many pilots had trouble climbing onto the wing to get to the cockpits of the raised-tail F4U-1s, so in the redesign of the F4U-4, cockpit access was improved with the incorporation of a step in the starboard center section inner flap. This new step system allowed for the deletion of the nonskid walkway on the upper surface of the wing center section, which improved the airflow over the wing surface, increasing the F4U-4's speed by an additional 3mph.[114] The pilot's seat was divided into two sections: a lower pan and an armored seat back. Both moved as one unit for pilot comfort and visibility. The armored seat back was hinged, swinging down into the cockpit and allowing the mechanic access to the radio shelf without having to climb into the belly of the aircraft and then up behind the cockpit wall. A floor was added to the F4U-4's cockpit, in place of the foot channels in the earlier models, to prevent tools or other items from being dropped into the belly of the Corsair where they couldn't be retrieved and would shower the pilot during inverted flight. The flooring also protected the pilot from hydraulic fluid baths if a line was shot out or ruptured. The rudder pedals were raised 10in in the F4U-4 to make the seating position more com-

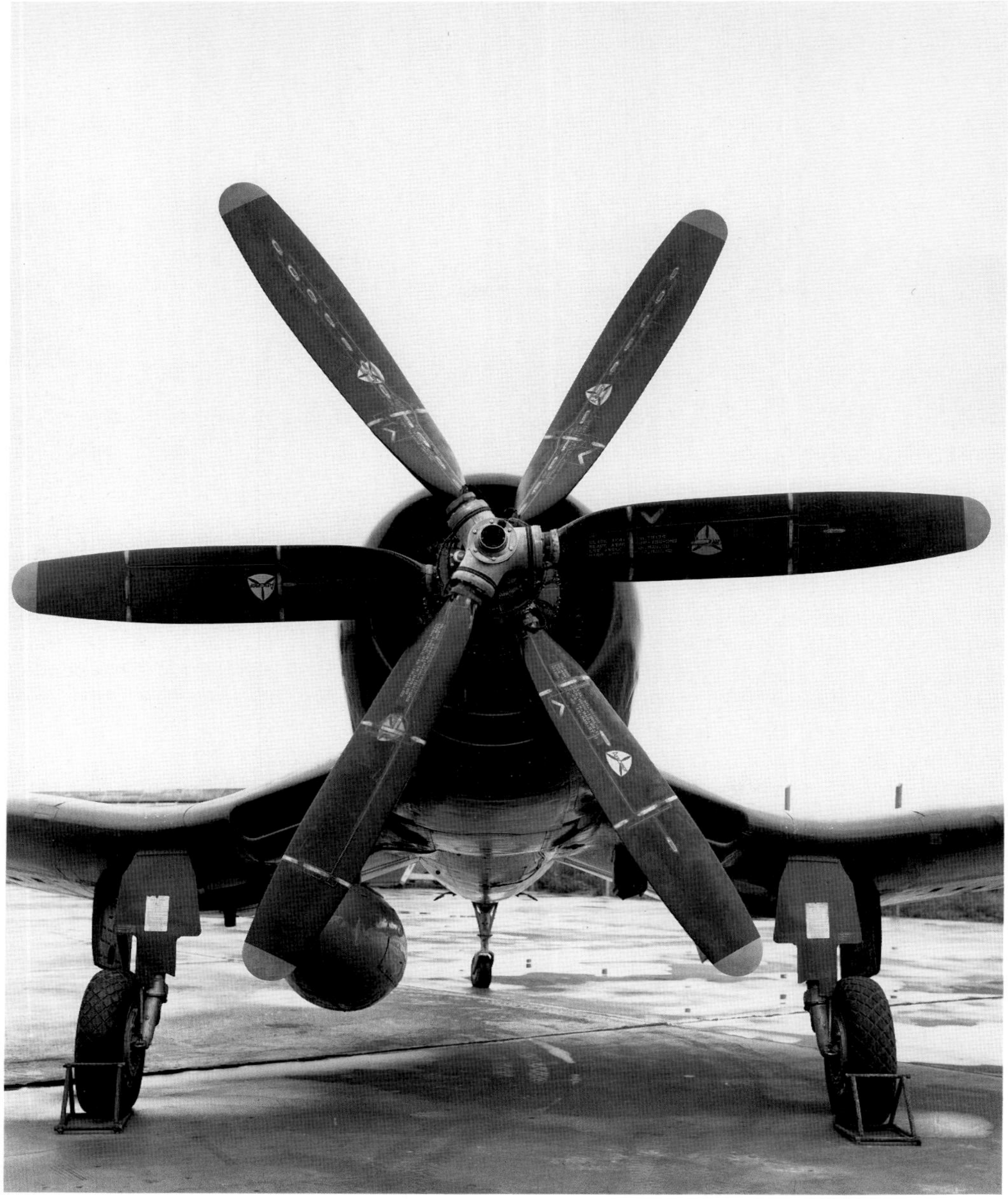

Engineering work was begun in October 1943 for an experimental F4U-4 with counter-rotating propellers. Designed to increase speed and climb performance over the F4U-1, the aircraft was tested but its performance did not exceed the new F4U-4's by a large amount, so the project was dropped. Vought Aircraft

fortable, and the control stick was shortened by raising its pivot point 18in, reducing the stick's interference with the pilot's legs during full-deflection maneuvers.

The F4U-4 featured a console-type cockpit. In the F4U-1 each control was mounted in its own box on the cockpit side walls, whereas, in the F4U-4, each side wall had "control shelves" with horizontal and vertical panels. The left shelf housed the controls for the fuel tank selector valves, landing gear, arrester hook, and flap levers. The right-hand console was devoted to electrical and radio installations as well as the circuit breaker box. The right-hand console could be removed as one unit and quickly replaced if necessary, eliminating down time while troubleshooting electronic problems. Instrumentation on the main panel was regrouped, centering around the artificial horizon, to reduce pilot fatigue. F4U-4s from BuNos 81759–81778, 81829, and subsequent incorporated flat bulletproof windscreens.

Goodyear Version of the F4U-4

The BuAer had contracted with Goodyear to build the F4U-4 under the designation FG-4. Goodyear had begun construction of the first FG-4s when the Japanese surrendered on August 14, 1945. All 2,371 FG-4s ordered were canceled and the seventeen aircraft under construction were scrapped on the assembly line.[115]

F4U-4B

The need for upgraded offensive firepower brought about the model change to the F4U-4B. Previously the F4U-4B has been reported as an export version, such as the F4U-1B built for the RN. Also, the cannon-equipped model of the F4U-4 has been reported as the F4U-4C with a reported 300 built as such. After a thorough search of the Records of Aircraft History Cards, the F4U-4 pilot's manual, and other sources, the authors have determined that no F4U-4Cs appeared in the Navy's inventory, thus the 297 20mm cannon-equipped F4U-4Bs built are the 300 aircraft referred to as F4U-4Cs.

The -4's six .50cal machine guns and 2,400 rounds of ammunition were replaced in the F4U-4B with four M3 20mm cannons and 984 rounds. The external stores load remained the same as the F4U-4: eight 5in rockets, two 1,000lb bombs, or two 11.75in rockets. A number of F4U-4Bs were modified to launch and control a single radar-guided BAT glide bomb, the world's first operational homing missile. The BAT bomb was successfully tested in combat on April 23, 1945, when one of the glide bombs was launched from a PB4Y-2 Privateer of VPB-109 against shipping targets in Balikpapan Harbor, Borneo. Although the bomb was test launched and directed from F4U-4Bs after World War II, it was never used in combat again.

F4U-4Bs BuNo 97486 and later, constructed after August 16, 1946, were built with the R-2800-42W engine. Although similar to the R-2800-18W, the -42W developed higher performance ratings with 115/145 octane fuel.

This F4U-4B has been modified to launch and direct the BAT glide bomb shown on the centerline hardpoint. The BAT bomb, a bomb with a wooden wing and tail structure attached, would receive radio signals from the controlling aircraft capable of making slight changes to the bomb's trajectory. The BAT bomb was used against targets with extremely heavy antiaircraft fire concentrations. Note that the aircraft still carries eight 2.75in rockets in addition to the BAT bomb. This F4U-4B is in the hangar at the Naval Aviation Ordnance Test Station, Chincoteague, Virginia. Campbell Archives

N-F4U-4

During the post-war transition, a number of F4U-4s assigned to Naval Reserve units were given the N-F4U-4

Beautiful in-flight study of N-F4U-4 BuNo 81667 from Naval Reserve Air Base, Oakland, California, circa 1947. William T. Larkins

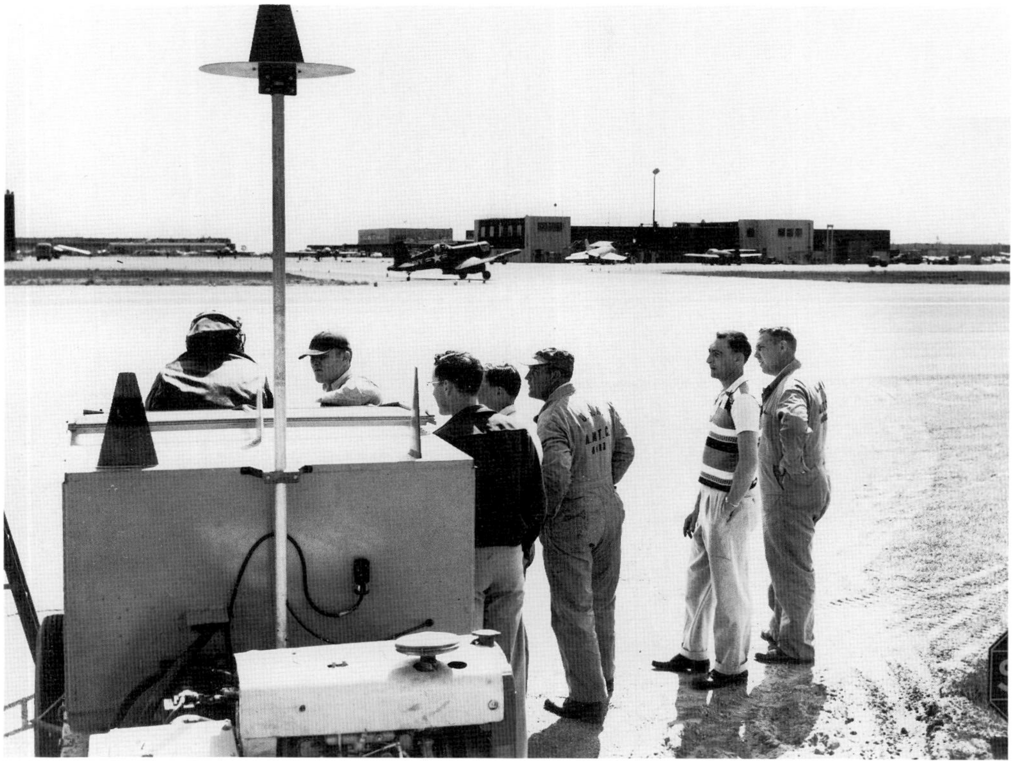

After being phased out of the fleet, a number of Corsairs were used as drones. This March 1956 photo shows the launch cart and the departure of the first unmanned Corsair drone at NAS Pt. Mugu. The F4Us met an undignified death as aerial targets for new generations of air-to-surface missiles. US Navy

designation denoting their training role. This designation only appeared on a limited number of aircraft while the Navy went through the process of sizing down its aircraft and the roles they performed.

F4U-4N

The F4U-4N was an F4U-4 with an updated APS-6 radar suite, which was

F4U-4 on display with the armament used in World War II: six .50cal machine guns, eight 2.75in rockets, one 11.75in Tiny Tim rocket on the starboard center wing hard point, and one 150gal napalm bomb on the port center wing hard point. Campbell archives

A factory fresh F4U-4B with two 11.75in Tiny Tim Rockets on the center wing hard points. Employed first during the Battle of Okinawa, the Tiny Tim weighed 1,200lb and carried a 150lb warhead of TNT. The Tiny Tim had a range of about a mile. Tiny Tim's were used extensively in Korea. Vought Aircraft

a vastly improved unit that was based on the AIA radar in the F4U-2. BuNo 97361, the sole F4U-4N, was accepted on March 3, 1946, and was retained at Stratford for testing. The standard F4U-4 armament of six .50cal machine guns and eight zero length rocket rails, four under each wing, was retained. In May 1947, 97361 was transferred to Electronic Test at NAS Patuxent River, Maryland. Eight months later, 97361 was assigned to the aircraft pool at Cherry Point, South Carolina. It served only three months before being stricken in March 1948. The F4U-4N served as a test bed for the later F4U-5N and -5NL Corsairs.

Photo Four: F4U-4P

Twelve F4U-4s were equipped with K-25 aerial cameras to allow them to take low-level poststrike reconnaissance photos.[116] These armed-reconnaissance Corsairs carried the K-25 in a rubber, shock-absorbing mount in the belly baggage compartment access door. The F4U-4P was fitted with a 90 degree lens prism, which enabled the pilot to fire rockets, strafe, or drop bombs, and then activate the camera during pull out to record the damage done by his and previous attacking aircraft.

During Korea, the twelve F4U-4Ps built served with VC-61 and VC-62. VC-61 had aircraft detachments aboard the USS *Valley Forge* from July 3 through November 23, 1950; and the USS *Philippine Sea* from August 1 to March 28, 1951. VC-62 flew F4U-5Ps from USS *Leyte* from October 9, 1950, to January 19, 1951.

The F4U-4Ps saw extensive combat in Korea. On February 20, 1951, Lt. Bernard F. McDermott of VC-61, detached to CAG-2, was on a low-altitude reconnaissance 10 miles inland from Wonsan Harbor, Korea, in F4U-4P 97527, when he took light antiaircraft fire in his oil cooler. The F4U-4P, not equipped with an oil cooler shut off, lost oil pressure as the remaining oil leaked overboard. McDermott immediately headed for the coast and friendly shipping. Upon reaching Wonsan Harbor the engine quit. He ditched, boarded his life raft, and was immediately rescued by a small boat from the destroyer USS *Lind*.[117]

The F4U-5P was phased out of front line service by mid-1951 in favor of the faster jet-powered Grumman F9F-2P.

F4U-4s in World War II

The F4U-4 made its combat debut during the opening shots of the Battle of Okinawa. Okinawa is a 60-mile-long island located 300 miles from the Japanese mainland. An estimated 80,000 loyal Japanese troops defended this stepping stone to Japan with a vengeance, and some of the worst fighting of the war would take place here. At this point in the war, the make-up of the carrier's air groups was being changed, gone were the squadrons of single-purpose dive and torpedo bombers. They were replaced with -1D Corsairs flown in the fighter-bomber role and the new F4U-4s in the fighter role.

F4U-4s and the new cannon equipped F4U-4Bs flew into combat for the first time on April 7, 1945. While launching Corsairs of MAG-31 from the decks of the escort carriers USS *Sitkoh Bay* (CVE-86) and USS *Breton* (CVE-23), a Japanese Kawasaki Ki-48 Lily bomber on a Kamikaze mission was reported 10 miles from the carriers at an altitude of 500ft. The Corsairs engaged the Lily, firing into the bomber's engines and fuselage. Five pilots from VMF-311 riddled the bomber with 20mm cannon fire. Although heavily damaged, the Lily continued its attack on the *Sitkoh Bay*. About 50 yards from the ship, the Lily's starboard wing failed, and the bomber crashed short of the carrier.[118] During the two days of April 6 and 7, 1945, the Japanese hurtled 355 Kamikaze attacks at the American fleet off the island's coast.[119] From April 6 though June 22, the Japanese sent an estimated 1,900 Kamikaze attacks against the fleet supporting the invasion of Okinawa.

Corsairs spent the remaining 100

F4U-4 Number 17 of VF-74 misses the wires and attempts to go around, but lands in the water on the port side of the carrier on March 19, 1946. Vought Aircraft via Jim Sullivan

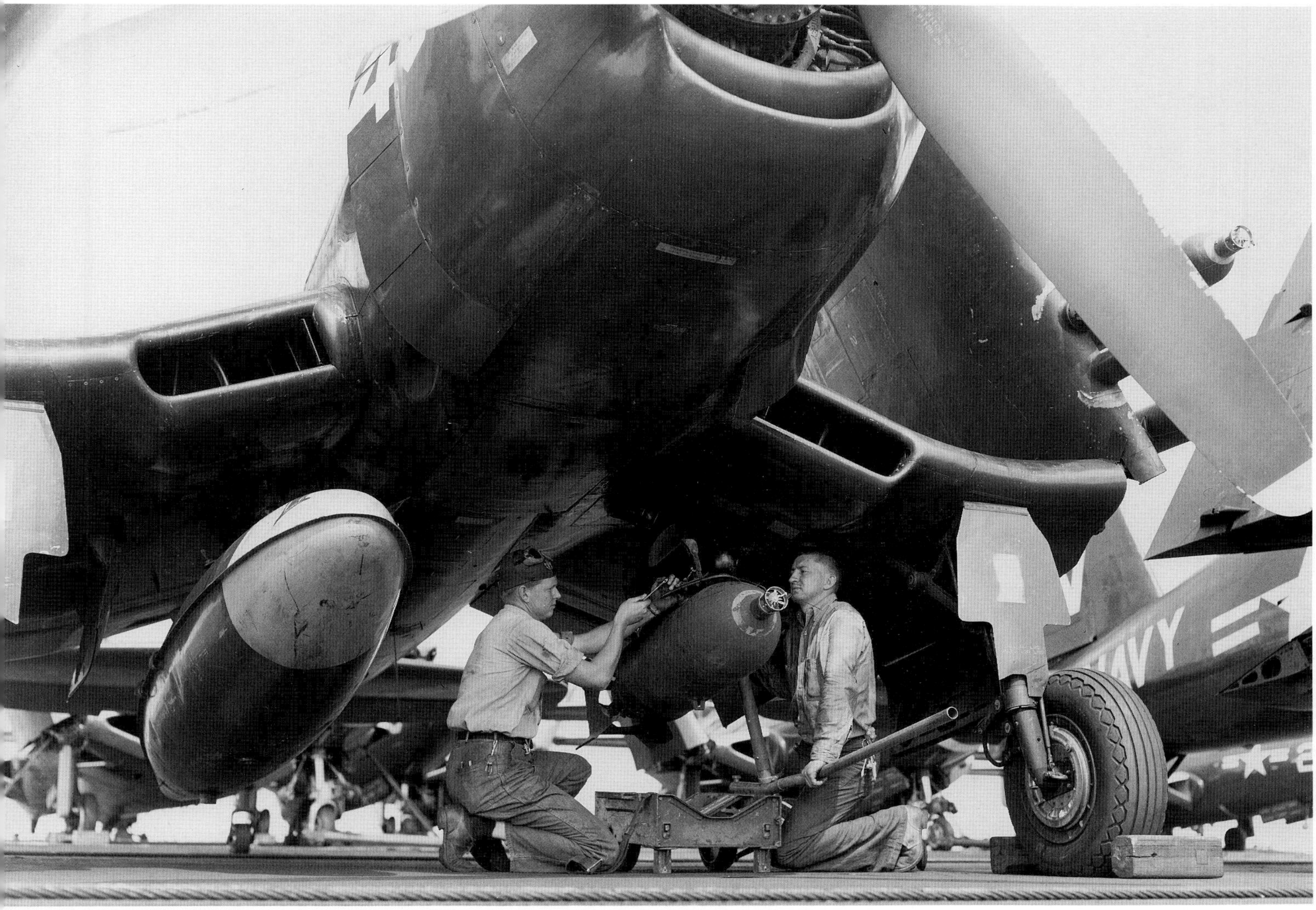

days of the war in the skies over the Japanese home islands from Tokyo south, raining destruction on the Japanese. The Corsairs also intercepted and repelled hundreds of Kamikaze attacks. From April 1 to July 1, combined Allied forces lost 763 aircraft—384 to enemy antiaircraft fire, 74 in air-to-air combat with Japanese aircraft, and 305 during takeoff, landing, or destroyed on the ground. The Japanese lost 7,800 aircraft either in the air or on the ground.[120]

Marine F4U-4s in China

Civil war in China began in 1927 as Chiang Kai-shek's Nationalist forces fought against Chinese forces. When the fighting was interrupted by the Japanese invasion of mainland China in 1937, the Chinese turned from fighting each other to attempting to repel the Japanese army. After the Japanese surrender, the United States sent Marines in to assist Chiang Kai-shek's Nationalist Chinese government in disarming the remaining Japanese soldiers as well as to aid in stabilizing the region.

Communist Chinese forces seized the opportunity to fill the power vacuum left by the defeated Japanese and quickly renewed their efforts to overthrow the Nationalist Chinese government. The USMC was sent to the country in an attempt to assist the Nationalist Chinese in keeping open the supply routes and lines of communications.

Marine Air Wing One arrived on October 6 with a headquarters squadron flying the Convair OY-1 Sentinel, a cousin to the Army Air Forces' Stinson L-5, used for observation duties. On October 21, MAG-32 arrived at Tsangkon. MAG-32 was comprised of VMSB-343 flying Curtiss SB2Cs in the aerial reconnaissance role, and VMF-224 and VMF-311 flying F4U-4 Corsairs. Two days later, MAG-12 and MAG-24 arrived at Peking. MAG-12 brought the F4U-4s of VMF-323 and the night-fighting F4U-5Ns of VMF-542, while MAG-24 brought the F4U-4s of VMF-115 and VMF-211, and night-fighting Grumman F7F-2N Tigercats of VMF-533. MAG-25 arrived on October 28 to

D. O. Bray and L. A. Wigley mount a 500lb bomb to the port center wing hard point of an F4U-4 aboard the USS Philippine Sea *prior to a September 5, 1950, strike on Korea.* US Navy via Robert F. Dorr

provide transport assets to the Chinese and to the Marines. MAG-25's two squadrons of R4Ds, VMR-152 and VMR-253, and VMR-153 flying R5Cs were based at Tsingtao.

The Corsairs supported the Nationalist Chinese by flying cover for rail and truck convoys as well as ground-attack missions while the Marine transport airlifted the Nationalists.

Communist forces fought the Nationalist Chinese using guerrilla warfare tactics. Seeing very limited combat primarily in a ground-attack role, the Marines' aviation assets were withdrawn. MAW-1, MAG-32, and the transports of MAG-25 were pulled out of China in June 1946. The Corsairs of MAG-12 remained in China until September 1946. MAG-24 was the last Marine aviation unit to pull out of China in April 1947.

Less than two years later, in January 1949, the Nationalist Chinese were pushed out of Peking, and had to set up their government on the island of Formosa. Nine months later, in October 1949, the Communists set up the Chinese People's Republic.

F4U-4s in Korea

When the United States came to the aid of the South Koreans after the June 25, 1950, invasion by North Korean troops, the US Navy's primary fighter aircraft were the Grumman F9F Panther jet fighter and the F4U-4 and F4U-4B Corsair. The F4U-5N was the Navy's primary nightfighter.

The USS *Valley Forge* (CV-45) was the first US Navy carrier on station, arriving July 3, 1950, to begin operations against the North Koreans. *Valley Forge* had sailed from the Philippines

Top
An F4U-4B of VMA-323 after landing accident in Korea. Campbell archives

Center
An F4U-4 from USS Princeton *about to be lifted by crane to a waiting barge, then transferred to shore.* Robert A. Rice

Bottom
Even aboard ship they have to plow snow. Here crew members of the USS Philippine Sea *clear snow from around an F4U-4 off the coast of Korea.* Robert A. Rice

with CVG-5 (VF-51 and VF- 52 flying F9F-2s, VF-53 and VF-54 flying F4U-4Bs, VA-55 flying AD-2 Skyraiders, and VC-61 flying F4U-5Ps).

Corsairs were flown primarily in a ground-support role. The F4U-4's eight 5in rockets, two 1,000lb bombs, or two 11.75in rockets were capable of knocking out bridges and destroying fortified positions and enemy airfields. The Corsair was also used against shipping targets, either by strafing the small coast freighters or by dropping napalm bombs on them. During the second year of the war, the Corsairs mainly attacked troop concentrations and supply lines.

One of the most amazing actions of the Korean War occurred on January 15, 1951. Ens. Edward J. Hofstra, Jr., USN, of VF-64 aboard USS *Valley Forge* (CV-45) was strafing coastal roads when his F4U-4, BuNo 96865, struck the ground in a flat attitude, shearing off his belly tank, napalm bomb, and wing bombs. The engine was also stopped when the propeller made contact with the ground. Following impact, the Corsair bounced back into the air. The remaining inertia carried the aircraft about 1,000 yards, 500 yards out to sea. Hofstra was able to ditch the F4U-4 and get into his life raft. He was rescued by a RN Sunderland flying boat about three hours later.[121]

The only use of aerial torpedoes during the Korean War occurred on May 1, 1951. Eight Skyraiders and twelve Corsairs from USS *Princeton* attacked the Hwachon dam. The dam was breached, releasing a flood of water into the Pukhan River, which prevented the Communist forces from making an easy crossing.[122]

Corsair Bags a MiG

An F4U-4B was the first and only US Navy propeller-driven aircraft to

The propeller of an F4U-4 of VF-791 aboard the USS Boxer *creates a vapor trail on the takeoff roll for a July 6, 1950, raid over Korea.* US Navy via Robert F. Dorr

Lower three

F4U-4 BuNo 96771 veers off the deck of the USS Philippine Sea *on January 1, 1949. Things really start to go wrong as 96771 torque rolls to an inverted attitude and crashes into the drink. It is believed that the pilot survived the mishap.* National Archives via Jim Sullivan

score a kill over the North Korean MiG jets. Although slower than the Soviet-designed jet fighters, the Corsair could easily outmaneuver them, and Capt. Jesse Folmar did just that. Folmar and his wingman, Lt. W. L. Daniels of VMA-312, departed USS *Sicily* (CVE-118) on September 10, 1952, and were jumped by four MiGs, which attacked in pairs near the mouth of North Korea's Taedong River.

After avoiding the first pair of MiGs, Folmar squeezed off a 5-second burst of 20mm cannon fire as the second element passed by, pulling up into a climbing left turn. His 20mm cannon fire struck one of the MiGs, which began trailing black smoke. The MiG's pilot quickly ejected, sending the fighter into the sea below.

Four additional MiGs joined the fight as Folmar and Daniels began diving for the safety of the sea. Daniels was able to chase one MiG off Folmar's tail, but a second scored numerous 37mm cannon fire hits on his left wing The damage to Folmar's wing made the aircraft uncontrollable, so he was forced to bail out. Daniels called air-sea rescue and circled while Folmar floated down to the sea. Folmar was quickly rescued by an Air Force SA-16 Albatross and returned to duty.

Medal of Honor Winner

Lt. (j.g.) Thomas J. Hudner was the only Corsair pilot awarded the Medal o Honor during the Korean War. Hudne and Ens. Jesse L. Brown, the firs African-American commissioned Navy pilot, took off from the USS *Leyte* (CV 32) on the morning of December 4 1950, in company of two other VF-3 aircraft.

While attacking ground targets in

Top
An F4U-4 of VF-152 hits another F4U-4 of the same squadron aboard the USS Princeton *on February 12, 1953.* National Archives via Jim Sullivan

Lower two
F4U-4 BuNo 81792 with VF-75 aboard USS Franklin *ditches off the port side of the carrier. The pilot, Ensign Porter can be seen standing on the wing of 81792 after a successful crash landing at sea.* National Archives via Jim Sullivan

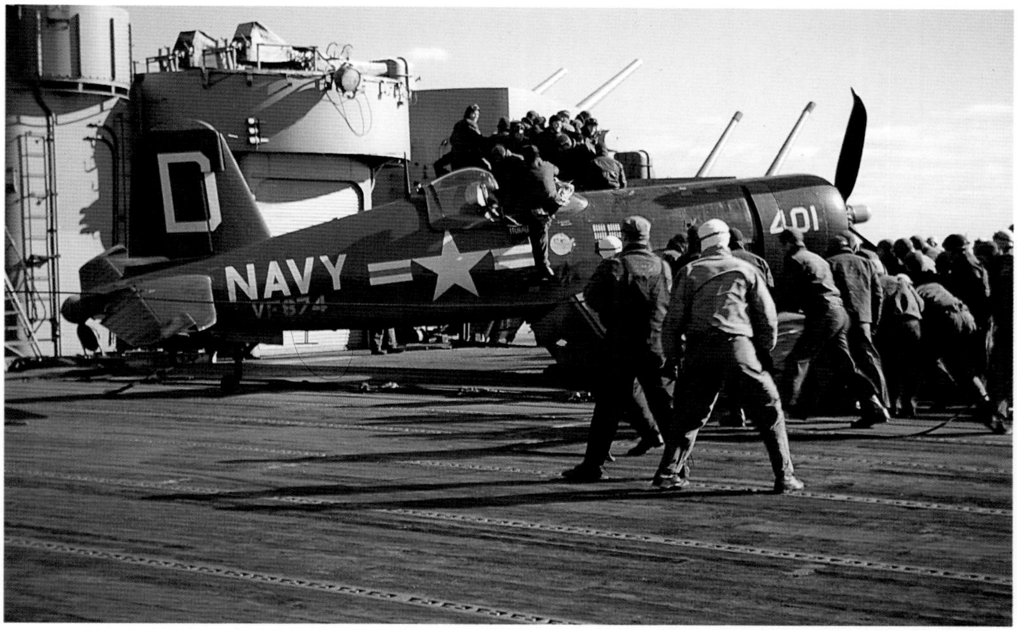

This F4U-4 Corsair belonging to VF-874 had to take the barrier on USS Philippine Sea *(CV-47), was wrenched abruptly around, and suffered a minor collision with the carrier's island. Damage is evident to the right horizontal stabilizer and to the propeller. Tightly cinched into his cockpit, the pilot was able to climb out and walk away, leaving plenty of work for the hard-pressed maintenance personnel on the ship.* William T. Barron via Robert F. Dorr

Wearing rare nose art which tells us that it's named Peggy, *this Vought F4U-4 Corsair belongs to Reserve squadron VF-783 from NAS Los Alamitos, California, and is returning from a combat mission in Korea. The squadron was called to active duty in August 1950 and wore the code letter* D *while operating as part of CVG-102. VF-783 was redesignated VF-122 when its carrier air group was redesignated CVG-12 during 1953.* William T. Barron via Robert F. Dorr

En route to a combat cruise in Korean waters aboard USS Princeton *(CV-37) which lasted from March 21 to November 3, 1952, CVG-19 under Capt. P. D. Stroop enjoyed a brief pause in Honolulu. Two Vought F4U-4 Corsairs from the group's fighter squadron VF-192 make a low-level pass over the Oahu shoreline and Hickam Field. Soon afterward, these Corsairs were flying air-to-ground sorties against the communists in Korea.* Gene Tissot via Robert F. Dorr

BuNo 97385, loaded with bombs and outboard 5in HVAR (high-velocity aircraft rockets) is ready to launch from USS Princeton *(CV-37) during the carrier's 1952 Korean combat cruise. During that cruise, the* B *tail code identified all of the squadrons of CVG-19. The group's two squadrons of F4U-4s were VF-192 (with 200-series modex numbers) and VF-193 (300-series). With no side number visible in this portrait, we can be certain only that the Corsair belonged to one of these two squadrons.* Gene Tissot via Robert F. Dorr

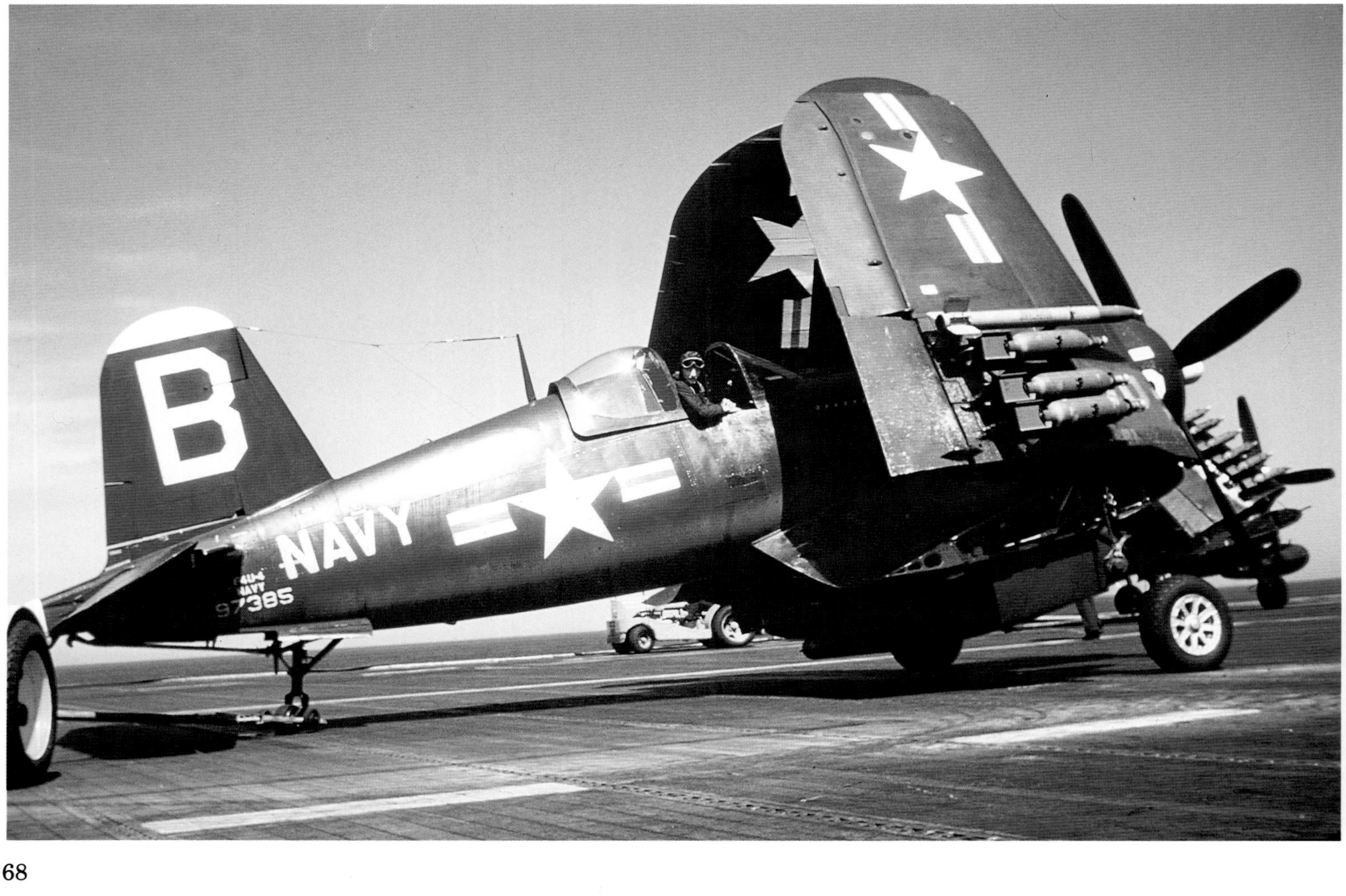

support of US troops, Brown's F4U-4 was struck by antiaircraft fire. Hudner and fellow VF-32 pilots watched as Brown belly-landed his Corsair behind enemy lines. Brown was visibly alive, but made no attempt to exit the Corsair's cockpit.

Hudner's Medal of Honor citation picks up the story: "Quickly maneuvering to circle the downed pilot and protect him from enemy troops infesting the area, Lt. (j.g.) Hudner risked his life to save the injured flier who was trapped alive in the burning wreckage. Fully aware of the extreme danger in landing on the rough mountainous terrain, and the scant hope of escape or survival in subzero temperature, he put his plane down skillfully in a deliberate wheels-up landing in the presence of enemy troops. With his bare hands, he packed the fuselage with snow to keep the flames away from the pilot and struggled to pull him free. Unsuccessful in this, he returned to his crashed aircraft and radioed other airborne planes, requesting that a helicopter be dispatched with an ax and fire extinguisher. He then remained on the spot despite the continuing danger from enemy action and, with the assistance of

Top
This air-to-air view of an F4U-4 Corsair belonging to VF-192 illustrates a typical weapons load for a 1952 Korean combat mission. The gull-winged bird carries a 1,000lb bomb on the left side of the centerline and a 360gal auxiliary drop tank under the right centerline. Under the wings, this Corsair carries six bombs, apparently 250lb in displacement, and a pair of outboard 5in rockets. Gene Tissot via Robert F. Dorr

Center
F4U-4 Corsairs of VF-192 aboard USS Princeton *(CV-37) during the Korean War.* Gene Tissot via Robert F. Dorr

Bottom
Oops! 5in rockets were intended to be fired at the enemy. This mishap with Ginger II *upon landing on USS* Bon Homme Richard *(CV-31) shows why pilots didn't like to bring the HVARs back to the boat. Both five-inchers have released from this F4U-4 of VF-783, part of CVG-102, and have plunked down on* Bonny Dick's *wooden surface. It was, unfortunately, a frequent occurrence.* Ron McMasters via Robert F. Dorr

This happened much too often and it could be fatal. A 5in rocket which was shaken loose, apparently from another Corsair during a hard carrier landing, lies just ahead of this F4U-4 Corsair taking the trap on the wooden deck of USS Princeton *(CV-37) in May 1953. It was so dangerous to land with HVARs still attached that pilots sometimes thought up excuses to jettison these rocket projectiles, even though each cost a couple of thousand dollars, a fortune at the time.* Tom Randall via Robert F. Dorr

F4U-4 Corsairs from VF-44, part of CVG-1 aboard USS Boxer *(CV-21) share the deck with "guppy" AD-4Q Skyraiders as they prepare for combat operations off the Korean coast in June 1953. During* Boxer*'s combat cruise beginning on March 30, 1953, and ending in the postwar era on November 28, 1953, the F4U-4s of VF-44 were joined by F4U-5N Corsairs from "Howe" detachment of VC-3. Though it had been designed to fight the Japanese in World War II, the propeller-driven Corsair was still in production at Vought's Dallas plant the year the Korean War ended.* Robert Edington via Robert F. Dorr

"Not all landings were perfect," remembers Ens. Richard E. "Dick" Brown, who flew F4U-4 Corsairs with reserve squadron VF-874 aboard USS Bon Homme Richard *(CV-31) during a Korean combat cruise that ran from May–December 1952. Statistics show that mishaps in and around the aircraft carrier caused as many aircraft losses as enemy action, but the landing gear on the Corsair was generally regarded as sturdy and not prone to accident.* Richard E. Brown via Robert F. Dorr

the rescue pilot, renewed a desperate but unavailing battle against time, cold, and flames. Lt. (j.g.) Hudner's exceptionally valiant action and selfless devotion to a shipmate sustain and enhance the highest traditions of the US

Midway through their 1950-1951 Valley Forge *cruise, F4U-4s of VF-64, part of CVG-2, suddenly acquired red propeller spinners. This F4U-4 is ready to taxi on the carrier's deck in Korean waters.* Bill Crouse via Robert F. Dorr

Naval Service."[123] Brown died, trapped in the cockpit of his downed Corsair.

The Ultimate Corsair

In all, Vought delivered five XF4U-4s, 2,042 F4U-4s, 297 cannon-equipped F4U-4Bs, one F4U-4N nightfighter, and twelve F4U-4Ps, for a total of 2,357 F4U-4s. Near the end of World War II, the BuAer had canceled orders for an additional 3,743 F4U-4s with BuNos 63072–63914, 105176–106875, and 114529–115728. Production was scaled back to complete the remaining uncanceled aircraft on contract.

Vought test pilot Bill Horan summed up the F4U-4 best by saying, "I think the F4U-4 was the best airplane that ever flew. The F4U-4 had everything. It was a goer. It had a good engine, good airplane. This airplane was without question the finest, the greatest and the best of the Corsair series. Ask anyone that has flown the F4U-5."[124]

Top
High over its target, an F4U-4 Corsair of VF-871 from Essex *forms a silhouette against a Korean background.* Bruce Bagwell via Robert F. Dorr

Lower two
Vought F4U-4 Corsairs of VF-871, from USS Essex *(CV-9), on a combat cruise in Korea.* Bruce Bagwell via Robert F. Dorr

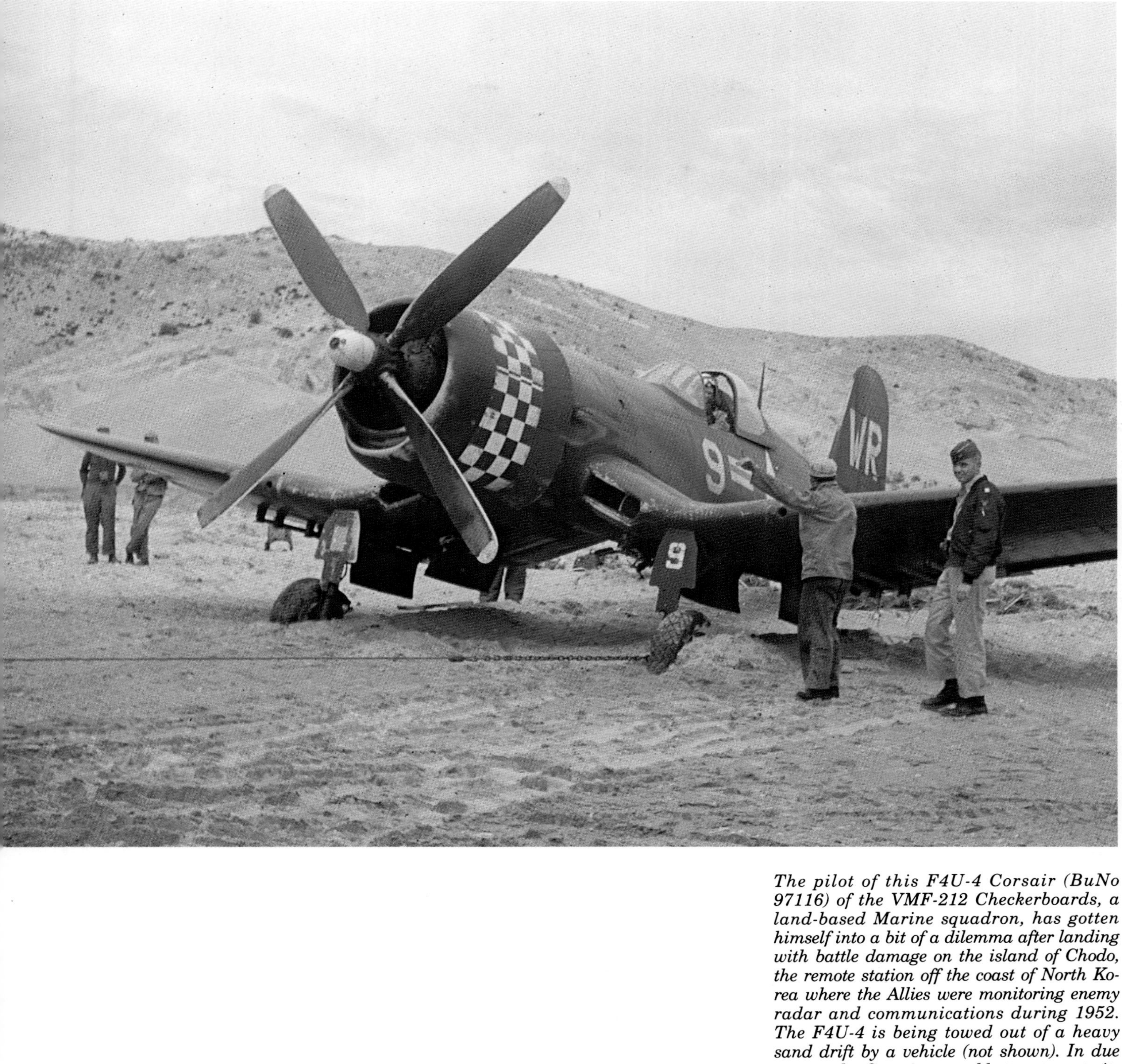

The pilot of this F4U-4 Corsair (BuNo 97116) of the VMF-212 Checkerboards, a land-based Marine squadron, has gotten himself into a bit of a dilemma after landing with battle damage on the island of Chodo, the remote station off the coast of North Korea where the Allies were monitoring enemy radar and communications during 1952. The F4U-4 is being towed out of a heavy sand drift by a vehicle (not shown). In due course, the Corsair was able to return to its base in South Korea. Franklin B. Love via Robert F. Dorr

Chapter 8

F2G: Goodyear's Corncob Corsair

Don Armstrong is at the controls of XF2G-1 BuNo 14691 on April 29, 1945, over Goodyear's Akron, Ohio, factory. Goodyear Aircraft via A. Kevin Grantham

After the successful conclusion of a series of tests with the proof of concept F4U-1WM, the Corsair Wasp Major program was turned over to Goodyear.

The BuAer Engineering Division, Fighter Design, drafted a letter of intent to contract on February 7, 1944, for the development of the F2G from the basic FG-1 Corsair. This letter, Directive 4705, assigned contract number 2971 to the F2G program.[125]

The F2G would be powered by a 3,000hp, twenty-eight cylinder Pratt & Whitney R-4360 Wasp Major engine and would feature a bubble canopy. The F2G-1 would be a land-based fighter while the F2G-2 would be a shipborne air-superiority fighter stressed to handle up to 4.7gs during a catapult launch.[126] The F2G was designed as a high-speed, fast-climbing air-superiority fighter to combat the Japanese Kamikaze threat.

On March 22, 1944, the BuAer issued a cost-plus-fixed-fee contract for the F2G. Contract Number 2971 specified a total cost of $39,094,097.12 for 418 aircraft.

It also stipulated that the first aircraft, BuNo 14691, be delivered, set up, and ready for flight at NAS Patuxent River, Maryland, in March 1945. Two more airplanes were to be delivered in April 1945; five each in May, June, July, and August; ten each in September, October, November, and December; and the balance of 355 aircraft were to be delivered in 1946 at a schedule to be agreed upon at a later date.

Publicity photo of Don Armstrong in front of an F2G-1 taken September 13, 1945, the day Goodyear was awarded the Army-Navy "E" for excellence. The Army-Navy "E" was awarded to less than 5 percent of US industries for meeting production and quality quotas. Don Armstrong

Aircraft performance specifications set out in the contract included a maximum speed of not less than 428mph for the F2G-1 and 426mph for the F2G-2, both at 16,500ft. Takeoff distance in a 25kt wind should not exceed 332ft for the F2G-1 and 323ft for the F2G-2. The F2G would also retain a high degree of interchangeability with the FG-1 and F4U-1.

Seventeen Goodyear-built aircraft would receive the XF2G or F2G designation: seven preproduction (XF2G-1 BuNos 13471, 13472, and 14691–4695), and ten production aircraft (F2G-1 BuNos 88454–88458 and F2G-2 BuNos 88459–88463).

The Goodyear flight-test department contributed nine aircraft that were involved in supporting the F2G project. The flight-test-support aircraft did not receive the XF2G or F2G desig-

Right side view of the Pratt & Whitney R-4360 Wasp Major engine. The Wasp Major was the largest piston engine ever to enter production. The R-4360 weighed in at 3,400lb and developed almost 1hp/lb of engine weight. The F2G-1's R-4360-4 featured a single-stage, variable-speed supercharger. Archives United Technologies Corporation

nation as each plane was given only specific F2G modifications, none of which alone brought the aircraft up to F2G configuration. For example, BuNo 12992 has been reported as an XF2G, but it was actually an FG-1A that had been stricken from the Navy's inventory and was used by Goodyear as a "shake test" airframe for static tests only, and BuNos 14091 and 14092 were both FG-1s that were modified with the F2G-style bubble canopy and cut down turtle deck. FG-1 BuNo 14091 was delivered to Goodyear on April 17, 1944, and was retained by Goodyear's flight test division for the duration of the proof of concept testing.[127] After modification and flight testing at Goodyear, BuNo 14092 was delivered to Anacostia NAS for Navy evaluation on October 11, 1944. BuNo 14092 was returned to Akron in February 1945 and was finally stricken from the Navy's inventory on November 30, 1945.[128] FG-1D, BuNo 13703, was assigned to Goodyear's flight test department for F2G weighted stability and spring tab tests before it was delivered to the Navy in September 1945.[129] BuNo 13374, also an FG-1D, flew as the F2G simulated scoop proof of concept ship.[130] Later, 13374 was used to test the single-disk-brake installation.[131] FG-1D, BuNo 13007, was employed as the preliminary spin demonstration aircraft.[132] Goodyear flight test employed British Corsair KD554 in the carbon monoxide tests. To check for firewall carbon monoxide leakage, smoke was forced from the engine accessory compartment into the cockpit under pressure. Any leaks were noted and corrected when the production aircraft were fume-proofed on the line.[133] FG-1 BuNo 13704 was used for brake testing and as the dive practice airplane. It was later turned over to the Navy. BuNo 14062 was flown to check the cooling characteristics of the engine and induction systems.[134]

BuNos 02312 and 02460 supported the R-4360 conversion at Pratt & Whitney.[135] The initial ground run of the XR-4360 engine mated to a F4U-1WM Corsair was completed on May 23, 1944.[136] Five months later, Pratt & Whitney was having trouble delivering the R-4360 engines to Goodyear due to production delays. On October 17, 1944, Goodyear sent a letter asking the BuAer to ensure the rapid delivery of engines so as to minimize the delay in obtaining F2G performance data.[137]

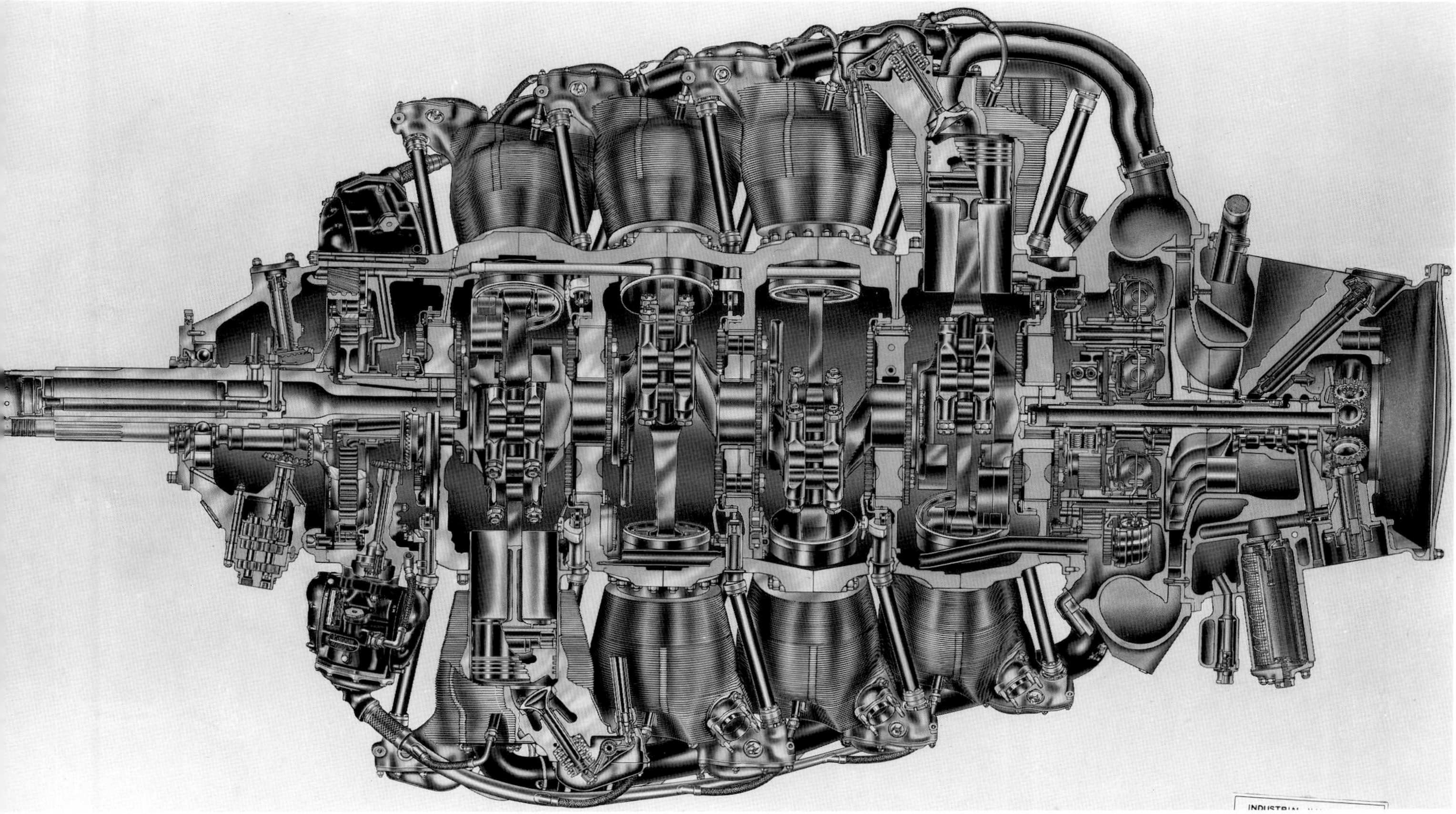

Left side cutaway of the Pratt & Whitney R-4360 powerplant showing the twenty-eight cylinders set in four rows of seven each. The R-4360 developed 3,000hp and pulled the F2G to speeds in excess of 450mph. Archives United Technologies Corporation

The first two aircraft designated in he Goodyear program as XF2G-1s were BuNos 13471 and 13472. Donald Armstrong was the chief engineering test pilot for Goodyear, the supervisor of all test pilots and flight-test programs. Armstrong made the first flight in 13471 on August 26, 1944. Both of hese aircraft started down the Akron, Ohio, production line as FG-1s. All of he F2G modifications were incorporated into them before delivery. BuNo 13471 was tasked with completing the following developmental tests: engine power development and powerplant emperature surveys; additional carbon monoxide tests; speed calibration; automatic cowl flap and automatic oil cooler door control tests; powerplant vibration surveys and fuel consumption tests; and limited performance tests including maximum speed, rate of climb, akeoff distance, stability checks, and stalling speeds. BuNo 13472 would complete the propeller vibration survey and test the performance of the Hamilton Standard, Curtiss, and Aero Products propellers; test the automatic cowl flap control; test the automatic oil cooler control; complete the air scoop and induction system tests; and perform a comparison of oil coolers.[138]

Upon completion of the above tests, 13471 was delivered to the Navy at NAS Patuxent River, Maryland.[139] After tests at Patuxent River, 13471 was brought back to the Goodyear factory at Akron on February 25, 1945, and its engine was removed for installation in BuNo 14691. BuNo 13472 completed its assigned tasks and on December 10, 1945, XF2G-1 BuNo 13472 was delivered to the Naval Air Technical Training Center (NATTC) Memphis. On February 11, 1946, 13472 was flown to NATTC Pensacola and was stricken from the records on April 30, 1946.

The third XF2G-1, BuNo 14691, was accepted by the Navy on September 29, 1944. This was the first aircraft manufactured completely as an F2G-1, and Armstrong took it on its uneventful first flight on October 15.

On October 21, 1944, Armstrong flew the new XF2G-1 to the joint Army-Navy fighter conference at NAS Patuxent River. Here he demonstrated the new fighter type in an impressive aerobatic routine. "I flew a short acrobatic demonstration at the Joint Army Navy Fighter Conference with the same airplane on October 22, seven days after its first flight," said Armstrong. "It shows you that the airplane was that good to begin with. It was just an amazing machine. I nicknamed it right away: 'The Homesick Angel.' It was that kind of an airplane. It just wanted to go up. At the Akron airport, I don't remember the length of the runway, but it was about 5,000ft, and I could takeoff and have 5,000ft underneath me by the end of the runway."[140] While at the fighter conference, in addition to the XF2G-1, Armstrong flew the Spitfire, P-51, Firefly, P-59, Mosquito, F7F,

Pratt & Whitney R-4360s being assembled for the F2G program. Archives United Technologies Corporation

P-38, P-63, and a captured Zero. Of all these aircraft, Armstrong said, "Nothing could climb with the F2G. Let's face it, the F2G had, conservatively, 50 percent more power and it was a decent performing airplane to begin with. Top speed didn't make that much of a difference. Nothing would outclimb it, but that was its designed purpose."

BuNo 14691 was delivered to the Navy on November 27, 1944. In January 1945, it arrived at NAS Patuxent River for a brief shakedown. In February it returned to Akron for nine months of flight test at the factory. In November 1945, it departed the factory for the last time and arrived at the Tactical Test Center, NAS Patuxent River, Maryland, to begin service trials. On April 18, 1947, BuNo 14691 departed for NAS Norfolk, Virginia, where it flew until June 30, 1947, when it was stricken from the inventory and is presumed to have been scrapped.

The fourth XF2G, BuNo 14692, was accepted on September 29, 1944. This aircraft was used to test new wing fuel tanks and a number of different rudder installations and to fly the final dive tests for the Navy.

The final and most successful modification of the vertical stabilizer was one in which a 12in pedestal was added to the fin and a supplemental rudder was installed underneath the standard rudder. This "split rudder" was automatically deployed 12.5deg to starboard when the tail wheel was extended. "Without the pedestal, when you were in a carrier wave-off position—gear down, flaps down, slow speed, canopy open—if you applied full power, it would take full right rudder to keep the aircraft straight," said Armstrong. "And that was marginal control because the torque of the R-4360 was probably 60 percent greater than the torque of the R-2800. We simply raised the vertical fin without any deflection—leaving it in the normal F2G position and then, behind it, installed what in essence was a huge trim tab. It was the size in chord length of the rudder and 12in high." When the split rudder was deployed, according to Armstrong, "It would give you a neutral rudder position when you applied full power. At slow speeds, even at carrier approach speeds with the nose up in the air and everything dirty, the split rudder didn't make a damn bit of difference. Actually you never noticed it. The pilot in essence didn't know that anything had happened, but when you poured the coal to it and you gave it full 3,500 or even higher horsepower, the increased slipstream hit this vertical fin, deflected the nose to the right, which offset the torque of the engine. It was a fantastic thing. The average Navy pilot said after he flew it, 'Carrier wave-off...no problem!'"[141] Before the split rudder, a carrier wave-off to the right was considered impossible as full rudder with full power would not turn the F2G to the right.

Don Armstrong belly-landed XF2G-1 BuNo 14695 on December 12, 1945. Armstrong, closest to the leading edge of the wing in flying helmet, walked away with only minor bruises after suffering a hydraulic failure that prevented him from extending the landing gear. Don Armstrong

BuNo 14693, the fifth XF2G, was also accepted on September 29, 1944. This aircraft was bailed to Pratt & Whitney, East Hartford, Connecticut, and was used to test the performance of a water injection system and to check WEP performance. The water injection system consisted of a 65gal fuselage tank holding a water-alcohol mixture, a water pump, and a regulator. This aircraft was also used in an attempt to cure the engine's "rough" feel and its propensity to "cut-out" during high-speed glides with low manifold pressures. In an attempt to correct these problems, this aircraft was fitted with an extended carburetor air scoop and the Stromberg carb was replaced with a Ceco unit, because of the latter's availability. The carburetor air scoop's inlet was extended from the rear of the cowling to the leading edge. This allowed air to enter the scoop undisturbed, without having to flow over the top of the cowling to the original intake. The extended scoop was abandoned in favor of the original style scoop at the top rear of the cowling—with internal changes made to control the airflow down to the carburetor. Less than three years later after four F2Gs found their way into civilian hands as air racers, the Navy would aid the racing attempts by providing an extended scoop. The extended scoop did increase the amount of undisturbed airflow to the carburetor, thus increasing horsepower. After the Pratt & Whitney tests, 14693 was transferred to NAS Patuxent River, Maryland, for flight and service tests. It was stricken from the Navy's inventory on July 31, 1949.

The sixth ship, XF2G-1 BuNo 14694, was test-flown at the factory until October 1945 when it was delivered to NAMC Philadelphia (Mustin Field) for carrier platform tests. During one of these arrested landings, the diagonal ribs of the inboard wing section failed. An investigation was conducted while repairs were being carried out at the NAF in Philadelphia. In order to continue the tests, BuNo 88460 was assigned to continue the data collection. In March 1946, BuNo 14694 was back at Mustin Field for continued testing. In April, 14694 was delivered to Patuxent River where it served until May 31, 1947.

The seventh and final prototype F2G, BuNo 14695, was flown on its first flight on December 4, 1945. Its second and final flight would be on December 12, 1945.

December 12, 1945, was not a good day for XF2G-1 BuNos 14692 and 14695. Within 20 minutes of each other, both aircraft experienced hydraulic failures. Armstrong took off on an instrument shakedown flight in 14695 and Arthur Chapman followed shortly after in 14692. After a few minutes of testing, Armstrong noticed that "Chapman's landing gear was 1/3 down and that he was having difficulty."[142] All attempts to lower the landing gear were unsuccessful. Chapman blew the emergency CO_2 bottles, which succeeded in locking the left wheel down fully extended, while the right main wheel was still 1/3 down. Armstrong then "organized the crash crew by radio and directed them to the point where Mr. Chapman had selected to bail out of his aircraft. At this point [Armstrong] noticed that the hydraulic pressure on his aircraft [14695] suddenly went to 0, automatically extending the tail wheel. Immediately upon noticing that the pressure was falling, [Armstrong] attempted to lower the main wheels without success."[143] Armstrong stayed with Chapman until he was safely on the ground. After having consulted with the engineering department, he elected to belly land 14695. He "reported to the Tower the conditions that existed at the time of his hydraulic failure. These were: landing gear retracted, air speed

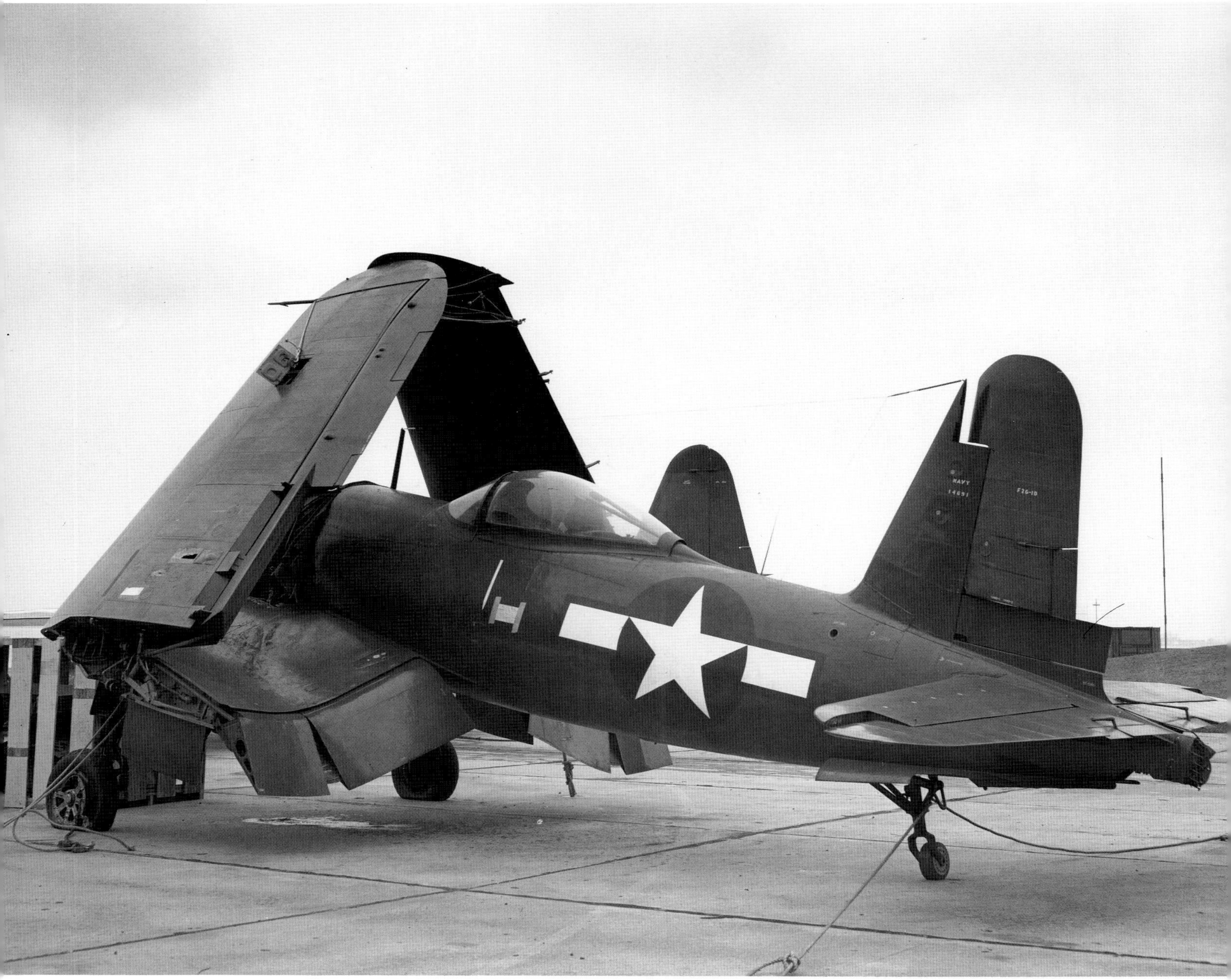

F2G-1 BuNo 14691 sits in storage at NAS Patuxent River in early 1948. Note the F2G's bubble canopy which provided better all-around visibility and the split rudder, which acted like a large rudder trim tab. When full throttle was applied to the engine, the lower rudder deflected the slipstream, offsetting the torque of the engine. H. G. Martin/Robert J. Pickett Collection via Kansas Aeronautical Historical Society

200mph, 30lb manifold pressure, 2100rpm, and that no use of the hydraulic system was being made at the time of the failure. He advised hand pump apparently had no effect on extending the landing gear."[144] Armstrong made a belly landing without flaps, without incident, and was unhurt although "considerably bumped around."

A mobile crane moved 14695 to a hangar for further investigation of the hydraulic failure, and the aircraft was suspended 6in off the ground. The aircraft was raised an additional 18in so jacks could be placed under the wings. It was realized that the jacks were for FG-1s, and 14695 remained 24in off the ground while the correct jacks were brought in. In the meantime, the hoisting cable broke, and 14695 crashed to the hangar floor followed by the crane's boom, which broke the F2G's back, striking the fuselage between the firewall and windshield. The hydraulic system failure was caused by the hyraulic pump stoppage due to the failure of the three-way accessory drive on he engine, one of which is used for the ydraulic system.[145] After the full investigation, the aircraft was scrapped.

Production Aircraft

On May 8, 1945, two months before he first production F2G-1s would roll ff the assembly line, the BuAer partially terminated the contract for F2Gs. The amount of production aircraft on he contract was reduced by 408, leaving only ten aircraft to be delivered. The letter terminating the contract did pecify that the first five aircraft, BuNos 88454–88458, would be F2G-1 land-based configuration, while the second five, BuNos 88459–88463, would be n the carrier-based configuration with wing folding mechanisms, shorter propellers, and arresting gear.[146] Production F2Gs maintained the same cockpit arrangement and instrumentation as n the Vought F4U-4.[147] The terminated contract called for the completion of he service-acceptance trials, the Navy's complete evaluation of the fighter, but it made no provisions for the fighter after that point. By the time esting of the F2G was complete, the R-4360-powered Corsairs were seen as obsolete reminders of the propeller driven age of naval aviation. The new jet fighters such as the Phantom were on ine and the F2G was quickly forgotten about. The type never saw squadron service.

The first production F2G-1, BuNo 88454, was accepted on June 30, 1945, and delivered to NAS Patuxent River on July 15. The aircraft was tested here until January 1948 when it was transferred to the Naval Electronic Project to test the aircraft's radios and IFF equipment.

In April 1948, BuNo 88454 was delivered to the Naval Ordnance Test Station Chincoteague, Virginia. Less han one month later, 88454 was transferred to the aircraft pool at NAS Norfolk and stricken from the Navy's inventory on May 31, 1948. (This aircraft was containerized for a preservation est and apparently forgotten only to be discovered by Capt. Walter Ohlrich in he early 1960s. The aircraft is now on display at the Champlin Fighter Museum, Mesa, Arizona.)

BuNo 88455 was accepted on August 31, 1945, and remained at the factory until May 1946. Subsequently it was delivered to Patuxent River for evaluation of the aircraft's armament. After tests were completed, the aircraft was declared obsolete, was stricken from the Navy's inventory on August 31, 1946, and was scrapped.

The third production F2G-1, BuNo 88456, was first flown on September 20, 1945, by Don Armstrong. On September 30, 88456 was delivered to the Navy at Port Columbus, Ohio, and quickly flown to Patuxent River for mechanical and servicing tests. When the tests were completed in March 1946, 88456 was transferred to NAS Norfolk. It was stricken on May 31, 1947.

BuNo 88457 made its first flight on September 27, 1945. It was delivered to Electronic Test at Patuxent on October 10, 1945, and was then transferred to the Tactical Test branch on July 26, 1946. Pilots at the Tactical Test branch were tasked with comparing the F2G's performance with other contemporary carrier- and land-based fighters (F6F-5, F4U-4, F7F-3 F8F-1, and XF8B-1). On January 9, 1947, Tactical Test concluded that "the F2G-2 aircraft meets the tactical demands for which it was designed and may be considered acceptable as a carrier-based fighter, fighter bomber, and medium altitude interceptor aircraft; similarly the F2G-1 may be considered acceptable as a land-based fighter, fighter-bomber, and interceptor."[148] BuNo 88457 was stricken from inventory on April 30, 1947, and released sold by the War Assets Administration one month later to racing pilot Cook Cleland.

BuNo 88458 was delivered to the Navy at Port Columbus on October 26, 1945. It served with the Armament Test branch at Patuxent until July 1946 when it was transferred to the Service Test branch. BuNo 88458 was stricken in January 1948.

The first F2G-2, BuNo 88459, was retained at Goodyear after delivery on October 31, 1945. On June 25, 1946, 88459 joined its fellow ships at NAS Patuxent River. It ended its service life at the Naval Proving Ground, NAS Dahlgren, Virginia, most likely as a ground target.

BuNo 88460 was delivered to Mustin Field for operational testing on December 10, 1945, where it flew until March 1947. It joined Tactical Test in mid-March. One year later it was transferred to NAS Norfolk, and it was stricken from the records on May 31, 1948.

Delivered on February 11, 1946, F2G-2 BuNo 88461 and the two aircraft to follow would get to see the fleet. BuNo 88461 was delivered to CASU-5 (a carrier aircraft service unit). In April 1946, 88461 was flown to the Tactical Development Unit at NAS North Island, San Diego. It remained on the West Coast until January 1947 when it was stricken from the Navy's inventory.

BuNo 88462 was delivered February 11, 1946, to NAS North Island, San Diego. It made the rounds with the Pacific Fleet flying with Fleet Air Service Squadrons 1 and 11 and was stricken in May 1947 and is presumed to have been scrapped.

The last F2G built, F2G-2 BuNo 88463, was delivered to the Instructional Aircraft Training Unit at NAS Jacksonville, Florida, on February 7, 1946. This aircraft remained at Jacksonville until stricken on February 28, 1947, and was bought by Cook Cleland for his racing team.

Don Armstrong summed up his opinion of the "Homesick Angel" with these words: "It was a fantastic airplane. You had a rugged aircraft that had been wrung out for years and years and to get something into production using as much as you could from an existing airframe, I believe the Corsair was probably the most logical place to stick the 4360 engine. It would have done the job as a Kamikaze killer, I believe, had they not dropped the atomic bomb. If they would have needed it, it would have filled the bill—because it got out quick, it got up quick, and had a little bit better performance than the FG, and the visibility was fantastic with that full bubble canopy.

"It was a beautiful airplane to fly....You could come over the field at 450 [mph] and pull it on up in a 60deg climb and just put full aileron on it and it just kept rolling its way up to 7,000 or 8,000ft. When you poured the coal to that thing, you knew you had power. It was an amazing machine."[149]

Chapter 9

F4U-5: The First Postwar Corsair

The BuAer authorized Vought to submit a proposal for the advanced F4U-5 on March 15, 1944, even though the F4U-4 had not yet flown. The Navy, still facing a long road ahead in the Pacific including the planned invasion of the Japanese home islands, was looking to increase the Corsair's overall performance, armament, and serviceability. Vought submitted design V-351 on July 27, 1944, and was awarded a contract for five prototypes of the F4U-5 on December 21, 1944.

The F4U-5 featured the R-2800-32W radial engine, which boasted 2,300hp at sea level and an automatically controlled two-stage, variable-speed supercharger. The F4U-5 was capable of a maximum speed of 480mph at 26,800ft and a rate of climb of 5,240fpm. For improved longitudinal stability and increased forward vision for the pilot, the engine installation was offset 2deg lower. The most noticeable outward difference distinguishing the -4 from the -5 was the cowl air-inlet scoops. The -5's scoops were in the cowl cheeks at the four and eight o'clock position. Four wing-mounted M3 20mm cannons were mounted in the all-metal wings, which now featured heated gun and pitot tubes. The metal wing surfaces reduced aerodynamic drag (until the F4U-5, the Corsair's outer wing panels were fabric covered). The F4U-5 incorporated a Mark 8 gyroscopic gun sight, and rearranged cockpit consoles headed up the modernized cockpit. To reduce pilot workload, the cowl flaps, intercooler doors, and oil cooler doors were now automatic. Elevator and rudder controls had spring tabs. To further increase pilot comfort, a new adjustable seat with folding armrests and swing-down brake pedals that could serve as leg rests rounded out the cockpit modifications.

Factory fresh F4U-5NL. The external differences from the F4U-4 to the F4U-5 are quickly visible, note the cheek air intakes and revised exhaust arrangement. The F4U-5NL also featured the right-wing radar nacelle, flash suppressers on the 20mm cannons, and deicer boots visible on the wing leading edges. Vought via Robert F. Dorr

Three aircraft—two F4U-4s and one F4U-4B—were used as the prototypes for the XF4U-5. First to be converted was F4U-4 BuNo 97296. This aircraft was accepted as an F4U-4 on December 6, 1945, but had not been delivered to the Navy when selected for conversion. BuNo 97364, accepted on March 15, 1946, was the second XF4U-5. Bill Horan took 97296 up for its first flight as an XF4U-5 on July 3, 1946.

Reflecting on flying the prototype XF4U-5, Bill Horan said, "Personally I didn't like it. The supercharging system never seemed to work right. It was supposed to be automatic, it would shift for you when you gained altitude. They finally got it working, but I just never liked the airplane. It wasn't so much the airplane as it was the engine."[150]

During a routine test flight on July 8, Dick Burroughs was killed and 97296 was completely destroyed when he attempted a dead stick landing at Stratford, Connecticut.

Subsequent to this crash, the third XF4U-5, BuNo 97415 was accepted on July 18, 1946. Both of the remaining XF4U-5s were accepted by the BuAer Representative at Stratford. The aircraft remained at the Vought plant for test work during the duration of the F4U-5 program.

The contract for production F4U-5s was awarded to Vought on February 6, 1946. The first flight of a production F4U-5 was on October 1, 1947, when Bill Horan took BuNo 121796 up in the skies over Stratford.

F4U-5N Nightfighter

Airborne intercept radar had come a long way since the early F4U-2 nightfighters flown in the South Pacific. The F4U-5N was the same aircraft as the F4U-5 except for the addition of radar equipment. The AN/APS-19 radar was installed in BuNos 121816–122206 and the updated AN/APS-19A set was installed in all F4U-5 and -5NL after BuNo 123144. The AN/APS-19A featured adjustment knobs to allow the pilot to dim or increase the brilliance of the radar scope and the radio altimeter limit light.

The radar sets could be operated in four modes: Beacon, as an aid to navigation; Search, for the long-range detection of surface targets such as ships (up to 100 miles); Intercept, of an airborne target (within 20 miles); and Aim, to acquire and fire at an airborne target (within 1,500 yards). The aircraft also featured an automatic pilot. The radar screen mounted in the center of the instrument panel displayed a dot in the center of the screen that represented the Corsair. The contact aircraft would appear as "blips," presenting the pilot with a visual orientation to the target.

One of the most unusual pieces of auxiliary equipment installed on the F4U-5N was the aerial pinball device, which consisted of three trihedral prisms, one each on the wing tips and tail, that reflected light back in the exact direction from which it came; a gun

Hunter/killer: F4U-5N BuNo 123187 and a Skyraider from VC-3 on a training mission near their home base of NAS Moffett Field, Sunnyvale, California. Aside from performing night air-superiority missions, the F4U-5s would guide the Skyraiders to targets over Korea, dropping flares and leading the attack. US Navy

camera in its normal right wing leading edge position; and a light beam projector that sent out an 80-candlepower light.

When using the aerial pinball device, the pilot of the attacking F4U-5N would press his gun trigger and a light beam would shine on his target. If the pilot was on target, the light beam would be reflected from all three prisms at the target aircraft. If only one prism returned light, then the attacking aircraft was off to one side, or too high or low. The results were recorded on the gun camera.[151]

F4U-5NL Night-Fighting Cold-Weather Corsairs

Fitted out for operations in the cold Korean theater, the F4U-5NL was an all-weather nightfighter featuring the AN/APS-19A radar set and deicer boots on the outer wing panels, horizontal and vertical stabilizers, deicer shoes on the propeller blades, and a windscreen deicing system. The propeller and wind screen deicing system used a glycol mixture to prevent ice from forming, but as was later found during operational use, the mix was ruining the rubber seals around the windscreen and causing the plastic canopies to become cloudy.

Pilots were cautioned not to dive the F4U-5NL or land with the deicer boots inflated. "With boots inflated, the airplane in the clean condition will roll to the right at airspeeds above 240kt; at airspeeds less than 105kt the airplane will roll to the left first and then to the right. In the landing condition (with boots inflated), control is satisfactory down to 80kt with power on; at speeds lower than 80kt, control effectiveness is reduced, and rapid and large

Top, Ens. Fred Blechman brings F4U-5 3uNo 122158 of VF-14 aboard the USS Kula Gulf *on November 8, 1951, after a CAP nission. After taking the cut, Blechman losed the aircraft over, diving for the deck. The aircraft bounced once. Blechman is ıbout to pass the number five wire but does ıot have his tail down to engage. Bottom, 3lechman was able to engage the number-ight cross-deck pendant and struck number wo and three barriers, damaging the pro-ɔeller and causing minor dents to the cowl-ng speed ring. Following this landing a novie camera was set up on the USS* Kula Gulf, *which filmed each landing from the ime the aircraft was picked up by the LSO. The films were reviewed by all pilots each vening.* Fred Blechman

.mounts of lateral stick displacement vill be required to maintain the wings evel. Flights at speeds lower than hose specified here should be avoided vhen the boots are operating."[152]

Even with these restrictions, the '4U-5NL was a very successful air-raft, and seventy-two were built. The 5NL saw extensive combat in Korea lying primarily with VC-3 operating letachments from land bases as well as he carriers USS *Boxer* and USS *Philippine Sea*. The only US Navy Ko-ean War ace, Lt. Guy P. Bordelon, flew he F4U-5NL on a number of his five ills.

F4U-5P Photo Five

A photo recce version of the F4U-5 vas brought into production after the 88th F4U-5 started down the assem-ly line. The F4U-5P was introduced at 3uNo 122167 and built on the line con-ecutively through BuNo 122206.

The cameras were mounted in low-r midfuselage, in front of and below he star and bar when viewed external-y. Entrance to the camera bay was hrough the radio access door. The cam-ras, one vertical and two oblique, were nounted behind closeable doors that eatured slipstream deflectors to pre-ent oil from fouling the camera ports. 'o accommodate the camera bay, the emote indicating compass was relocat-d to the vertical stabilizer.

The F4U-5P was designed to ac-ommodate either the K series (K-17 or K-18) aerial cameras or the S-7S con-inuous strip camera in a rotating camera conversion kit." To control the ameras, master switches were mount-

Top, F4U-5 M-117 of VF-21 crashes and catches fire aboard the USS Coral Sea *on June 15, 1949, after a training flight. Bottom, M-117, deemed unsalvageable, is pushed over the side. The pilot, Proctor, was uninjured.* National Archives via Jim Sullivan

ed on the top of the right and left cockpit consoles and an intervalometer was mounted through the instrument panel, below and to the right of the gun sight.[153] A large percentage of the forty F4U-5Ps built ranged over Korea photographing while striking targets as well as providing post-strike intelligence. Navy squadrons VC-60 and VC-61 operated the F4U-5P in theater while VC-62 flew the -5P from the decks of the USS *Leyte* from October 1950 through January 1951.

A Pilot's View of the F4U-5

Ens. Fred Blechman, who flew F4U-5 Corsairs with VF-14, describes flying the F4U-5: "The first thing I recognized when I got in the F4U-5 was that it was a lot heavier airplane [than the F4U-4. The F4U-4's normal gross weight was 12,500lb versus the F4U-5N and -5NL at 13,800lb]. The F4U-5 had cigarette lighters—actually a cigar lighter, and padded armrests that would swing down. The padded armrests would allow you to relax while flying. And in order to make it more comfortable, the airplane had rudder pedals that would swing back—you would stick your legs through the rudder pedals, and on the back of the pedals there were cushions. You could stick your legs through the rudder pedals and just sit there and be real comfortable.

"However, there were some other features about the plane that weren't so wonderful. It was about the time, in the early 1950s, when everything was getting automated. Computers in airplanes were coming on-line. Computerized controls were coming in. One of the first things Vought and the Navy did was they decided to use electric trim tabs. There were two things bad about electric trim tabs. It had a little joystick type arrangement so you could do left and right trim and up and down trim but what was particularly bad about it was that you had no feel at all [versus manual wheel set trim tabs]. So you had to get all the feel from the stick. When the stick was neutral, that was

t. There was always a certain amount of overrun in an electric trim tab. The mechanism has inertia, so you let the trim tab switch go, but the trim tab wouldn't stop right at that point. So you were constantly fiddling around. Because of all that fiddling around, every time you open and close a switch there is some sort of arc. It might be too small to be noticeable, but eventually the arc causes the contacts to wear and unfortunately sometimes weld together. We lost several pilots in our squadron who were pushing over in a dive, and as you push over your nose wants to come up as you're getting speed. So you are constantly feeding in down trim. As these guys were feeding in down trim, they would let the switch go and it wouldn't stop. They would get full down trim and go right into the ground. No way to pull out.

"So we were then told 'Well, we have this little problem with the trim tabs so when you are up at 10 or 20,000ft before you start your dive, feed in forward tab to where you think it should be, so you don't have to touch it on the way down.' The rules were don't touch the trim tab on the way down in a dive—just a terrible arrangement for a gun or bombing platform. You are fighting the airplane all the way down. I don't think I cared much for electric trim tabs."[154]

The F4U-5 was the first Corsair with automatic cowl flaps. "That's a nice feature," continued Blechman, "because if you don't open your cowl flaps when you are on the ground and the engine is running, you are going to burn up your engine. These things worked beautifully. They were tied to the wheels. Whenever the wheel struts were depressed because of the weight of the aircraft, the automatic cowl flaps would open. The cowl flaps were also tied in with the engine temperature when you were in the air. So here are two things that happened: You're flying along at normal speed in tight formation. The problem with this airplane was you had no control over the cowl flaps, there was a manual control, but if you had it on automatic, the cowl flaps would decide when they would open and close by themselves—dependent on the engine temperature. So you would be flying along in formation, pretty close, and all of the sudden the cowl flaps would open and you would drop behind. The worst part was if you were flying on somebody's wing and the cowl flaps were partly open and decided to close, now you would over run your wingman. So in the F4U-5 we would have to keep pretty far apart. Then, on landing, because of the landing gear switch, who bothered to pay attention to the cowl flaps as you were going back to the line? If the switch didn't work, the cowl flaps didn't open, and the engine burned up. Another nice feature of the F4U-5."

The F4U-5 had an automatic power unit (APU). This system had no override. The APU was kind of like a supercharger. "On the older airplanes we had a knob you could push forward and it would give you an extra ten inches of manifold pressure," Blechman said. "Manifold pressure, air temperature, atmospheric pressure, prop pitch, and a number of other parameters were fed into the APU's computer and it decided when it needed the extra power. You could not make formation takeoffs in the F4U-5 because nobody knew when their APU would cut in. When making a carrier takeoff, you would get off the end of the deck and get halfway down to the water and then the APU would decide to cut in.

"Then you would get up to about 19,000ft. If you were in formation, you would have to split. Between 19,000 and 23,000ft, the blowers would start cutting in and out. Nobody knew when their blower would cut in. So we had to separate a good distance apart. When all the blowers had cut in, everybody would report in and then we would rejoin in formation."

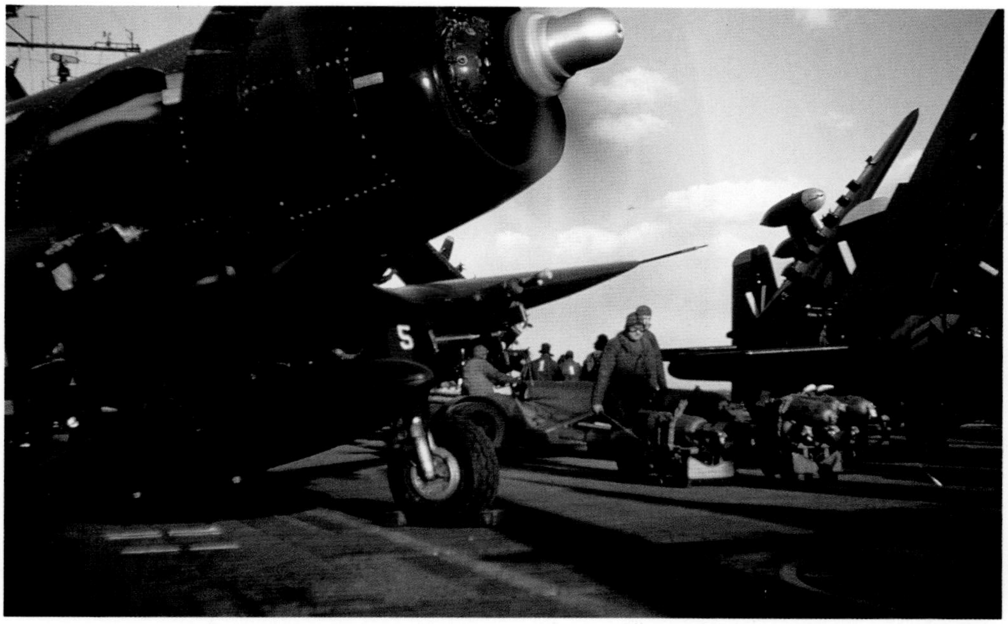

Armorers on board USS Philippine Sea *bring up an assortment of ordnance to waiting Corsairs preparing for a night-interdiction strike against North Korean road and rail traffic. The aircraft in the foreground with its engine turning over is F4U-5NL BuNo 123178* Nite Hawk *of VC-3.* Robert A. Rice

The F4U-5 also introduced the gyroscopic gun sight. The gyro gun sight was created to simplify the deflection shot. When attacking a target that is moving across your flight path, you have to lead the target so that the bullets leaving your guns will strike the target airplane. The gyro gun sight projected a recticle onto the windscreen. It had six diamond shaped "pips" that formed a circle that the pilot used to aim at the target. The throttle handle's knob rotated right or left to move the pips. According to Blechman, "Depending on how you moved that throttle knob determined how big the circle of pips was around the center. If you were perfectly stationary on the ground, it was simple. You turned it one way and the pattern would open up, the other

F4U-5NL warming up on the starboard deck of the USS Philippine Sea. *Note the Daisy Cutter bomb fuses protruding below the aircraft's 20mm cannons.* Robert A. Rice

way it would close down. The object was to encircle the wingspan of the target within the circle of pips. The closer you got to the target, the bigger the circle. As you were flying into the target, you were supposed to turn the control on the throttle to the right or left to circle the target, as well as move the throttle forward and backward as necessary, as well as operating the rudders while moving the stick all over the place. After all you were trying to home in on the target, but at the same time you were supposed to be feeding in this information to the computer by turning the knob, telling it how close you were to the target aircraft and what your rate of closure is. If you know the rate of closure and the wing span of the target aircraft, you can then calculate the rate of deflection. With this information, the circle of pips would move on the screen to tell you where to put your target. So as you are flying the aircraft, this thing is floating around the screen, you are constantly adjusting and trying to hold your target in the center. If you jerked the throttle a little bit, the whole thing would move off to one side. You would try and be as smooth as you could, but there is no way a human is going to be smooth enough to do this. It was a great idea. The trouble with the idea was that they were depending on an individual to do this smooth transition of ranging. In the F-86 Sabre jets they let a small radar set determine the range to the target and in fact the closure range. This was highly successful."

Korean Action

Corsairs were quickly committed to the Korean War, flying close-air-support, ground-attack, and antishipping missions. Later the night-fighting Corsairs were flown against Communist night raiders. Night interdiction missions against troop and truck convoys were also a major role of the Corsair. During "Firefly" missions, the Corsairs would orbit a target area as a PB4Y-2 Privateer would drop flares, illuminating the Communist forces. The Corsairs would push over into strafing and rocket attacks or drop napalm and iron bombs.

Night-fighting Corsair pilots faced fierce antiaircraft fire. The flares dropped to illuminate ground targets also lit up the strafing Corsairs for enemy gunners. Lt. (j.g.) David A. McCoskrie, USN, of VC-3, flying F4U-5N BuNo 124496, departed on a night mission on February 13, 1951. He was reported missing and presumed dead near Yontee-ri, Korea. On March 21, 1951, Maj. Scott G. Gier, USMC with VMF-212, flying an F4U-5, BuNo 121911, was hit by enemy antiaircraft fire on a close-air-support mission. He made an excellent forced landing and radioed the remainder of his flight that he was under fire from enemy troops in the area. Later that day, Gier was killed by small arms fire.

VMF-212's 2nd Lt. Alan Beers, USMC, was killed and his aircraft—F4U-5 BuNo 121931—was destroyed on a close-air-support mission over Korea on April 7, 1951.

After completing a glide-bombing run on enemy vehicles at 4:10 A.M., on April 13, 1951, Capt. John E. Van Housen, USMC, of VMF(N)-513, reported a complete loss of oil pressure. A short time later, Van Housen reported that he was bailing out of his F4U-5NL, BuNo 124512, fifteen miles northeast of Pyongyang—site of a North Korean airfield and rail yards, because of engine failure. Van Housen's aircraft was believed to have been damaged by an exploding vehicle or enemy antiaircraft fire. Van Housen was reported missing in action.

Capt. William Lesage, USMC, was on a VMF(N)-513 Firefly mission near Yang-gu in the early morning hours of May 20, 1951. Flying F4U-5NL BuNo 124531, Lesage last reported he was making an attack on vehicles below flares that had been dropped by other aircraft. Shortly thereafter fire was noticed on the ground. The fire was observed for about an hour but was not positively identified as that of an aircraft. A search of the area failed to locate the missing F4U-5NL. The pilot of the flare plane had previously reported heavy antiaircraft fire.

Capt. Arthur Wagner, USMCR, flying a VMF(N)-513 F4U-5N, BuNo 123204, was on an armed-reconnaissance mission May 27, 1951, in the vicinity of Mayhon-ni Kunwha. Wagner was flying at about 2,500ft when a bright orange flame appeared from his napalm tank. The plane was in a shallow glide to the left at the time, approaching a ridge at approximately 1,000ft above the terrain. Shortly thereafter, the pilot bailed out and his chute opened partially at a low alti-

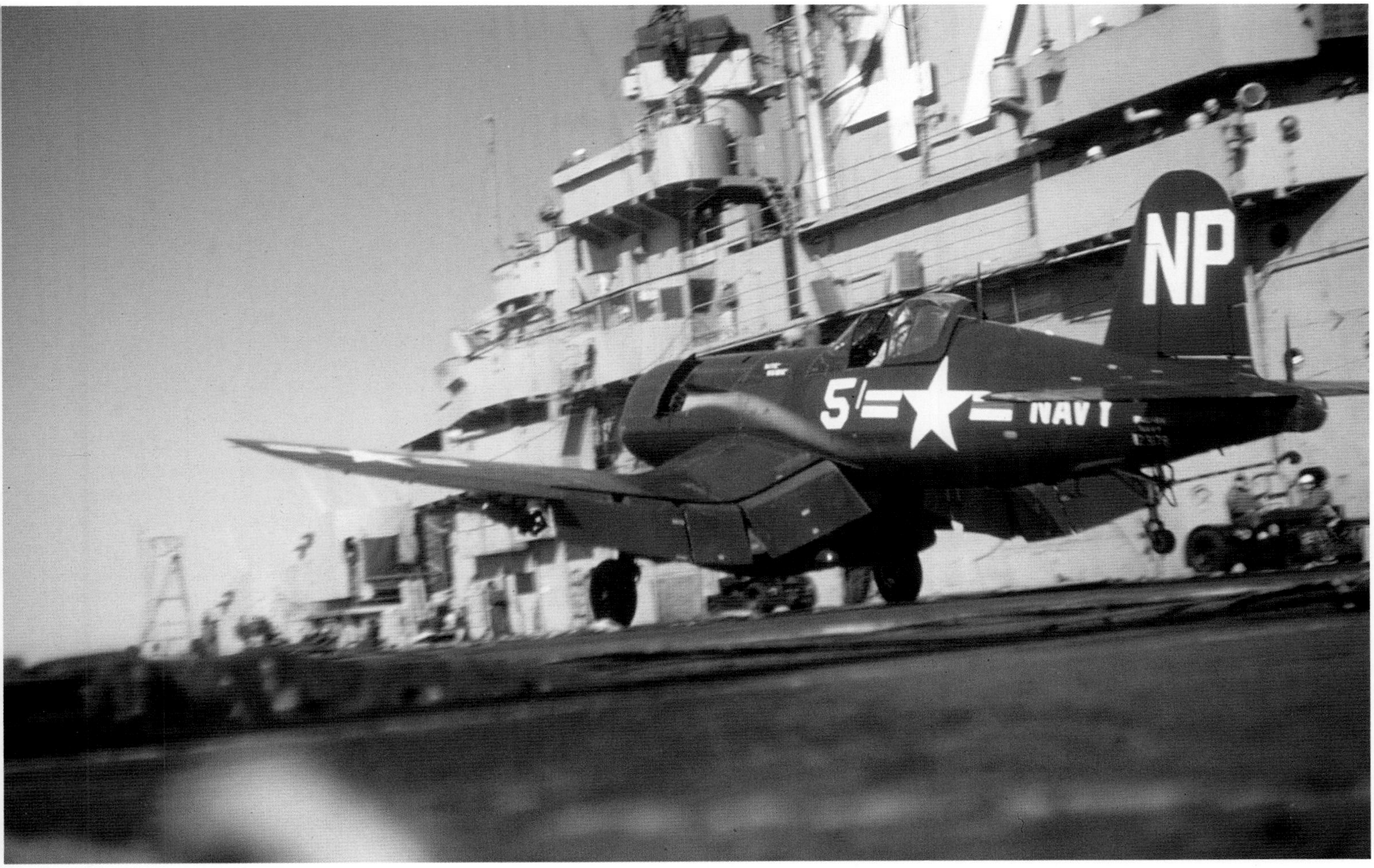

Nite Hawk *departs the deck of the USS* Philippine Sea. Robert A. Rice

tude. No activity on the ground was observed by pilots covering the area. The chute, although in plain view initially, disappeared from sight shortly after it hit the ground. Wagner was reported as missing in action.

On July 13, 1951, at 3:15 A.M., 1st Lt. William K. Garmany, USMC, flying a VMF(N)-513 F4U-5N, BuNo 124518, crashed after dropping napalm bombs on Hanp'o'ri, Korea. Garmany was last reported making a napalm attack on vehicles below flares that had been dropped by other aircraft. Shortly thereafter a double explosion was observed on the ground, one obviously napalm, the other presumed to be 124518. A search of the area the following day revealed wreckage of Garmany's F4U-5N. Other pilots reported small arms ground fire.

1st Lt. Arnold Olson, USMC, of VMF(N)-513 was dropping napalm from F4U-5N BuNo 124528 on July 13, 1951, at 4:36 A.M., near Namchon-jom. About a minute later a second explosion was observed and no further communication was made by Olson. The second explosion was assumed to have been the crash of Olson's aircraft. A search of the area the following day failed to locate any wreckage. Olson was listed as missing in action.

Lt. Samuel B. Murphey, USN, of VC-3 Detachment D was flying his F4U-5NL, BuNo 124553, over North Korea on January 29, 1952, at 7:35 A.M. During this predawn heckler mission, Murphey was hit by 37mm or 40mm antiaircraft fire in his engine upon recovery from a bombing run on a railroad bridge. His engine caught fire immediately and lost all power. He made a successful wheels up landing in some rice paddies, crossing three irrigation ditches in the process. The Corsair was engulfed in flames when Murphey abandoned it. He was rescued 1 hour after the crash landing, 3–4 miles from the crash site after being chased by two enemy soldiers and receiving a gunshot wound to the neck. A successful helicopter rescue was accomplished and he returned to his ship later that same day.

Routine operations in theater also took their toll on the F4U-5s. On April 22, 1951, Maj. Joseph Mackin, USMC, was returning to Kangmung Air Field in F4U-5 BuNo 121823 from a reconnaissance mission. Unable to reduce power below 1,500rpm and forced to land in a crosswind, his aircraft nosed over, inverted. Mackin escaped with minor head injuries.

During the takeoff roll in his F4U-5N, BuNo 124449, on May 11, 1951, 2nd Lt. John C. Jones, USMC, of VMF-

F4U-5NL armed and ready to go on the port catapult for an early evening mission against North Korean targets. Robert A. Rice

212 suffered an engine failure. Departing on a reconnaissance mission from K-3 Airfield, Korea, Jones swerved left off the runway. His left wing struck a pile of cement bags, and the wing was ripped off at the root. His napalm and belly tanks tore loose and caught fire. The aircraft did a half roll to the left into the missing wing and came to rest inverted and on fire. Jones was dragged from cockpit by two bystanders, escaping with minor cuts and bruises.

Nine days later at K-3, another VMF-212 pilot, Lt. Dock H. Pugeus, USMC, lost power on takeoff flying F4U-5 122041. Quickly dropping his napalm and belly tank on the runway, he was able to settle the aircraft back down but was unable to keep it on the runway. The aircraft swerved to the right and nosed over on its back. Pugeus escaped with minor injuries.

On July 19, 1951, at K-3 Air Field, Korea, during a late ground-controlled approach waveoff, Capt. Raymond W. Baker, USMCR, flying F4U-5 BuNo 121834, struck a US Air Force T-7 parked on the ramp 40ft to the left of the head of the runway. The T-7 was warming up awaiting clearance onto runway for takeoff. Baker's left landing gear was sheared on impact with the T-7. The Corsair then hit the runway and swerved right. Continuing parallel to the runway in the dirt for a short distance, Baker swerved back on the runway and ground-looped. He walked away from the incident.

One of the last F4U-5 pilots to perish in the Korean War was Capt. Francis Kelly, USMC, flying F4U-5NL BuNo 124537. While the airstrip was under alert at Kimpo, Kelly made a normal ground-controlled approach to the field, and after a three-point touchdown one-third of the way down the runway, attempted a waveoff. Witnesses testified that it appeared he could not obtain full engine power. The aircraft hit the top of a 100ft hill, one-eighth of a mile off the end of the runway.

Only about thirty F4U-5s of all models were lost to direct enemy action in Korea. A greater number of -5 Corsairs were lost from 1950 to 1953 during training and carrier landing accidents.

The Navy's Only Korean War Ace

The F4U-5's major success story comes from the flying skills of Lt. Guy P. Bordelon Jr., USN. Flying with Task Force 77 aboard the USS *Princeton* as a member of VC-3, the Navy's only all-weather combat fighter squadron at that time, Bordelon was transferred to Kimpo under the command of the Fifth Air Force to intercept Communist night hecklers. The North Koreans were flying a mixed bag of biplanes and trainers that were too slow for the Air Force's jet interceptors to engage.

On June 17, 1953, a four-plane detachment from VC-3, including Bordelon, was transferred from Task Force 77 to the Air Force's K-14 airfield near Seoul to begin night operations against the Communist "Bed Check Charlies." From K-14, the VC-3 detachment was transferred to K-6 at Pyongtaek, 30 miles south of Seoul. K-6 was a big USMC air base, better able to maintain the VC-3 Corsairs.

During the early morning hours of June 30, Bordelon was given instructions to launch. "Local radar had picked up aircraft in the area. Two of us were launched. The other aircraft had some radar trouble, but I had good radar placed on the enemy," Bordelon said.[155] "It was a nice moonlit night and I had a good chance to see the exhaust stack pattern. When I finally got a visual—we had to get a visual because there were friendly aircraft in the area too—I soon reported that it was obviously an enemy aircraft, a Yak-18. So they said 'go shoot,' and I shot. He immediately banked hard right and I kept right on him and poured about fifty or sixty rounds into him and he exploded. I was using high explosive incendiary 20mm cannon fire. One of those rounds could have blown him out of the air. The Yak-18 was a utility aircraft they had equipped with a gun mount in the rear seat. This aircraft had a rear gunner who was firing off to the right whereas I was to his left."

Shortly thereafter, ground control radar vectored Bordelon on to another target, which he identified as a second Yak-18. "I got in back of him and he started firing right away," Bordelon said, "but he was firing in the wrong direction again. I let loose with a long burst of 20mm and he caught fire, his wing came off, and he exploded on the ground."

During the night of June 30–July 1, Bordelon again encountered enemy aircraft. He was up running a control barrier north of Seoul to keep the enemy from flying aircraft into the area. While patrolling seaward of Inchon, Bordelon said he was vectored by JOC, Joint Operations Center, Korea, onto an enemy aircraft. "When I got in, there were several aircraft. I got in back of one (an La-11) and managed to shoot him down. It sounds easy, but it wasn't. They were twisting and turning and [while pursuing the second aircraft of the same type] we ended up over North Korea. When I finally shot him down I was being fired on by antiaircraft. I had pulled in close enough to him, under 200 yards, that when he finally leveled out I gave him a long burst," Bordelon said. His total was now four confirmed air-to-air kills.

A few nights later, Bordelon made his fifth and final kill of the war. "I was in the air heading north to go up to Seoul when one of our aircraft reported he had a bogey. Shortly thereafter he reported that his radar had gone out. So I was vectored in to take over, picked him up, and had a long chase. I finally got on his tail. It was dark, black dark, but I was able to pick up the exhaust pattern. It was the same exhaust pattern as the previous two aircraft, Lavochkin La-11s, which are high-performance fighters. He again led me right over the antiaircraft positions at Kaesong. They started firing and I pulled in closer because they were firing to the rear of his aircraft. The closer I was to him the safer I was. I pulled up and started firing and he made a turn to the right as if he was going to really give me fits trying to get away—and exploded. The blast took my night vision away. I had to reach up and grab the auto pilot switch, switching it on. I had already set it so that the auto pilot would come in easily. And it cracked right in and I could have given her a kiss! She was so good to me. I flew around until I got my eyesight back and the plane was burning on the ground. I probably put more rounds into my last kill than the others combined. I was down to about 50 rounds, and I carried a total of 200 rounds for each of the four guns."

The Air Force corroborated each of Bordelon's kills. For his efforts he was awarded the Navy Cross.

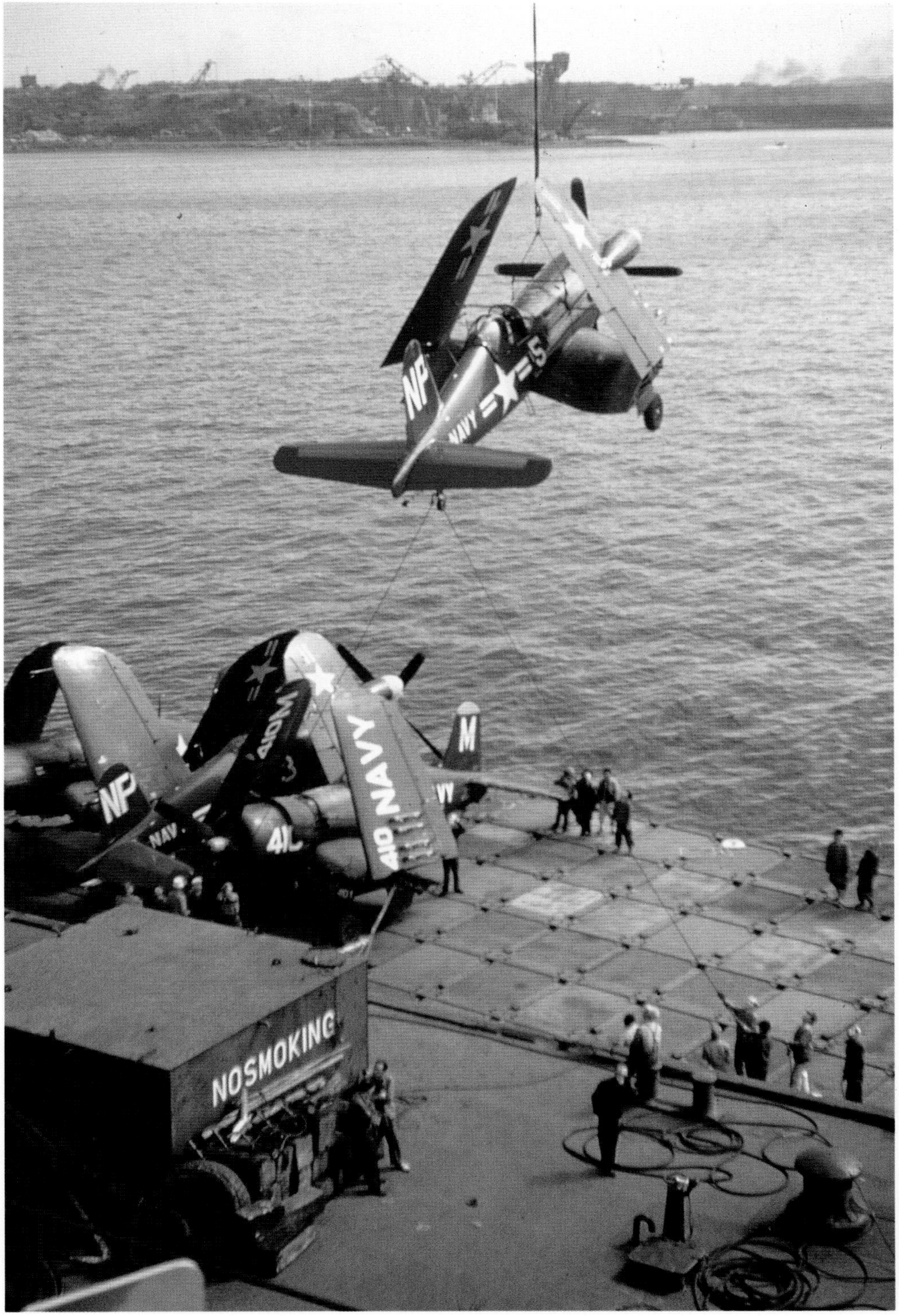

Aircraft of VC-3 being transferred from the deck of the USS Philippine Sea *after a tour flying night-interdiction missions.* Robert A. Rice

Final F4U-5 Flights, Final Thoughts

Ens. Fred Blechman, like many other pilots, did not like the F4U-5. Blechman describes his last flight in an F4U-5, which resulted in a barrier crash:

"It was a bright, clear dawn in the Caribbean on November 8, 1951, when eight of us in Fighter Squadron Fourteen [VF-14] were catapulted from the

A Vought F4U-5N Corsair nightfighter (note radar housing on folded starboard wing) stands in the foreground, not far ahead of a Grumman F9F-5 Panther, as the 5in guns of the USS Princeton *(CV-37) are fired off the Korean coast in March 1953. F4U-4 Corsairs did most of the air-to-ground flying in the Korean conflict, while the F4U-5N and F4U-5NL (with the* L *suffix for* winterized*) protected carriers or chased "Bedcheck Charlie" biplanes at night.* Tom Randall via Robert F. Dorr

escort carrier USS *Kula Gulf* (CVE-108). Our F4U-5 Corsairs were part of an annual training exercise called LANTFLEX (AtLANTic FLeet EXercise), and we were the Red Squadron, flying CAP to protect our small task force from any Blue [enemy] raids.

"Nothing happened. We just flew around in large, lazy circles in loose formation some distance from the carrier and its support vessels. After a couple of hours of occasional vectoring by the carrier CIC [Combat Information Center], we came back in, landed, and hit the ready room. The Acey-Ducey and card games came out, and we relaxed. I was not scheduled for any other flights that day after our early launch.

"Things changed suddenly when our radar spotted a 'snooper,' apparently a Blue patrol plane approaching our ships. 'Pilots, man your planes!' was called for those scheduled on standby. Although I was not scheduled to fly, the deck was not spotted for launch, so I was called up on deck to help taxi some planes around. I climbed into one of our Corsairs (#405) without even a plotting board, since I was only going to taxi. I had the regular flight gear—a hard hat, G-suit and parachute, standard procedure in case of standby launch—but no plotting board, and no briefing.

"But the last of the eight planes being launched for this search-and-destroy mission had engine trouble. All planes were being catapulted since the wind over the short deck was not sufficient for a safe deck launch, not that cat shots were all that safe! They took the dud Corsair off the port catapult, put me on, and shot me into the gathering clouds! Equipped with an extra gas tank, we were off for a 3-hour search flight.

"This turned out to be a long, boring, very tiring flight. The flight leader, to make things more interesting, put us in a 'tail chase,' and I was the last plane in this whipping tail as the leader performed mild aerobatics. Following was relatively easy if you were in one of the up-front positions in this tail chase, but got progressively more difficult if you were further back in the stack. I was in position number eight, the end of the tail, and was using full throttle, full rudder, and lots of elevator and aileron movement, to try to stay in position.

"The F4U-5, the heaviest in the Corsair series, did not have boosted controls, and didn't need them for normal flight. But it took a lot of physical effort to horse it around the sky. Also, we had gone up above the cloud layer, and the sun was beating through the bubble canopy. Combined with the natural high humidity of the Caribbean, the inside of that bird was hot and sticky! I recall popping the canopy back a few inches several times to try to cool off.

"Finally, we were called back to land. There had been another unscheduled launch while we were airborne, and now the deck was spotted again for our recovery. These were still the days of straight-deck carriers, when reshuffling of planes on deck was a common and necessary procedure.

"As we approached the landing pattern in right echelon formation, flying upwind along the starboard side of the carrier for the break-off, I reflected about how well I had been doing. I mentally patted myself on the back for my good ordnance scores, and, although there had been a rash of accidents on this cruise, my slate was clean.

"Landing an F4U-5 on a small escort carrier was inherently marginal. Escort carriers (CVEs), with a flight deck under 500ft long, were small compared to the larger 800ft and 1000ft light (CVL) and battle (CV) carrier decks. Escort carriers had fewer arresting wires—six, compared to eight for CVLs and thirteen for CVs—and the decks had a much greater tendency to pitch, yaw, and roll even in light seas. Every landing was a challenge.

"As I set my interval and peeled off for the downwind leg, I looked forward to getting down. I was very tired and sweaty. Getting back on deck, into a shower, and then sacking out was what I was planning.

"I came around the base leg, with wheels, flaps, and hook down, and throttled back enough to hold the nose-up attitude and about 90kt, hanging on the prop. I began slowly dropping altitude on the base leg by reference to where the horizon cut the bridge. I put the nose of the Corsair on the aft starboard deck for an intercept course and held it there. As the ship moved forward at about 20kt, I pulled the Corsair around to the left, watching the LSO for paddle instructions.

"There was no luxury of any straightaway in landing on those old straight-deck carriers when you were flying a long-nose Corsair in a nose-up attitude. You just couldn't see ahead of you, only off to the side. We essentially pyloned counterclockwise around the LSO in order to keep him in sight at his port fantail location.

"As we got close in, we pulled the nose left toward the ship's centerline. This was effected by the wind over the deck, which was never straight down the deck, but about 15deg to port so the turbulence from the ship's stacks and bridge did not appear in the flight path of the landing planes. This made for a very tricky last few seconds. . . .

"It took a lot of back stick, considerable power, and almost all my right rudder to hang in there. As I approached the ramp in a left turn, the LSO's paddles and my own perception was that I was drifting to the right of the deck centerline. Too much right rudder. I cross-controlled a bit and slipped to the left just as I approached the ramp and got a cut.

"'Ah, home at last,' I thought as I relaxed, dropped the nose, and pulled back to drop the tail so my hook would catch an early wire. But I relaxed too soon! Perhaps I was more tired than I realized and didn't pull back soon enough, or perhaps the deck lurched up at that time. Whatever the reason, my wheels hit the deck and bounced. I was flying over the arresting wires, tail up, and drifting to the left!

"I heard the crash horn just as I popped the stick forward to get back on deck, and then quickly pulled back, to get my arresting hook down. I caught Number Five wire, but on this ship with a heavy Corsair the arresting cable pulled out just enough for the prop to catch the uplifted barrier cables. Strike two prop blades!

"The moral of the story? Don't relax at the wrong time. The flight isn't over until the wheels are in the chocks and the prop has stopped."[156]

In all, 468 F4U-5s of all models were built. Three hundred fifty-one F4U-5s, forty-five F4U-5Ns, and seventy-two F4U-5NLs. The F4U-5 was the last Corsair type flown in US Navy squadron service. VC-4 flew F4U-5Ns until December 31, 1955.[157]

MARINES

Chapter 10

AU-1: Ground Attack Corsair

A Marine Corps AU-1 runs up prior to a mission over North Korea, late 1952. Campbell archives

Taking a page from the lesson book of early Korea air operations, the Navy contracted Vought to build the F4U-6, later known as the AU-1. The AU-1 (Attack, U [military designation for Vought], -1, first Vought attack aircraft) was designed as a low-level daylight ground-support aircraft. Survivability from small arms and light antiaircraft fire were incorporated into the design. The oil coolers were surrounded with armor plate and relocated to the wing roots.

The AU-1 had the same outward appearance of the F4U-5 but its engine was changed to the single-stage, single-speed supercharged Pratt & Whitney R-2800-83WA radial, which was designed for operations at lower altitudes. The engine was capable of 2,100hp at 2,800rpm at 3,000ft, but the power output quickly dropped off to 1,700hp at 2,800rpm at 16,000ft.

The aircraft's armament consisted of four M-3 20mm cannons, and up to ten 5in rockets or bombs on wing hard points plus additional fuel or bombs on the aircraft's centerline pylon. The heavy punch delivered by the AU-1's heavy offensive armament was exactly what the Marines needed in Korea.

F4U-5N BuNo 124665 was converted to become the first XF4U-6/AU-1. The first production AU-1 made its first flight on January 31, 1952. In all, 111 AU-1s were constructed: BuNos 129318–129417 and 133833–133843.

A factory fresh AU-1 in flight. Designed primarily for the ground attack role, the AU-1 was powered by the Pratt & Whitney R-2800-83WA radial engine. The R-2800-83WA was a single-stage supercharged engine that gave superior performance at low altitudes. Vought Aircraft

The AU-1 was delivered exclusively to the USMC beginning in the summer of 1952. VMA-323 took the AU-1 to Korea flying out of K-6 Airfield, Pyongtaek, South Korea, and VMA-312 flew AU-1s from K-3 Airfield, Pohang, South Korea. Although heavily armored, sixteen AU-1s were lost to enemy ground fire during the Korean War.[158]

As the Korean War was coming to a close, the situation in French Indochina was rapidly deteriorating. Indochina was comprised of five French colonies: Laos, Cambodia, and the three provinces that made up Vietnam (Tonkin, Annam, and Cochin-China). After World War II, the French were granted control of Southern Vietnam and began the process of "recolonizing" the remaining provinces. Fighting the Communist-backed Viet Minh for control of Vietnam, the French were fighting a point defense—defending forts and camps in the countryside, while the Viet Minh were on the offensive using guerrilla tactics.

By 1954, the French garrison had retreated to a defensive position at Dien Bien Phu. They were surrounded by four divisions of Viet Minh infantry and one artillery division. Dien Bien Phu sat in the center of a 2-mile-wide by 7-mile-long valley that was ringed

The Navy and USMC need for a close air support aircraft for the Korean War led Vought designers to modify an F4U-5 to XF4U-6 configuration, later becoming the AU-1. Increased armor plating was provide for the pilot and the fuel and oil tanks. The AU-1 was delivered exclusively to the Marines beginning in the summer of 1952. Vought Aircraft

with Viet Minh troops, artillery, and antiaircraft batteries. The Viet Minh began their attacks in the Dien Bien Phu valley on March 13, 1954.

Pilots and ground crews of 14 Flotille, Aeronavale, were rapidly deployed from Karouba, Tunisia, to Tourane, Indochina, to aid the beleaguered French paratroopers at Dien Bien Phu. Traveling to Indochina aboard US Air Force aircraft, the arriving Aeronavale pilots took delivery of twenty-five AU-1s from USMC aircraft stocks in Japan. Aeronavale pilots flew ground-support mission in the AU-1s from Bach Mai. On July 21, a cease-fire was arranged between the French and the Viet Minh. Six AU-1s had been lost at the cost of two Aeronavale pilots. The remaining AU-1s were returned to

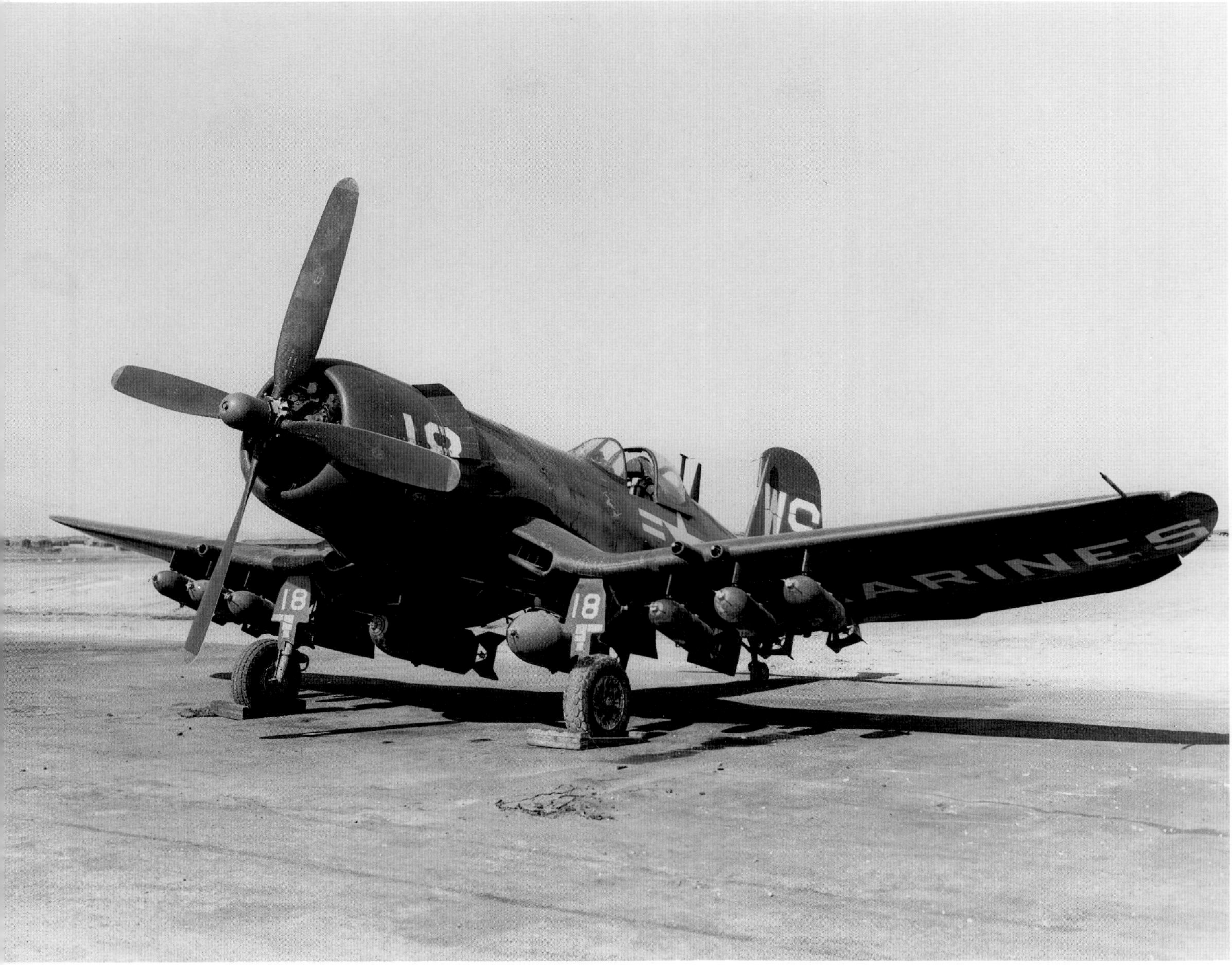

he USMC, and the 14 Flotille personnel returned to fight again in the French colonial uprising in Algeria.[159]

Operations with the AU-1s were short lived. After the Korean War cease-fire, propeller-driven aircraft were quickly phased out of front-line USMC squadrons, flying with reserve units until the type was finally phased out of US service in 1957.

AU-1s from the Marine Air Wing One's VMF-323 Deathrattlers is bombed up for a February 20, 1953, mission over Korea. Very successful in the ground-attack role, AU-1s suffered heavily with sixteen aircraft being lost to Communist antiaircraft fire from the time they were introduced in Korea, July 1952, to the end of the conflict in July 1953. USMC via Robert F. Dorr

Chapter 11

French Corsair: The F4U-7

The F4U-7 was essentially an F4U-5 fuselage mated to an overhauled F4U-4 two-speed, two-stage Pratt & Whitney R2800-18W engine. The availability of war surplus R-2800-18W engines made the powerplant an economical choice for the US government when supplying aircraft under the Military Assistance Program (MAP). The R-2800-18W was an excellent powerplant for the air superiority role the F4U-7 was envisioned to perform for the French.

Ninety-four F4U-7s were built specifically for the French Aeronavale under the MAP. The aircraft carried serial numbers 133652–133731 and 133819–133832. The basic design was 95 percent complete on December 15, 1951, and the first flight of an F4U-7 was on July 2, 1952.

After becoming an ace in the Korean War, Lt. Guy P. Bordelon, Jr., was assigned to instruct the French in their newly acquired Corsairs. "I went over and instructed them for awhile," said Bordelon, "but it was totally unsatisfactory because they had a terrible maintenance procedure: 'If it's loose, tighten it as tight as it will go.' They usually had one aircraft out of sixteen up. On a day when we got two or three up it was really unusual. I got some maintenance people in and an ordnanceman and we helped them to set up a maintenance program.

French Corsairs saw combat in Algeria, Tunisia, and in the brief Suez conflict. The crews of 14 Flotille were deployed from North Africa to Indochina while their aircraft remained in Tunisia. Although the French Corsairs never achieved an air-to-air kill, they did support their troops until the type was retired in 1964 and replaced with another Vought aircraft, the F-8 Crusader. Most Corsairs of the Aeronavale were scrapped; only three survive today. Vought Aircraft via Robert F. Dorr

The French Aeronavale received ninety-four Corsairs beginning in 1952. Here a Corsair comes aboard the carrier Bois Belleau. Vought Aircraft

"They had never fired the guns when I got there and they'd had the aircraft for months. I went up and fired the guns three times on three different hops. After each hop that I made, one of their top pilots would take the airplane up and could not get the guns to fire. When I'd take them up they would fire just perfectly. We never could figure out what they were doing wrong. We tried everything with them. I have an idea they didn't want them to fire. But later on they replaced their 20mm guns with .50-calibers, I believe. The 20mm cannon we used was a unique weapon and it required perfect head space setting on the guns and perfect belting on the ammo, and their ordnancemen apparently did not maintain these adjustments. They were a good bunch of guys and a lot of fun to be with." [160]

While flying with the French, Bordelon was based in North Africa and

The Vought-built F4U-7 closely resembled the F4U-4 in outward appearance and featured a cockpit similar to the F4U-5. The F4U-7 was powered by the R-2800-18W water-injected two-stage supercharged engine, which developed 2,100hp at takeoff. The R-2800-18W also powered the F4U-4. Vought Aircraft

also flew aboard the carrier *Bois Belleau,* formerly the US Navy carrier USS *Belleau Wood* (CVL-24).

F4U-7 into Battle

On May 8, 1945, at the end of World War II, a victory parade was held in Setif, Algeria, then a French colony. Algeria's population of almost ten million Arabs and Muslims was ruled by less than one million French colonists. During the victory parade, extremist Muslims demonstrated and a number were shot and killed by policemen. The Muslims retaliated by killing over 100 colonists. To quell the Muslim uprising, the French began naval bombardments of the Muslim villages. After the bombardments, the situation stabilized.

In November 1953, the Aeronavale deployed F4U-7-equipped 12 Flotille and 14 Flotille to Karouba, Tunisia. The crews of 14 Flotille were deployed to Indochina in October 1954, while their aircraft remained at Karouba.

The Muslims began a new round of attacks on French government installations in November 1954, and the Algerian battle for independence was on. 15

Flotille and 17 Flotille joined in the fight in 1958. Both squadrons flew from Karouba, Hyeres, and later Telergma, Algeria. The Corsairs were flown in the ground-attack role against villages near Muslim terrorist activities.

On July 26, 1956, while the French were fighting in Algeria, Egyptian President Nassar nationalized the Suez Canal, a vital economic link to the Far East for France, England, and Europe. The English and French governments planned a joint invasion of Egypt to regain control of the canal, and in August 1956, French and English nationals were evacuated from the area. During the last days of September 1956, Israel joined in the attack plans.

The Israelis began their drive across the Sinai Peninsula toward the Suez Canal on October 29. The British and French joined the fray on October 31 and November 2 respectively. The French attacked the bridge at Damietta and other targets of opportunity in the Suez and Port Siad areas. F4U-7s of 14 Flotille aboard the carrier *Arromanches* and 15 Flotille aboard the carrier *La Fayette* flew close-air-support and air-defense sorties.

After much international pressure, a cease-fire was ordered on November 7, 1956. United Nations forces began to arrive eight days later to supervise the withdrawal of the Israeli, French, and British forces. The Egyptians suffered tremendously with almost 1,600 dead or wounded, and the country's air force was decimated by the combined French, British, and Israeli air power. One French Corsair was lost in five days of fighting at the Suez canal.

Retirement

During the 1950s, the French government was waging war in Algeria, Indochina, and at the Suez Canal. The Suez incident ended with the loss of one F4U-7, and while Aeronavale Corsair pilots flew in Indochina, no F4U-7s operated there. Fighting in Algeria, the French F4U-7s were flown on ground-attack missions against rebel Muslim positions until a cease-fire was declared in March 1962. Four months later the French granted Algeria its independence.

Two years later, the Aeronavale retired their F4U-7s and replaced them with the Vought F-8 Crusader. A few F4U-7s went to technical schools in France and eventually wound their way into the hands of American warbird collectors by the mid-1970s. The remainder of the French Corsair fleet was scrapped.

The F4U-7 was the end of the propeller-driven Corsair line, a line that began in February 1938, lasted fourteen years, and produced 12,582 aircraft.

201
FAS

Chapter 12

Corsairs South of the Border

After World War II, numerous surplus American fighter, bomber, and transport aircraft were supplied to third world countries to help stem the tide of communism and to create a balance of power between neighboring nations. Three nations were to receive Corsairs through various military assistance programs: Honduras, El Salvador, and Argentina.

Under the MAP the Fuerza Aerea Hondurena (FAH) received at least five Bell P-63E Kingcobras and four Lockheed P-38 Lightnings (three P-38L models and one P-38M nightfighter) between October 1948 and September 1949.

The FAH flew these complicated Allison-engine-powered World War II fighters for the next twelve years. Slowly they cannibalized the aircraft to keep the small fleet flying. Under the MAS (Military Aid Sales) program, the FAH purchased ten US Navy surplus F4U-5s, -5Ns, and -5NLs Corsairs in early 1956.

Although the FAH P-38s and P-63s were virtually grounded and considered useless, their value as civilian "warbirds" was increasing in the United States. The late Bob Bean, a noted and eccentric warbird collector of the late 1950s and early 1960s, entered into a trade agreement with the FAH in 1959. In exchange for the four flyable P-38s and two flyable and two wrecked P-63s, Bean would trade the Hondurans ten F4U-4 Corsairs.[161]

Two years earlier, in June 1957, the Fuerza Aerea Salvadorena (FAS) purchased twenty Goodyear FG-1D Corsairs under the MAS Program. Each aircraft cost $8,700 and was sold from surplus Corsair stocks at NAS Litchfield Park, Arizona.[162] Fifteen aircraft were to be delivered in flyable condition with five aircraft grounded for use as spare ships. The US military advisors were attempting to maintain a balance of power in the region and felt that the presence of additional fighter aircraft could escalate tensions between the neighboring Central American countries. For political reasons the US military mission's objections were overruled. The five spares aircraft did not arrive in El Salvador until October 1959, and when they did arrive they were F4U-4s, not FG-1Ds. The FG-1Ds being earlier models, although having some commonality of parts with the F4U-4, were quickly grounded for a lack of necessary spare parts.

FG-1D BuNo 92460 of the Fuerza Aerea Salvadorena (FAS) at Blythe, California. The FAS acquired twenty Goodyear FG-1Ds from surplus US Navy stocks in June 1957. FAS Corsairs were on the losing end in the July 1969 Soccer War with Honduras. On July 17, 1969, FAH Capt. Fernando Soto, flying an F4U-5N, downed two FAS FG-1Ds in air-to-air combat. The 1969 Honduran-El Salvador Soccer War was the last armed conflict the Corsair would participate in as well as the only Vought-built versus Goodyear-built Corsair engagement. Gary Kuhn via Robert F. Dorr

FG-1D versus F4U-5: Last Piston-Engine Air-to-Air Combat

During the late 1960s tens of thousands of El Salvadorans had illegally migrated across the border into underpopulated Honduras. Anti-El Salvador sentiment was running high in Honduras, and by June 1969 the pot was coming to a boil.

The two countries were matched in the World Cup soccer tournament, and the tournament would become the breaking point, as well as the popular name by which the coming border war would be known. Radio Honduras broadcast anti-El Salvador propaganda as the soccer match drew near.[163] The Hondurans emerged victorious from the first soccer match, which was played in Tegucigalpa, Honduras. For the second match, held June 15, 1969, the Honduran team traveled to San Salvador and lost. The final game of the best two out of three match was held in neutral Mexico City, Mexico. Here the El Salvadoran team won and tensions between the two nations escalated. On June 26, Honduras and El Salvador broke diplomatic relations.

The "Soccer War" began on July 10 when 12,000 El Salvadoran army troops crossed the border into Honduras. The cross-border incursion was billed as an attempt to secure the safety of the Salvadorians who had settled in Honduras, yet the action had expansionist overtones. The ground troops were followed by an attack of FAS aircraft against the FAH base at Tocontin, outside of Tegucigalpa. The FAS had a number of North American P-51D Mustangs, Goodyear FG-1D Corsairs, Douglas C-47s, as well as a solitary Douglas A-26B Invader. The FAS Corsairs were flying primarily in the ground-attack role. Laden with bombs, they were escorted to their Honduran targets by P-51Ds.

The FG-1Ds of FAS would do battle with the F4U-4s and -5s of the FAH. On July 17, FAH Capt. Fernando Soto was on a ground-attack mission when one of his two wingmen were jumped by a pair of FAS Mustangs. Soto, in FAH609, an F4U-5N, quickly downed FAS Capt. Humberto Varela, who per-

Formation flight of Fuerza Aerea Hondurena (FAH) Corsairs returning to the United States. The Hondurans acquired twenty-two F4U-4 and F4U-5, -5N, and -5NL Corsairs between 1956 and 1959. The Hondurans flew their Vought-built Corsairs in air-to-air combat during the 1969 Soccer War with neighboring El Salvador's Goodyear-built FG-1Ds and P-51 Mustangs. The Hondurans sold eight of their nine remaining Corsairs to an American warbird collector in 1979. Vought Aircraft

ished in the attack. Later in the day, Soto and his wingman were en route to attack San Miguel, El Salvador, when they spotted a pair of FAS FG-1Ds. Now the Goodyear Corsairs would do battle with the later Vought-built Corsairs. Soto dropped his bombs and began to climb for an altitude advantage over the FG-1Ds. Diving on the FG-1Ds, Soto quickly flamed one, its pilot parachuting to safety. Soto overshot the second. His wingman had been bounced by an additional pair of FAS bandits and was unable to aid Soto. After maneuvering behind his second FG-1D, Soto was able to hit the aircraft's port wing, exploding the Corsair and killing the pilot.[164] lost on the ground, Soto's three kills on July 17 were the only air-to-air victories of the Soccer War.

On July 18, Honduras and El Salvador accepted the Organization of American States' peace plan. Although the peace plan had been accepted, both sides sporadically attacked each other with Honduran forces drawing the last blood on July 27 when they made a number of attacks across the border. El Salvador began to withdraw its troops from Honduras on July 29, thus ending the last aerial battles of the former World War II fighter types.

The End of the Operational Corsairs

The FAS flew its last Corsair in the summer of 1971. FAS201 was donated to the Sikorsky Memorial Airport, Connecticut, where it serves as a memorial to those who built and flew the Corsair. At least three other FAS Corsairs have been returned to the United States and are now being restored to flying condition.

The FAH retired their Corsairs in favor of the Korean War-vintage North American F-86 Sabre jet in the 1970s. The Corsairs were parked in the weeds at Tegucigalpa awaiting an uncertain future.

Enter Jim Nettle. Nettle was co owner and mechanic on a DC-4 hauling freight in Honduras. Nettle's partner the late Andres Paz Leiva, a Honduran national, had some excellent connec tions in the military and the two men tioned that they would like to purchase the Corsairs when the government nc longer needed them.

A few years passed and Nettle solc his interest in the DC-4. While wonder ing what to do next, the Corsairs were offered to Nettle and his partner by ar FAH general in late 1978. Nettle quick ly formed Hollywood Wings as the com pany under which all of the Corsai business would be transacted. The dea would take two years from the day i began until the day they had disposec of the last of the Corsair parts.

The Hondurans had nine flyable Corsairs of different models. Hollywooc Wings was able to purchase eight of the aircraft along with five to six containe loads of parts—each container was 40f long—which would later yield a trea sure trove of Corsair parts. The Cor sairs all had low airframe times, rang ing between 1,200 and 2,000 hours, ex cept for FAH614 (F4U-4 96995), which had 2,649.55 hours.[165]

The ninth Corsair, FAH609, wa Captain Soto's aircraft in which he downed the three Salvadoran aircraf during the 1969 border war. It was re tained by the Hondurans and currently sits in outside storage awaiting a suit able display space.

Nettle hired and contracted the pi lots who would ferry the Corsairs to the states. Six of the eight aircraft were flown as an "unarmed squadron of ob solete military fighter aircraft" from Tegucigalpa, Honduras, to Houston Texas, via Guatemala City, Guatemala Veracruz, Mexico; and Brownsville Texas; with final delivery to customer at Houston. The fighters were thor oughly checked out on the ground anc flight-tested while in Tegucigalpa. Net tle, who performed most of the mainte nance checks himself, says the Corsai is "just a tank. It's built to change ma jor parts with just a crescen wrench."[166]

The Corsairs had only VHF radios no navigational aids, and one-third hac no compasses. This did not present a problem as Nettle was to lead the fligh of six F4Us in a Cessna 340 from which

The late Ed Real flying an FAH F4U-4 back to the states after the aircraft's purchase by Hollywood Wings of Long Beach, California. Vought Aircraft

ıe could navigate and conduct all radio ransmissions for the flight. Nettle had prearranged the overflight permissions and fuel stops with the various governments en route.

Pilots for the flight included the ate Ed Real; the late Lou Remshner; Harold "Bubba" Beale; Mike Penketh; Bob Forbes; and the late Orrin Carr.

Mike Penketh flew FAH615, BuNo 97280, in the six ship formation from Tegucigalpa. At the time, Penketh was a PBY fire bomber pilot and had been a USMC captain flying Douglas A-4 Skyhawks with the famous VMF-214 "Black Sheep" squadron. Flying the Corsairs from Honduras to the US was not only a fitting aside to his aviation career, but the fulfillment of a dream for Penketh because his father had served in VMF-214 during Korea when the squadron flew F4U-4 Corsairs.

The crew flew commercial from Los Angeles to New Orleans, then boarded a Sasha Airlines—the national airline of Honduras—flight to Tegucigalpa. Penketh said of the Sasha flight, "About midway down on the flight to Tegucigalpa, the captain of the airliner came back to visit with us. On his shirt it said 'Fernando Soto.' He was flying the airliner down there. He didn't say anything about the Corsairs, but obviously he knew who we were and what we were doing. After that we never saw him again. Then as we were rolling out on the runway [at Tegucigalpa], on one side of the plane I could see eight Corsairs sitting there and my heart kind of skipped a beat.

"They finally let us on the military

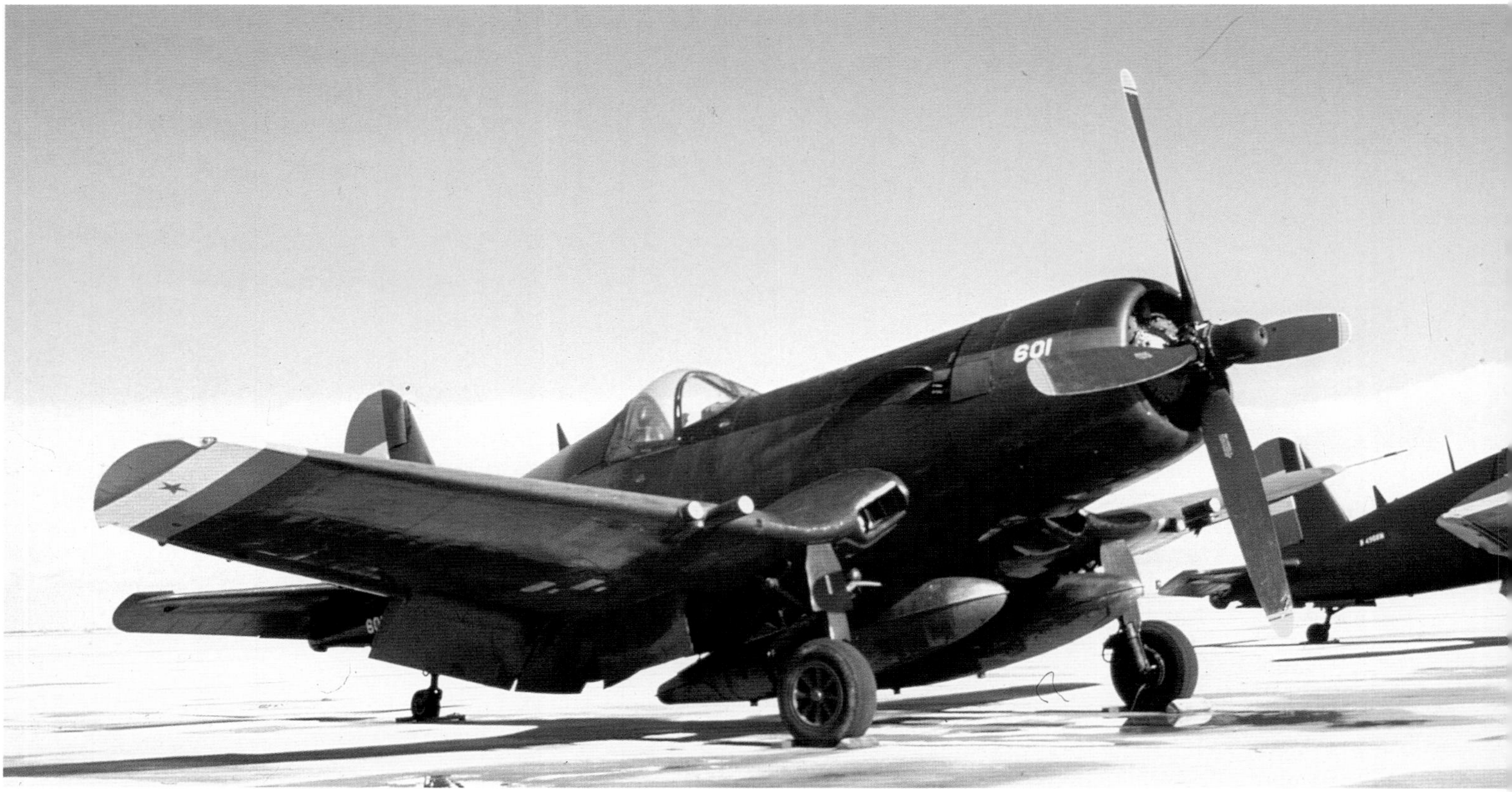

A line-up of Honduran Corsairs on the ramp before their return to the United States. Hollywood Wings bought eight of the nine FAH Corsairs, along with several 40ft containers of spare parts. Mike Penketh

base and we walked around, each guy picked out an airplane, climbed in 'em, fired up, and went out and flew 'em. It was just that simple. We had no training in the airplanes, no check outs in the airplane. We had one book written in English that one guy had read. If we had a question, we just asked him. I got an F4U-4 and just went out and flew it.

"The airplanes all flew good, they all worked well. Cosmetically the airplanes were real shabby looking. But mechanically, they were really nice. When we got down there all the airplanes had drop tanks on them, rocket racks, armor plating, gun sights, they were the real airplane. In fact the aircraft had guns in them, but they were removed shortly after we arrived.

"I'd never flown anything like it before. I'd flown the T-6 a little bit, have an awful lot of Pitts Special time, and time in general aviation tail dragger types. I was really aware of all the nasty stories you hear about the Corsair. Of course if you're aware of that stuff, you're probably not as surprised. It's not nearly as scary as the stories you hear, if you're prepared for it. I remember that you had to trim the rudder 8deg, right wing down 6deg, and zero on the elevator for takeoff. After flying a Pitts Special for about a thousand hours, you could push the power up and by the time the throttle got to the stop you were climbing at 3,000fpm. In the Corsair, if you push the power up, the tail wheel doesn't come up. You just roll down the runway. To this day I still remember rolling down the runway at Tegucigalpa and pushing the stick forward trying to get the tail wheel up, and having nothing happen. I remember trying that three times in the takeoff roll and nothing happened until I got enough speed to get the tail flying. When the tail flies, you roll on the main gear for what seems like forever—in reality a pretty short distance—and the airplane flies off when you have sufficient flying speed. You can't fly off on shear power like you can in the Pitts.

"Then you have the three-axis trim in your left hand: the rudder, elevators, and aileron trim wheels. As the airplane accelerated, it took trim changes in all three axis to keep the airplane flying hands-off. A very, very busy airplane. I thought about the guys who flew these things in combat that went from 400mph to 50mph in air combat maneuvering; they either had a right arm that was bigger than a horse, or they had real fast left hand fingers on those trim wheels. The trim changes on the airplane were incredible.

"As far as flying it, the Corsair flew just like any other airplane. It's a real long airplane. When you sit in the cockpit, you sit so far aft, and sit so high, and the nose sticks so far out in front of you, that if you breathe on the rudders you can see the nose yaw. It was very easy to be coordinated in the airplane as you could see what the airplane was doing from where you were sitting.

"The airplane flew real nice. After you got the airplane up to 200kt, it became a different airplane. It wanted to

An FAS FG-1D at San Miguel prior to the start of the Soccer War. Basset via Ethell

go faster. The faster you flew, the better it handled. Real docile. Beautiful loops. Beautiful rolls. Just a very nice flying airplane.

"I don't think the Corsairs had been flown in quite a while. When we went up to fly these things for the first day I swear to God that the entire town of Tegucigalpa turned out to watch the airplanes fly. There were road jams leading to the airport. I landed and taxied up the civilian side of the runway. The airport terminal was a four-tiered open air affair, and it was packed with people watching the airplanes. I don't know why the people were out watching unless they thought the war was on, or they came out to see the Corsair fly and say good-bye to them, or what.

"The flight back was uneventful, except I made an unscheduled landing due to a fuel leak. Three of the guys went on, while two other Corsairs landed with me. We caught up with the others in Brownsville after dark." [167]

After clearing customs in Brownsville, Texas, the six aircraft arrived in Houston on December 19, 1979, where Hollywood Wings turned the Corsairs over to their new owners.[168] Howard Pardue, of Breckenridge, Texas, and his partner Bob Ferguson, of Wellesley, Massachusetts, took delivery of FAH601 (F4U-5NL 124560), FAH604 (F4U-5N 122179), FAH605 (F4U-5 122184), FAH606 (F4U-5N 124486), FAH612 (F4U-4 97288), and FAH615 (F4U-4 97280).

Ferguson retained FAH601 and Pardue kept FAH605, selling the balance of the aircraft to recoup their investment. Ferguson sold his aircraft by 1983 and replaced it with a North American P-51D Mustang, while Pardue kept his until 1987.

Five of the pilots went back to their full-time flying jobs while Ed Real returned to retrieve the last F4U-4, FAH 614, BuNo 96995. Real flew this aircraft back unescorted.

Real was then sent back to Tegucigalpa one more time to retrieve the aircraft Hollywood Wings had decided was special—F4U-5NL BuNo 124724—and he flew it back to the states unescorted. This plane was the last -5NL built, many claim the last true Corsair built, as the AU-1 was primarily a ground attack aircraft and the F4U-7 did not see service with the US Navy or Marines. While flying from Tegucigalpa, Real was to land in Belize for fuel. As he set up for his landing, the spring-loaded tail wheel dropped, but the main gear failed to extend. After attempting to shake the gear out of the wheel wells with high-G maneuvers, Real elected to belly-land FAH600. After dropping the external fuel tanks and stopping the engine, Real dead-sticked the Corsair in and slid to a safe landing. The F4U-5NL slid on the propeller and drop tank hard points, limiting the damage to these items and the inboard flaps. The necessary parts to repair the Corsair were sent from Long Beach, California and the Corsair was quickly on its way back to the United States.

Hollywood Wings held onto 124724 until it sold the winterized nightfighter to Ralph Parker of Wichita Falls, Texas. Parker sold the aircraft in 1986 to the well-known French aeronautical collection Amicale Jean-Baptiste Salis, headed by Jean Baptiste, who then registered the aircraft F-AZEG. The last F4U-5NL is maintained in flyable condition and is flown regularly from its base at La Ferte-Alais, France.

After disposing of the flyable aircraft, Nettle began to open the containers of parts shipped up from Honduras to Long Beach, California. From the treasure chest of parts, Nettle was able to piece together three complete aircraft, which Hollywood Wings sold as "kits." These kits included FAH602, an F4U-5NL BuNo 124447, which was rebuilt, registered N100CV, and passed through a couple of owners before ending up on display at the USMC Command Museum at El Toro, California. The second kit was FAH606, an F4U-5 BuNo 124486, which was rebuilt by Phil Dear of Jackson, Mississippi, and was registered N49068. 124486 is now owned and flown by Dick Bertea of Chino, California. The last kit, FAH610, is an F4U-4, BuNo 97388, which is currently under rebuild with Gerald Beck at Wahpeton, North Dakota.

Hollywood Wings donated a number of parts to restorations being undertaken by the National Air and Space Museum and LTV Aerospace. It then sold off the balance of the parts to other F4U owners and went out of the Corsair parts business.

Argentinean Operations

In May 1956 the government of Argentina acquired ten flyable F4U-5 and -5NL Corsairs for use with Commando Aviacion Naval Argentina (CANA). One year later an additional sixteen aircraft, again -5s and -5NLs, were purchased with two or three nonflyers to be used as spare ships. Given CANA serial numbers 0374–0395 and 0432–0435, the -5 Corsairs operated from the carrier ARA *Indepencia* and were also shore-based at Punta de Indio.[169] Throughout the Corsair's service with CANA, the aircraft flew patrol missions and did not see combat.

Chapter 13

Air Racing Corsairs

Shortly after the end of World War II, t was announced that the National Air Races would resume at Cleveland, Ohio, over Labor Day weekend August 28–30, 1946. The first event of the National Air Races was the Bendix Trophy Race, a transcontinental speed dash from Los Angeles to Cleveland.

The Bendix Trophy Race was sponsored by the Bendix Aviation Corporation beginning in 1931. The race's prize money was to encourage the design and development of faster cross-country aircraft. The race could be flown nonstop with aerial refueling or with prepositioned ground stops. Additional prize money was awarded if the racer continued on and set a cross-country record flying to Bendix, New Jersey.

Prewar winners of the Bendix Trophy included such aviation luminaries as Jimmy Doolittle, Roscoe Turner, Ben O. Howard, Jackie Cochran, Louise Thaden, and Frank Fuller.

The fastest prewar time and speed for the Los Angeles (Van Nuys Airport) to Cleveland race was set by Frank Fuller in 1939 flying a Seversky SEV-S2. Fuller covered the 2,048 miles to Cleveland in 7 hours, 14 minutes, and 19 seconds. He continued on to Bendix—a total distance of 2,450 miles—setting a cross-country record of 8 hours, 58 minutes, and 8 seconds.

The field for the August 30, 1946, Bendix Trophy Race consisted of twenty-two aircraft, seventeen of which would finish. Entered in the Bendix race were fifteen Lockheed P-38 Lightnings, four North American P-51 Mustangs, one Bell P-63 Kingcobra, a Douglas A-26 Invader, and a Goodyear FG-1D, BuNo 88086, flown by Thomas Call. Registered NX63382, this FG-1D had Race No. 90 and the nickname *Joe*.

Kevin Eldridge rounds the pylons in the Super Corsair *at the 1992 National Championship Air Races. He finished the race in sixth place.* Nick Veronico

Paul Mantz was the first across the finish line in his P-51C, NX1202. Mantz beat Fuller's 1939 Bendix time by more than 4 hours, covering the distance in 4 hours, 42 minutes, and 14 seconds, for an average speed of 435.501mph. Mantz flew nonstop. In fifteenth place was Call and the FG-1D. Call flew the 2,043 miles in 6 hours, 17 minutes, and 29 seconds at an average speed of 325.612mph.

The field for the 1947 Bendix Trophy Race had thinned out. The race was again launched from Van Nuys Airport, and thirteen aircraft were entered: six P-51s of various models, three P-38s, a P-63, an A-26, and FG-1D BuNo 88086—back with a new number, 99, and a new pilot; this time Frank Whitton was at the controls.

Once again Paul Mantz won the race in NX1202. Mantz improved his time and speed over the 1946 race by 17 minutes and 25mph. The first six places of the Bendix race went to P-51 Mustangs. Whitton placed seventh, covering the course in 6 hours, 24 minutes, and 4 seconds, at an average speed of 320.025mph. After the 1947 Bendix race, it was obvious that the Corsair could not compete.

F2Gs Dominate the Thompson Trophy Races

After a rather poor showing in the Bendix distance races, the Corsair was to leave its mark in the record books of pylon racing at the Thompson Trophy Races, which took place each year in Cleveland after the Bendix race.

The Thompson Trophy Race began in 1929 as the Thompson Cup race—five laps of a 10-mile closed course. Doug Davis won the race at an average speed of 194.90mph flying a Travel Air-R Mystery Ship. Davis took home a $750 purse. Jimmy Doolittle won the race in 1932 flying the Gee Bee R-1 at a speed of 252.686mph. Roscoe Turner won the race in 1934 and 1938, and in 1939 he flew the Turner Special *Miss Champion* to victory at a speed of 282.536mph. He took home $16,000 in the last prewar Thompson Trophy Race.

The days of custom-built racers in the Thompson race were over. Thousands of surplus ex-military aircraft were up for sale at dozens of storage facilities across the United States. As the US military entered the jet age, numerous types of propeller-driven fighters were becoming obsolete. The aircraft chosen by the new breed of Thompson Trophy contestants ranged from P-38s and P-51s to P-39s and P-63s to FG-1Ds and F2Gs.

The 1946 Thompson Trophy Race covered a distance of 300 miles—twenty laps of a 15-mile closed course, with a race purse totaling $40,000. To qualify, pilots had to complete two laps at a minimum average speed of 300mph.

Twelve aircraft qualified for the September 2, 1946, Thompson: five P-51Ds, four P-63s, one P-39, a P-38, and an FG-1A—BuNo 13481, NX69900, No. 92 *Lucky Gallon*, flown by Cook Cleland. Cleland qualified fifth at an average speed of 361.81mph. "Tex" Johnston, in the P-39 *Cobra II*, was top qualifier at 409.09mph.

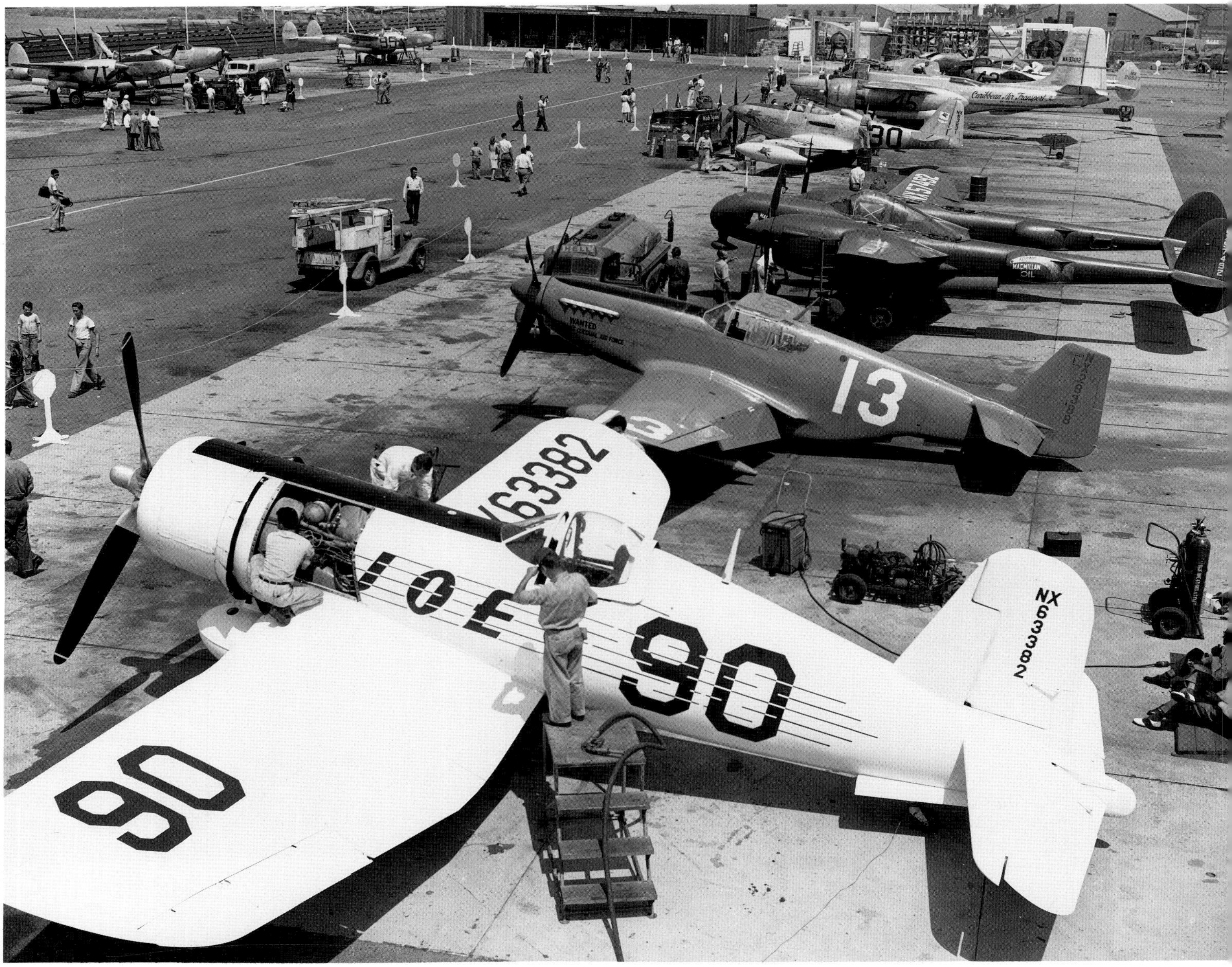

Thomas Call entered Joe, *an FG-1D, BuNo 88086, NX63382, No. 90, in the 1946 Bendix.* Joe *is seen at the Van Nuys Airport preparing for the start of the Bendix race to Cleveland, Ohio. Call flew Number 90 to a fifteenth-place finish.* Birch Matthews via A. Kevin Grantham

The Thompson featured a racehorse start. After the green flag was dropped, the field of twelve racers took off heading for the home pylon, turning, then entering the race course.

When the green flag dropped for the 1946 Thompson, Tex Johnston in *Cobra II* was the first off the ground and around the home pylon. Chuck Tucker was close behind, but could not retract his main landing gear and was forced out of the race. Cook Cleland and *Lucky Gallon* were flying in the middle of the pack. George Welch, flying a P-51D named *Wraith*, moved into second place, gaining on Johnston. Before he could complete the second lap, Welch was out of the race with cylinder problems. With Tucker and Welch out of the way, Tony LeVier and his P-38 *Fox of the Skyways* started moving up on Johnston. During the last lap, Johnston and LeVier were separated from Cleland by three P-51D Mustangs. Johnston finished the race in 48 minutes 8.41 seconds at an average speed o 373.908mph. LeVier was second a 370.193, followed by Earl Ortman in No. 2, a P-51D, with an average speed of 367.625mph. Cleland and the FG-1L finished sixth at an average speed o 357.465mph.

A new type of racing plane made its first appearance in the 1947 Thompson Trophy Race: the R-4360-powered F2C Corsair. Cook Cleland, who was able to obtain three Super Corsairs from the Navy, had flown SBDs during the war He had been on the USS *Wasp* when it was sunk at Guadalcanal and was then

ʾook Cleland qualified to race in the 1946 ʾhompson Trophy Race in Lucky Gallon, *an ʾG-1A, BuNo 13481, NX69900, No. 92. Cle-ɜnd flew* Lucky Gallon *around the 15-mile ourse at an average speed of 361.81mph in ʾualifying. Cleland and* Lucky Gallon *fin-shed the 1946 Thompson in sixth place at n average speed of 357.465mph.* Leo Kohn ʾia Tim Weinschenker

ransferred to the new USS *Lexington.* ʾuring the last year of the war he was test pilot at Tactical Test, Naval Air ʾest Center Patuxent River, Maryland, ʾhere he met then Ens. Richard M. ɜecker, his 1947–1949 racing team-nate. During his tour at sea, Cleland ad been highly decorated and even re-eived the Navy's highest award, the ɴavy Cross, for dropping a 1,000lb omb on the deck of a Japanese carrier. ɐfter placing sixth in the only Navy lane entered in the 1946 Thompson, ʋord reached Cleland that Admiral Ialsey had said he would like to see a ood Navy airplane win the race. "So I ʋent down to see Admiral Halsey in Vashington, D.C.," said Cleland. "I ʾalked in cold. I told him I wanted the uper Corsair. Admiral Halsey asked ne, 'Son, what do you want to win this ace for?' I could have said I wanted to y for fame and fortune, the Blue and ɜold, the big trophy, or the big money, ut I said, 'I want to put it to the Air orce.' He just came right out of his hair! That was at 9:30 in the morning. ʾhe Navy made a survey, declared the ircraft surplus, turned them over to Var Assets Administration. War As-ets put them out for bid, my bid was ccepted, and I owned the first airplane t 3:30 in the afternoon."[170] Things appen fast when a five-star admiral ushes the paper along.

"After we got the first airplane, the oor was kind of open," Cleland said. ʾhe F2Gs started arriving as surplus. Becker and I tried to corner the mar-et, but we missed out. Ron Puckett got ne. He flew the hell out of it too."[171] on Puckett had bid for one of the oth-r surplus F2Gs and was able to ac-

his rare photo shows Cook Cleland round-ɡ a pylon in F2G-2 BuNo 88463, N5577N, ɥring the 1947 Thompson Trophy races. H. . Martin, Robert J. Pickett Collection, ansas Aeronautical Historical Society

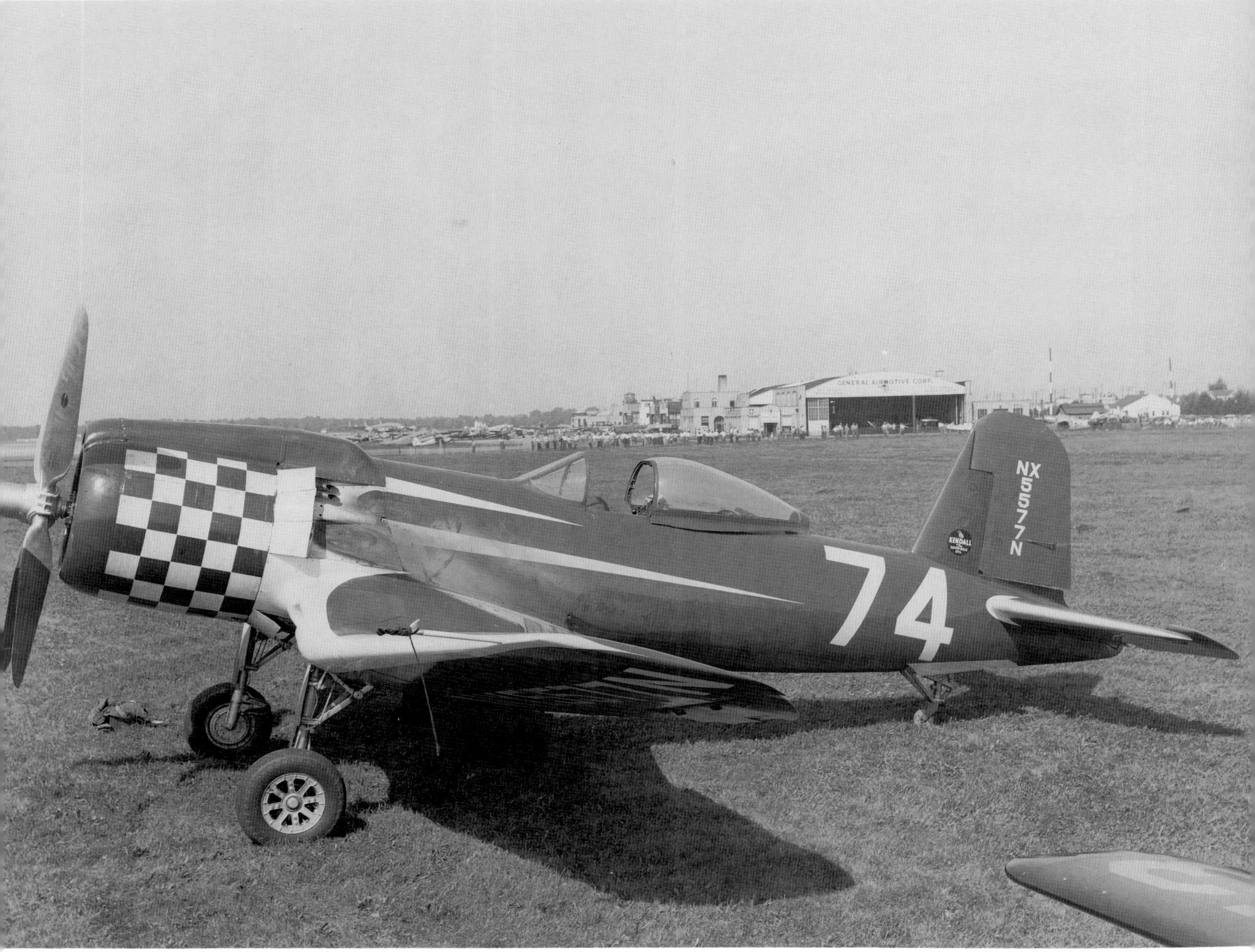

F2G No. 74, in which Cleland won the 1947 Thompson Trophy race at an average speed of 396.131mph, rests after the record-setting race. Note the lengthened Navy-designed carburetor air scoop, which increased the air flow to the carburetor allowing the R-4360 to develop a reported 4,000hp. Campbell Collection

quire XF2G-1 BuNo 14694, N91092, which he raced as number 18.

Dick Becker describes the formation of Cleland's all-F2G 1947 Thompson Trophy Race team, "In the original group of aircraft, Cook bid on and acquired three. Subsequently he bid on a fourth one and acquired it. At the time that he got these three airplanes, I had agreed that I would fly one, Cook was going to fly another one, and another fellow, Tommy Thomas [later an Admiral], who had been a test pilot with us in the Navy, had agreed to take some leave and come home and fly one for Cook also. But apparently the Navy found out what he was going to do and told him he couldn't. So Cook had to get somebody to fly the third airplane, and in desperation he took on Tony Janazzo, who was flying in the reserves down out of Akron. He was flying the standard Corsair, and Cook figured h could handle it, so Tony was sort of a fill-in choice."[172]

Cleland would fly F2G-2 BuN 88463, N5577N, while his teammate Dick Becker and Tony Janazzo would fly XF2G-1 BuNo 14693, N5590N, and F2G-1 BuNo 88457, N5588N, respectively. Becker's XF2G-1 had bee stricken on July 31, less than one month prior to qualifications.

The twelve planes for the 194 Thompson Trophy race were parke abreast for the horse-race start. Cleland, sitting in the pole position, said

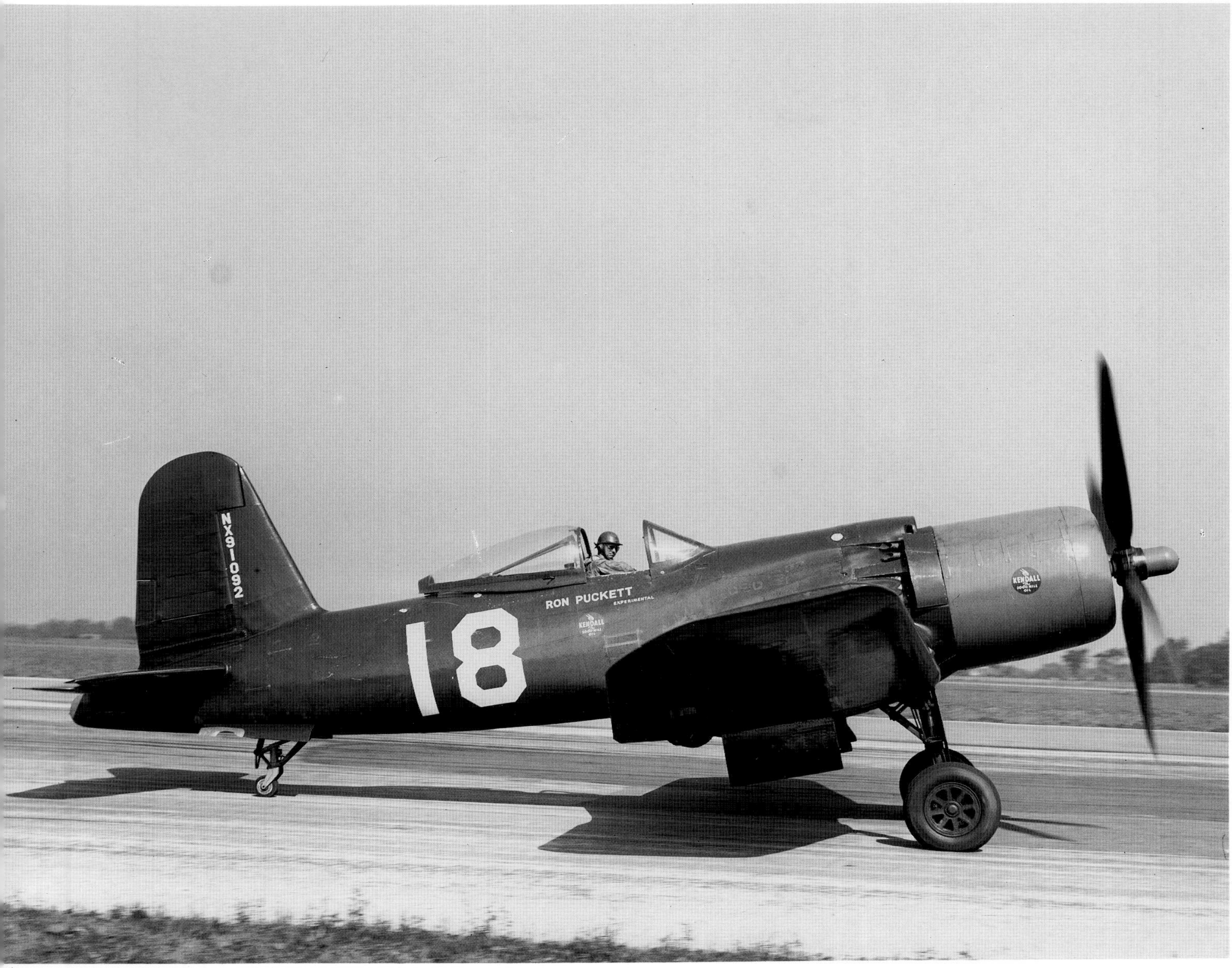

Dashing Ron Puckett finished the 1949 Thompson Trophy Race at an average speed of 393.527mph, placing him second behind Cook Cleland. H. G. Martin , Robert J. Pickett Collection, Kansas Aeronautical Historical Society

They dropped the flag, you took your oot off the brakes, pushed the throttle orward, and off you went. Then you ad to fight for the first pylon." Jay Demming (who flew the 1946 Thompson-winning P-39, *Cobra II*) was, as Cleland puts it, "temporarily ahead. Then we [Cleland and Becker] passed im and we stayed out in front. Old Becker was ahead of me and he and I ever talked over who's going to win. Finally I caught up to him and I got im on a pylon—he had to give vay."[173]

Cleland and Becker's teammate Tony Janazzo did not finish the seventh lap. Apparently overcome by carbon monoxide fumes, Janazzo was flying erratically before hitting the ground at almost 400mph. "We all had carbon monoxide in our cockpits. I think Tony didn't recognize the problem, or when he began to recognize the problem he cracked open the cockpit, which brought in more carbon monoxide," Becker said. "This is only speculation, we don't know exactly what happened. Also, the exhaust stacks would crack and break. This would let the engine exhaust fire right inside the cowling. The firewalls have various leaks where there is penetration of the instrumentation and the exhaust gases would seep in [to the cockpit]. By opening the canopy you would really ingest it. We think that's what he did, giving himself a fatal dose."[174] As a result of Tony Janazzo's death, wearing oxygen masks became a race requirement.

Cleland finished the race first, Becker second, and Demming third.

Dick Becker flew No. 74, N5577N, for the 1948 and 1949 Thompson Trophy races. Becker was unable to start the 1949 races when his propeller reduction gear stripped after he qualified in the pole position. H. G. Martin, Robert J. Pickett Collection Kansas Aeronautical Historical Society

The brute horsepower of the R-4360 dominated the first two finishing positions. Cleland and Becker were looking forward to winning the 1948 Thompson.

The horse-race start of the 1948 Thompson Trophy race featured four P-51Ds, a single P-51A and P-39, two P-63s, and the F2Gs of Cleland and Becker. This year the F2Gs boasted many modifications, the most visible were the aircraft's modified carburetor air-intake scoops.

Using a new special fuel blend, Cleland turned the second and third laps at 410mph! Becker described the new fuel: "Cook had learned about this fuel which was made by Shell. It was made specifically for Pratt & Whitney for engine-test-stand work to take the power section up to extremely high power output to look at the destruction of accessories. And Cook thought that if Shell would put this fuel together and we g some, it would really enhance our o portunities. At the time of the race, t maximum octane fuel available wa 150. This particular triptane that She put together was the equivalent of 21 octane. We ran it and tried it out. An under warmer conditions, it worke real well."[175]

The 1948 race was a somewh overcast, rainy, dull day—cooler tha the days on which Cleland and Beck had tested the new fuel. The fuel mi ture was so slow burning that spar timing had to be advanced to the poi that combustion was taking place whe

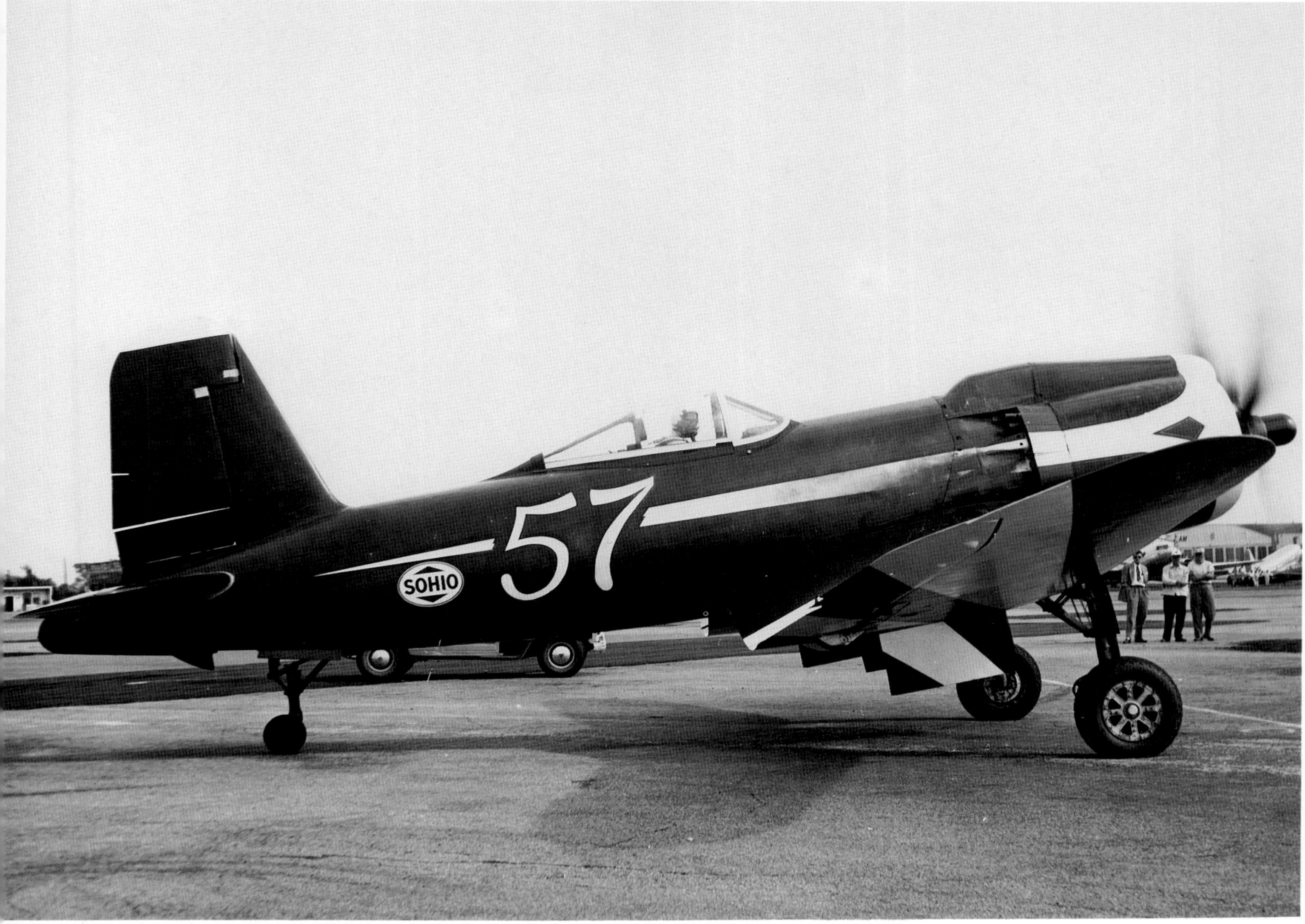

Ben McKillen placed third at the 1949 Thompson Race, behind the F2Gs of Cook Cleland and Ron Puckett. McKillen finished with an average speed of 387.589mph. Roger Besecker collection

the intake valve was opening and while the exhaust valve was closing, creating the potential for a catastrophic backfire through the intake system. On the third lap Becker's engine backfired, blowing off his carburetor air intake scoop, which forced him out of the race. On the fourth lap, Cleland experienced the same problem. Both of the Cleland team F2Gs were out of the race. "We had tested the carburetors with a mixture of triptane high-octane fuel said Cleland. "And instead of using water injection, we were using hydrogen peroxide. We found this information in captured German documents. They had experimented with it in World War II. The day of the race was cloudy and our rpms were high. It was just like someone tossed a hand grenade in the cockpit. It was a bad year. We won $200, lap money for two laps."[176]

The field for the 1949 Thompson Trophy race consisted of one P-51A, one P-51C, three P-51Ds, one P-51K, Chuck Tucker's highly modified P-63C, and the F2Gs of Cook Cleland, Dick Becker, Ben McKillen, and Ron Puckett.

McKillen was flying F2G-1 BuNo 88454, N5588N, the second aircraft to wear this registration number. McKillen was a flight instructor at Cleland's flight school, becoming the third pilot on the Cleland team after the death of Tony Janazzo. McKillen flew in Cleland's fourth Corsair.

For the 1949 races, Cleland cut 4 1/2ft off the wings of his racer and added tip plates. "You couldn't have flown without the tip plates," Cleland said. He was now flying with a 14ft diameter prop. "With a 20 percent depression in the tires, on takeoff, I had 2 1/4in of clearance," said Cleland. "We had to do something because Jackie Cochran had spent $150,000 bucks [on the P-51 *Beguine* piloted by Bill Odom]. She had cut off the belly scoop of her P-51 and put the radiators out in two wing-tip tanks. She picked up, I think, 46mph just on that one modification."[177]

For Dick Becker, 1949 was a repeat of the 1948 races. "I flew No. 74,"said

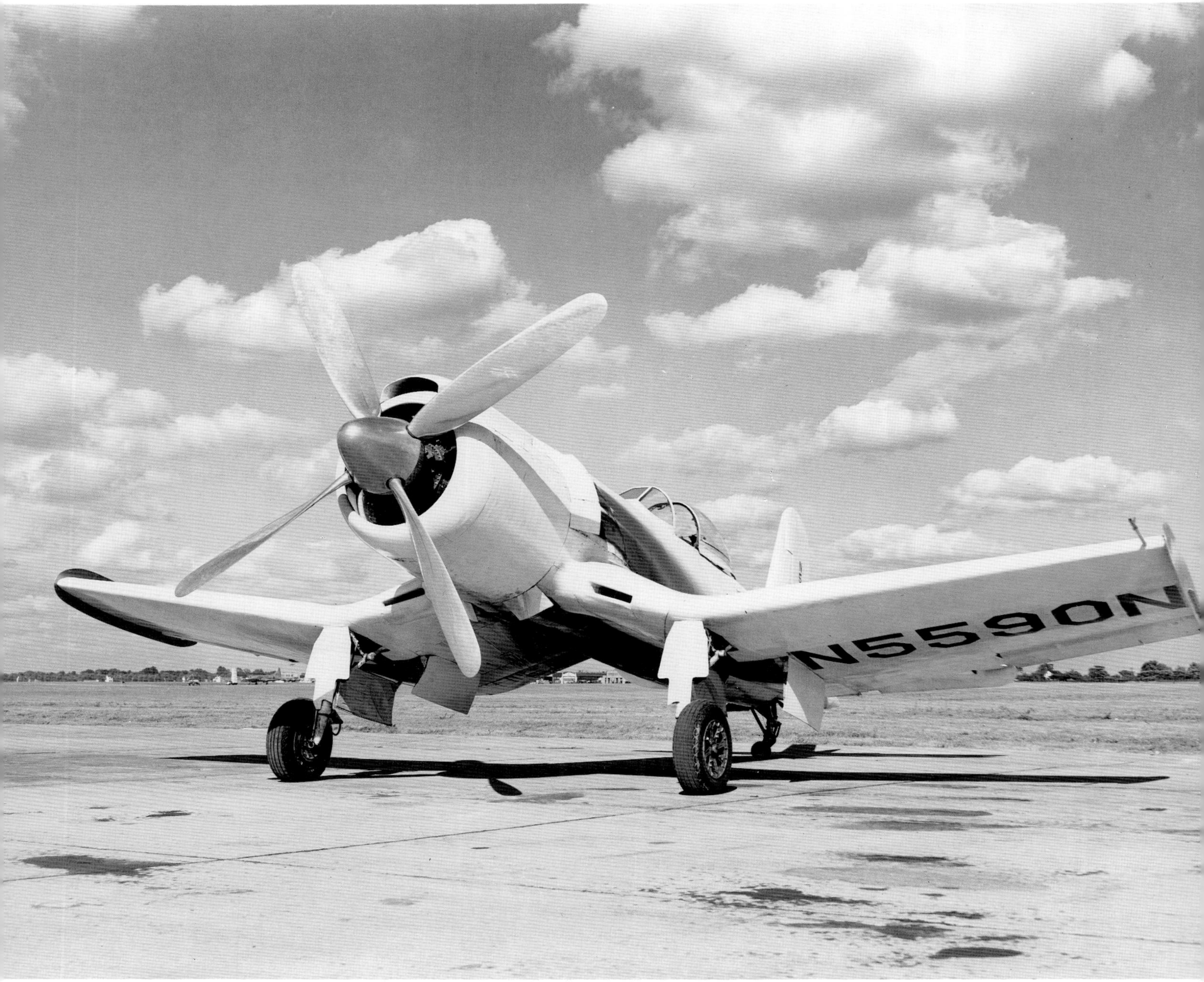

Cleland flew Number 94 to victory in the 1949 Thompson Trophy Race at an average speed of 397.071mph—a record that stood for twenty years until broken by Darryl Greenameyer in 1969. H. G. Martin , Robert J. Pickett Collection Kansas Aeronautical Historical Society

Becker. "Cleland was flying No. 94. I took No. 74 around for qualifying later in the day and later in the qualification week. The need to qualify was there and I just picked my day, went up, and did it. I had gotten frightened away from the triptane, so I went back to the 150-octane fuel and normal water injection. Somehow number 74 just responded so beautifully that day that I had the pole position being the top qualifier. I came in at around 415mph and Cleland was second, Odom was third. So I had the pole position. However, as I completed the second lap of the qualification run, the reduction gear stripped in the nose section of the airplane. In fact it disconnected the propeller and the engine just destructed. I had to do a dead stick landing. So even though I was qualified and on the records and did really have the pole position, I could not start the race."

The starter's flag dropped and the race was on. "I was out in front and this fancy Jackie Cochran airplane was on my tail," Cleland recalled. "A guy

Gene Akers was the first pilot to race a Corsair since the Cleveland days. Akers' F4U-4 BuNo 97259, N6667, is seen here at the 1967 National Championship Air Races at the beginning of its civilian modification program. The tail feathers and cowling have been painted while the fuselage remains bare metal prior to being painted. A. Kevin Grantham collection

named Bill Odom was flying it. He was quite famous and had flown around the world with Milton Reynolds. I tried to keep track of him for a while down on the southern pylons. The sun was getting low and you could see the shadows—kind of who's behind you. Then about the fourth or fifth lap I saw a house burning. He overshot a pylon, tried to snap back in and got into trouble." Odom crashed into a house near the second pylon, killing himself and a mother and her child.

Cleland won the race at an average speed of 397.071mph, followed by Ron Puckett in his XF2G-1 at an average speed of 393.527mph, with Cleland's teammate McKillen following in third place at 387.589mph. R-4360-powered Corsairs came in first, second, and third. Cleland was good to his promise to Admiral Halsey; he did "stick it" to the Air Force after all.

The Odom crash and the Korean War put an end to the Thompson Trophy races at Cleveland. Two-time winner Cleland returned to active duty as commanding officer of VF-653 flying F4U-4s.

Corsair Returns to Modern Air Racing

Billed as the National Championship Air Races, unlimited pylon racing was reborn at Reno, Nevada, in September 1964. Accompanying the pylon races, Harold's Club sponsored a transcontinental trophy dash similar to the Bendix race. These early years of post-Cleveland air racing were dominated by P-51 Mustangs and F8F Bearcats.

Eight months after the first Reno air races, a Corsair was back on the racing circuit, albeit with a shaky start. The Los Angeles National Air Races were held at Fox Field, Lancaster, California, from May 29–June 6, 1965. The race consisted of fifteen laps of a 9-mile closed course. An FG-1D, BuNo 92081, registered N4719C, and owned by Lou Kaufman, was entered into the race. Lynn Whinney was to fly the stock Corsair, No. 2. During the test hop one day prior to the time trials, Whinney crashed and was killed, dashing the hopes of a Corsair victory at the Los Angeles races. Chuck Lyford, flying a P-51D won the race with an average speed of 366.82mph.

Two years after the crash of Kauf-

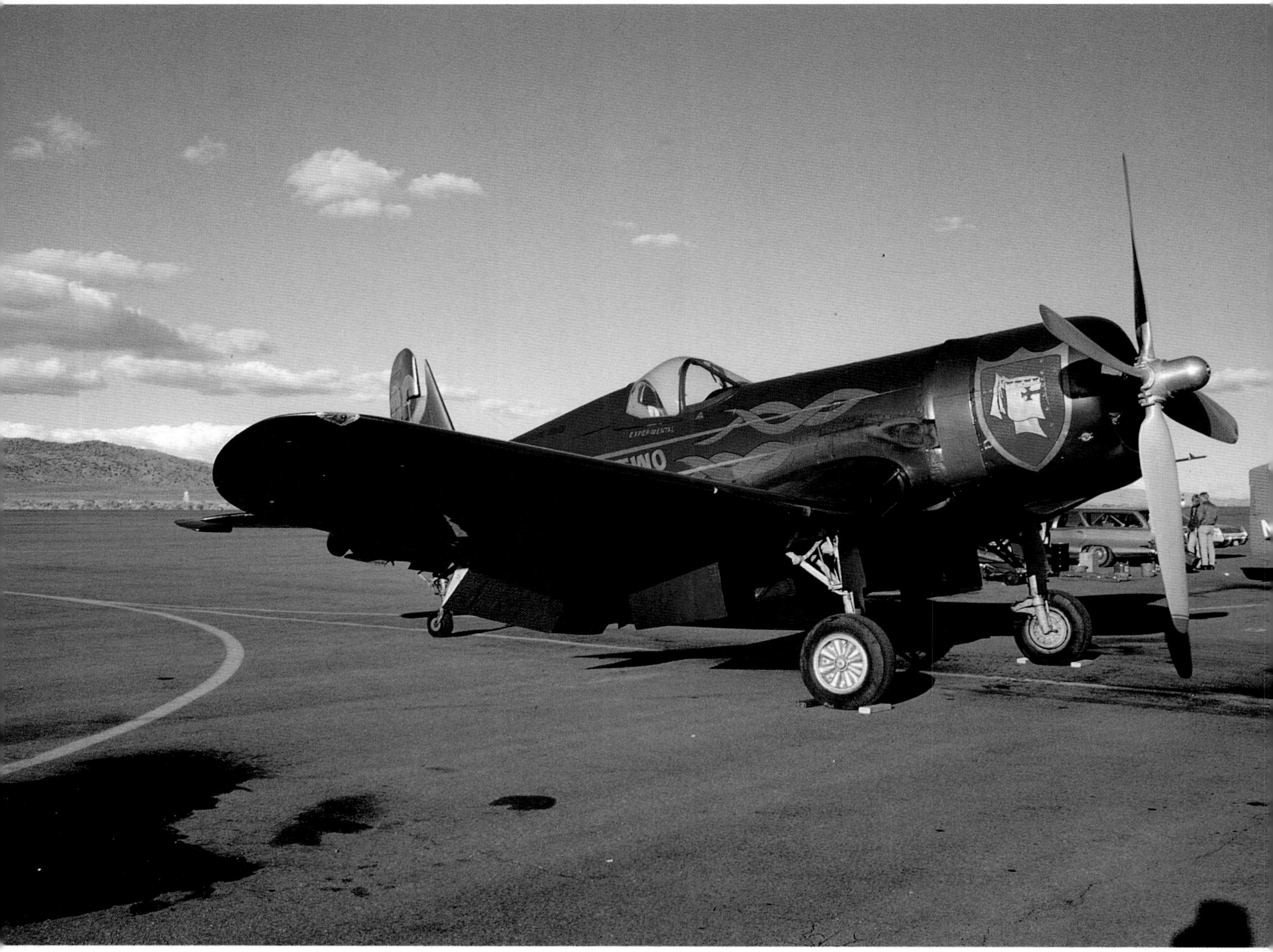

By the 1968 Reno races, Akers' Corsair had been fully painted and wore the name Lancer Two. A. Kevin Grantham collection

man's Corsair, former B-17 and current air-tanker pilot Eugene Akers successfully raced the first Corsair in a post-1964 event. Flying F4U-4 BuNo 97259, No. 22, Akers' first racing event was the National Championship Air Races held at Stead Field, north of Reno, September 21 to 24, 1967. Akers was sponsored by his employer at the time, Cal-Nat Airways of Grass Valley, California. His aircraft was just beginning the painting process. Only the cowling, tail, and wing tips had been painted, in a dark green, with red No. 22 on the tail. "Mac Mendoza and I were airplane nuts. He's a Navy mechanic. We just were old friends and we decided we wanted to go air racing. So we figured what's the best airplane for it and we decided on the Corsair. We just ran it stock," Akers said.[178]

Bob Mitchem also attended the 1967 Reno races in his FG-1D, BuNo 92050, registered N194G, and called *Big Hummer*. This stock FG-1D was flown in a natural unpolished aluminum and zinc chromate green an primer gray scheme with red No. 94 On final to Stead, Mitchem's engin seized. After a hair-raising landing Mitchem and his crew attempted t change engines before the deadline fo qualifications. Unable to meet th deadline, Mitchem and No. 94 were ou of the race.

The 1967 Reno course measured distance of 8.04 miles and the Unlimit ed class was to complete ten laps. Th Unlimited field of sixteen racers con sisted primarily of P-51Ds. Akers' F4U 4, Mike Carroll's Hawker Sea Fury and Greenameyer's F8F-1—which ha

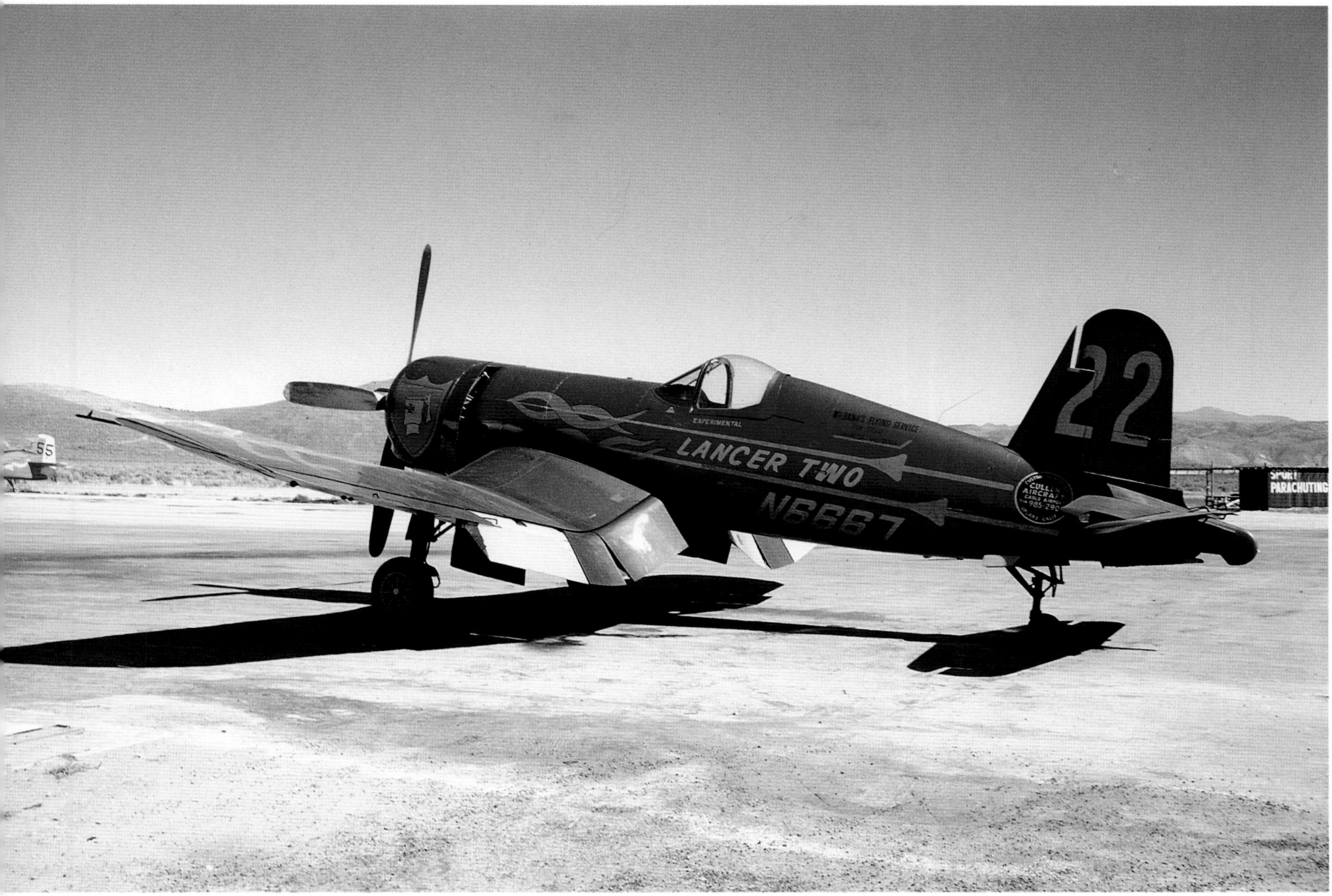

A profile of Lancer Two *showing the knight's helmet on the cowling and the jousting lances on the fuselage.* A. Kevin Grantham collection

von the two previous Reno races—ounded out the field. Having qualified enth at a speed of 316.67mph, Akers vent on to finish fourth in the Unlimit-d Consolation race with an average peed of 300.78mph. Around the py-ons, Akers said the Corsair flew "great. Vith that big long nose you didn't have o watch the ground at all. You just put he nose a couple inches below the hori-on, and it acted like a big old broom tick coming around the pylons. The ose didn't drop off or come up high ike some planes do. It was an ideal rac-r I thought. The Corsair just didn't ave enough power."[179]

For 1968, Akers returned to Reno vith the F4U-4 sporting a sharp look-ng green, gold, and red paint scheme. t was nicknamed *Lancer Two*. "We vanted something a little different han it came out. We got a sponsor for the paint job and it was supposed to be more of a metallic blue than a green. So we took what we got, it was free. I've always been sort of a white knight type. That's why we had the knight's helmet on the cowling. It was supposed to have been *Lancer's Two* for the two of us—the mechanic and the pilot—but they put *Lancer Two*. They dropped the 's off for some reason. I guess they thought we made a mistake on the sketch for the paint scheme. That's how it got that name," Akers said.[180]

The race pylons had been respotted for 1968, and the course now measured 8.5 miles. Akers arrived too late to qualify but was allowed to race in the twelfth qualifying position to round out the Unlimited racing field. Moving up one place from his 1967 finish, Akers and *Lancer Two* finished in the money at third place in the Unlimited Consolation race with an average speed of 301.54mph.

Lancer Two was busy in 1969. Dick Thomas flew the now veteran racing Corsair in the September 14 Harold's Club Transcontinental Trophy Dash from Milwaukee to Reno. Ten aircraft entered the 1,667-mile race including two F8Fs, six P-51Ds, Akers' Corsair, and a Beech Bonanza. Thomas finished the race in ninth place, taking 7 hours and 39 minutes to fly the distance with an average speed of 217.86mph.

Two days later the National Championship Air Races got underway at Stead Field. Akers qualified *Lancer*

The Corsair with the longest racing history is Bob Guilford's F4U-7 BuNo 133693, N693M. It began turning the pylons at the 1970 California 1,000 race held in Mojave and made its last racing appearance at Reno 1986. A. Kevin Grantham collection

Two at 281.25mph, twelfth in the field of fifteen racers. Competing in the second heat race, Akers finished sixth at an average speed of 296.11mph. The 1969 Unlimited races also saw an interesting turn of events. At the 1949 Cleveland air races Cook Cleland had flown his F2G to a closed course speed record of 397.07mph. Cleland's record stood for twenty years until Darryl Greenameyer broke the record during the 1969 Reno Unlimited Gold races, flying a highly modified F8F to an average race speed of 412.63mph.

Gene Akers and *Lancer Two* didn't make the 1970 races held September 14–20. Bob Mitchem did return to Reno in No. 94, and this year *Big Hummer* resembled its nickname. In three short years, the plane had gone from a stock FG-1D to a thoroughly competitive racer. The airframe and wings had undergone an intensive aerodynamic cleanup; the flaps were sealed; the cowl flaps had been removed and replaced with a cowl fairing; the FG-1D's wing-root carburetor air intake ducts had been skinned over and an F2G-style carburetor air intake scoop had been mounted above the cowling; and *Big Hummer* was now turning a propeller from a Skyraider with a P-51H prop spinner. *Big Hummer* placed fourth in the first heat race with a speed of 344.40mph. Advancing to the consolation race, Mitchem finished a very competitive third with an average speed of 357.95 mph.

The fall of 1970 brought an additional venue to air racing. Located in the high desert north of Los Angeles, the former Marine base at Mojave was to be the site of the California 1000

FG-1D BuNo 92509, N92509, was only raced once at the 1971 Cape May, New Jersey, air races. Ron Reynolds was the pilot and he lost the left aileron after the start of the first heat race. Robert F. Pauley via Tim Weinschenker

Held November 13–15, the race was to be sixty-six laps of a 15-mile course. Among the thirty-four aircraft entered were two Corsairs. Akers flew *Lancer Two*, which sported a new overall blue paint scheme, and Bob Guilford, in F4U-7 BuNo 133693, N693M, No. 3, *Blue Max*. Sherman Cooper won the California 1000 flying a Sea Fury. "The race was real strenuous to fly, especially the time in the 1,000-mile race. It was a 3-hour race and it really took everything out of you. You had to land once and we changed pilots for the remainder of the race. Captain Birdwell, Commanding Officer of China Lake's VX-5, took over in the middle of the race," Akers said.[181] Akers finished fourteenth having completed fifty-five laps, and Guilford was sixteenth after forty-seven laps.

Four Unlimited pylon races were slated for 1971. The first one of the year was held June 6 at Cape May, New Jersey. Six P-51Ds, a Sea Fury, two F8Fs, and a Corsair would fly ten laps of a 7.5-mile course. Registered to John T. Van Andel of Stamford, Connecticut, *Whistling Death*, an FG-1D BuNo 92509, N92509, No. 86, was flown by Ron Reynolds. Reynolds qualified at a speed of 310.71mph. After the start of the first Unlimited heat race as Reynolds entered the first turn, he lost the left aileron. After declaring a Mayday, he landed safely. Reynolds and No. 86 were out of the races for the weekend. Lyle Shelton won the Cape May Unlimited races in his Bearcat at an average speed of 360.15mph. Although Reynolds would go on to compete in other races, N92509 was retired from pylon racing.

The second race of the year was held July 18 at Brown Field, southeast of San Diego. This distance dash was 100 laps of a 10-mile course. The field of fourteen aircraft included Akers' F4U-4 and Guilford's F4U-7, which was flown in this race by Bob Laidlaw. Sherman Cooper won this 1,000-mile race while Akers finished sixth with an average speed of 276mph. Laidlaw did not finish the race.

September brought the Unlimited racers back to Reno. The course had been extended to 9.8 miles. Akers was absent from the field of qualifiers, but Bob Mitchem was back in *Big Hummer*, No. 94. Guilford, flying his F4U-7, rounded out the field of eighteen Unlimited racers. Guilford qualified his Corsair at 289.66mph and went on to take second place in the Unlimited Medallion (later referred to as the Silver) race at a speed of 264.77mph. Mitchem flew the Corsair like it was on rails. During qualifying he posted a speed of 342.19mph but was guilty of pylon cuts. Unable to requalify before the races, he was disqualified.

The California 1,000, held November 13, was the final race of 1971. Fourteen aircraft started the race and ten finished. Akers' and Guilford's Corsairs were on hand to compete. To keep spectator interest, the racing distance was reduced from sixty-six laps to forty-one of the 15.15-mile course. The late Frank Sanders won the race flying his Sea Fury at an average speed of 346.55mph. Akers brought *Lancer Two* in for a fifth place finish with a speed of 314.97mph, having completed thirty-eight laps. Guilford finished tenth. He completed thirty-two laps at an average speed of 264.16mph.

Competition for 1972 consisted only of Reno. Sixteen aircraft qualified for the race with Mitchem's *Big Hummer* the sole Corsair in the field. Mitchem qualified at a speed of 367.50mph. The Unlimited Championship (later referred to as the Gold) race would be eight laps of the 9.8-mile course. Gunther Balz won it, setting a new race record speed of 416.16mph, while Mitchem finished fifth with an average speed of 341.99mph.

Akers had wanted to replace the F4U-4's R-2800 with an R-4360 but did not have the money. He and his partner sold the aircraft, and Akers retired from racing. Bob Mitchem sold his Corsair shortly after the Reno races. This left Bob Guilford with the sole Corsair participating in pylon racing.

Robert Yancey flew this ex-FAH F4U-4 as No. 101 in the 1981–1987 race seasons. A. Kevin Grantham collection

From 1972 until 1978, Bob Guilford and his F4U-7 were the mainstay of racing Corsairs. Guilford turned the pylons in the neighborhood of 330mph at each event, thus keeping the Corsair in the race while he had a great time.

During 1978 and 1979, at Chino Airport, California, the late Jim Maloney and The Air Museum Planes of Fame campaigned an F4U-1, BuNo 17799, registered N83782, No. 0, nicknamed *The Chino Kids*. Maloney qualified at a speed of 314.968mph at Reno 1978, finishing in the heat races at a speed of 282.00mph, too slow to move up into the money races.

Air race pilot Don Whittington brought Unlimited-style racing to South Florida in March 1979. The Homestead Air Races, held at Homestead Airport, drew twenty-eight racers competing for a cash purse of $120,000. Two Corsairs were entered in the Stock class. Howard Pardue flew his FG-1D, BuNo 92095, registered N67HP, and Dennis Bradley flew the Canadian Warplane Heritage's FG-1D, BuNo 92436, registered C-GCWX. Bill Whittington won the Stock race flying a P-63 at a speed of 287.769mph. Bradley finished sixth at an average speed of 278.822mph, with Pardue following in seventh place at 250.447mph.

Reno 1979 saw the return of Jim Maloney and Bob Guilford. Guilford qualified at a speed of 330.702mph and placed sixth in the Bronze race turning a speed of 252.124mph. Maloney qualified at 319.64mph, but did not race.

Reno was again the sole air racing venue for 1980, and Bob Guilford's F4U-7 was the only racing Corsair. Guilford qualified at 312.950mph and finished sixth in the Bronze race at 239.598mph.

Guilford was back for Reno 1981 along with a new racing Corsair campaigned by Bob Yancey. BuNo 97280, ex-Honduran Air Force F4U-4, registered N49092, was purchased by Yancey in July 1980. Yancey qualified at a speed of 334.933mph, almost 11mph faster than Guilford's speed of 323.665mph. Both aircraft flew in the Bronze race, Yancey finishing third at 325.765mph followed by Guilford in fourth at 247.779mph.

Enter the Super Corsair

Beginning in 1982, things were going to change. Four Corsairs of different models arrived for the September races.

The Planes of Fame came to the 1982 Reno races with a new mount. Jim Maloney and Reno 1978 Unlimited Gold race winner Steve Hinton would share flying duties of their newly restored and heavily modified F4U-1, which boasted a 3,000-plus horsepower Pratt & Whitney R-4360. The aircraft is commonly referred to as the *Super Corsair*. Finally, the sleek Mustangs, powerful Bearcats, and Sea Furies would have some competition from a bent wing bird!

"Looking at the old books of the Cleveland air racers and thinking back, we asked, 'What was something we could do and what's really unique?' We have quite a bit of knowledge, talent, and motivation here at the Chino Airport," Steve Hinton said. "We had an F4U Corsair fuselage in the backyard and we just got to shootin' the breeze

The Air Museum's Planes of Fame F4U-1 Super Corsair *was modified to F2G configuration in the summer of 1982. The F4U-1's R-2800 was replaced by an R-4360 engine and a four-blade prop. Only three pilots have raced the* Super Corsair, *John Maloney, Kevin Eldridge, and Steve Hinton who won the 1985 Unlimited Gold Race at Reno.* Nick Veronico

'welve Unlimiteds showed up to race ncluding five P-51s, four Sea Furies, wo Bearcats, and the *Super Corsair*. on Hevle flew the modified P-51 *Dago ed* to a first place finish at 431.451 nph, followed by Lyle Shelton in his 8F-2 *Rare Bear* at 418.774 mph, with teve Hinton in the *Super Corsair* finshing third at 412.999mph.

Reno 1985 saw the return of five orsairs. Mike Wright did not return, ut Alan Preston took his place in the ineup flying an F4U-5NL. Out of a eld of thirty-two racers Hinton qualied fifth at 431.944mph. The top qualiying speed for 1985 was 443.129mph et by Neil Anderson flying the R-4360-owered Super Sea Fury *Dreadnought*. ob Yancey and *Old Blue* qualified at 68.062mph. The remaining three Corairs all qualified within 6mph of each ther: J. K. Ridley in *Big Richard* at 38.767mph; Alan Preston in No. 12, 4U-5NL BuNo 124569, N4901W, at 32.891mph; and Bob Guilford in *Blue lax* at 326.732mph.

The 1985 Bronze race was won by Viley Sanders in his P-51D *Jeannie oo* at a speed of 355.725mph. In fifth lace was J. K. Ridley in his F4U-4, folowed closely by Alan Preston. Bob Guilford's F4U-7 finished at the back of the pack.

Old Blue led the Silver race from the start until the final few feet when Tom Kelley dove down to pass him at the home pylon. Kelley's average speed was 374.418mph versus Yancey's second place finish at 374.392mph. It doesn't get any closer than that!

During the Gold race, Hinton and the *Super Corsair* steadily moved up through the pack into second place. The *Super Corsair* was putting the pressure on front-runner *Dreadnought*. Nearing the last pylon of the last lap, *Dreadnought*'s pilot Neil Anderson made a mistake. Hinton describes his Unlimited Gold victory: "During the race in '85 everything seemed to work pretty good and we were flying the plane as best as we could, hoping to get up close to the front of the pack. With a stroke of luck, the leader cut a pylon on the last lap. We won, which was great, and then we found out it was a course speed record too!"[184]

Hinton's average race speed record of 438.186mph would hold for two years. After his Unlimited Gold race victory, he moved on to fly the new custom-built Unlimited racer *Tsunami* at Reno 1986. John Maloney now took over full-time duties at the stick of the *Super Corsair*.

Since the *Super Corsair*'s win at Reno 1985, the speeds of the Unlimited Gold racers has steadily increased into the 450–480mph range. This increased competition has left the *Super Corsair* in the third to fourth place range at speeds averaging 430mph. Quite respectable for the bent-wing bird, but just not fast enough.

The Air Museum Planes of Fame continues the racing traditions of Cook Cleland, Dick Becker, Ron Puckett, and Ben McKillen, by campaigning the *Super Corsair* in the 1990s. The *Super Corsair* is now adding the likes of Steve Hinton, John Maloney, and Kevin Eldridge to the Corsair racing record books.

Chapter 14

The Corsair in Movies and Television

Corsairs flew across the silver screen for the first time in Republic's 1949 release *Sands of Iwo Jima,* starring John Wayne as Sergeant Striker. The film features many stock shots of Marines landing on Tarawa and Iwo Jima. Wartime footage of Avengers, Hellcats, and an SB2C Helldiver over the invasion beaches add to the film. Corsairs enter the movie toward the end; they are only in two scenes, and for all of 30 seconds.

After the Marines have captured Tarawa, they ship out for Iwo Jima. Nearing the beaches, the Marines board landing craft in preparation for the invasion. Hellcats and Avengers are shown warming up on a carrier deck, then the shot quickly turns to another carrier where, in rapid succession, two Corsairs are catapult-launched. The aircraft are wearing the fuselage codes FF-51 and FF-62 and the wing and tail codes ("G" symbols) of Carrier Division 27's USS *Gilbert Island* (CVE-107), possibly VMF-351.[185]

John Wayne and his Marines have hit the beach and a Corsair makes a low, head-on pass down the surf line. This ends the debut of the Vought fighter's film career.

Released two years later, RKO Pictures' *Flying Leathernecks* brought John Wayne and the Corsair together again. Wayne stars as Maj. Dan Kirby, the grizzled squadron leader. Robert Ryan costars as Captain Griffith, a flyer who has risen through the ranks with the squadron. The squadron, the fictitious VMF-247 Wildcats, expects Griff to take over the squadron and is surprised when Major Kirby is introduced as the new commanding officer. Kirby and Griff head out to the Pacific to "fight the enemy and each other."[186] As the movie gets underway, a brief scene of F4Us breaking to the left starts things out.

The plot bumps along, Kirby fighting Griff. Kirby makes his point, and Griff learns a lesson. The squadron is sent out against a Japanese fleet coming to the aid of the Japanese garrison on Guadalcanal. VMF-247 is sent up in the all-out attack to repel the Japanese fleet. After downing a number of Japanese aircraft, the pilots of VMF-247 go after the fleet, sending a num-

The Corsair appeared in seven full-length feature films and was the star of the television series Baa Baa Black Sheep. *Here, an almost perfect formation of Corsairs is caught on film for the made-for-TV movie* Flying Misfits. Armand Veronico collection

An F4U-4 taxis in after a film shoot for the movie Flying Misfits, *starring a number of Corsairs and Robert Conrad as World War II Ace Gregory "Pappy" Boyington.* Armand Veronico collection

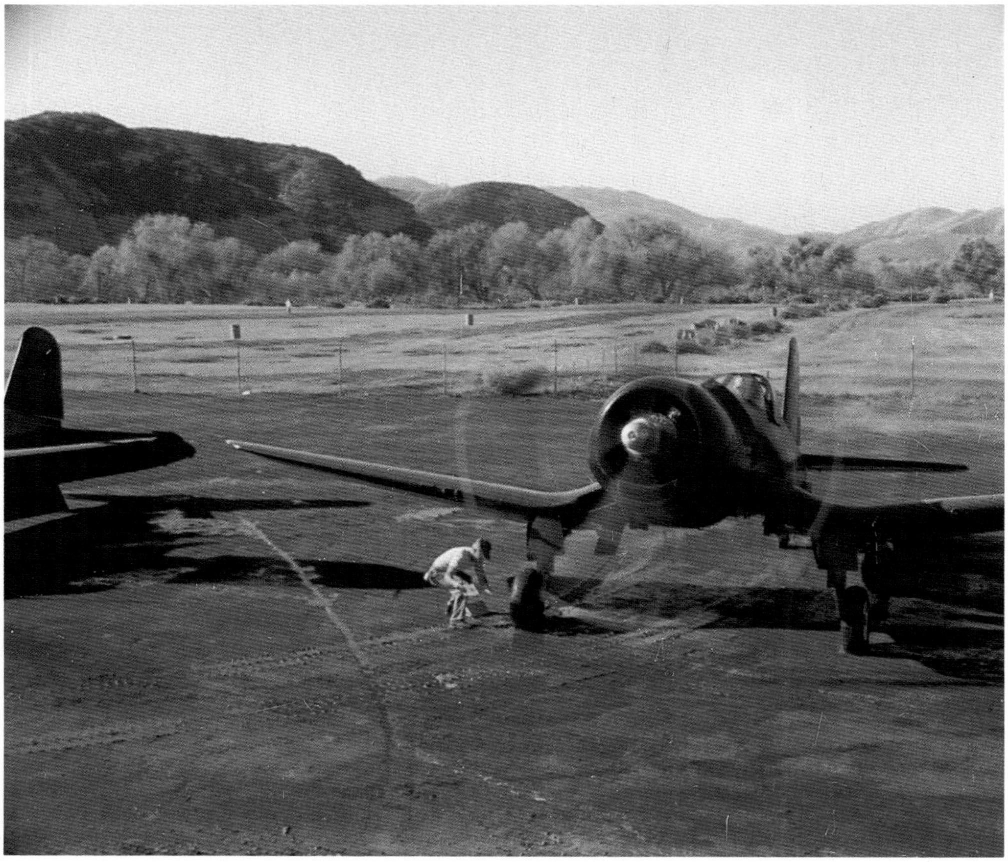

F4U-4 being chocked after flying an air-to-air photographic mission for Baa Baa Black Sheep. *A number of aircraft used Indian Dunes, north of Los Angeles, as a staging base. This location could be converted to resemble a forward area World War II airfield and was also close to the Pacific Coast and the very scenic Channel Islands off Ventura, California.* Armand Veronico collection

ber of ships to their watery graves. Excellent World War II gun camera film footage is spliced in with sound-stage shots of the Hellcats. After this mission, Kirby receives orders for stateside rotation. Prior to leaving, he recommends that Griff not be promoted to squadron commander.

After the standard stateside romantic reunion of Kirby and his wife Joan, played by Janis Carter, Kirby is offered command of a new squadron. This squadron is flying the Corsair and is dedicated to ground-support missions. To Kirby's surprise, Griff is appointed his executive officer. At this point in the movie, the Corsair makes its big appearance. Scenes of Corsairs being catapulted from carriers and formation shots grace the screen. When the squadron arrives at its new base, wrecked Hellcats painted as Japanese aircraft litter the field. The first mission of the new squadron is to help pinned down Marines. This scene features excellent footage of Corsairs strafing, firing multiple rocket salvos, and dropping napalm bombs to help clear the path for the Marines' advance. The next mission is to repel a Kamikaze attack on the US fleet. The Corsairs arrive and begin to down a variety of aircraft. Gun camera footage of numerous Japanese fighters, Betty bombers, a Mavis flying boat, and a Taffy (DC-3 copy) going down in flames shows the Marines' superior flying skills and aircraft. The attack is repulsed. In his last attack on a Betty bomber, Kirby's guns jam. So he rams the bomber, cutting its tail off. Kirby jumps from his ship and parachutes into the water. He is then reunited with his squadron, albeit with a broken arm. Kirby gets his stateside transfer and recommends that Griff get the squadron. The movie ends with a mass flyover of Corsairs. For Corsair enthusiasts, the last 20 minutes mak this film.

Monogram's 1952 release *Flat Top* brought the Corsair back into movi theaters. It stars Sterling Hayden a the hardened, experienced squadro leader and Richard Carlson as th squadron executive officer. The movi opens with an F9F Panther trappin aboard the carrier, which takes Hayde back to his 1944–1945 days flying th Corsair. The film winds its wa through a turkey of a plot: Hayden, ba guy to the squadron, Carlson, good guy

Technically the movie is not ver accurate. The pilots scramble to thei Corsairs, then scenes of SB2Cs bein launched are followed by Corsairs en gaging and destroying five Japanes fighters.

Flat Top uses a lot of World War I stock footage of Corsairs, SBDs Avengers, and gun camera footage. Al most all of the excellent deck-base shots of F4U-4 and -5 Corsairs bein launched and trapping were sho aboard the USS *Princeton* while it wa en route to the Korean War via Pear Harbor.[187] There is some great footag of Corsairs coming aboard ship as wel as a World War II vintage shot of a Corsair missing the wire and bouncin as high as Vulture's Row before crash ing on deck. Not an aviation classic, bu worth viewing once.

Twenty years later, filming of th 1976 Universal movie *Flying Misfits* brought the Corsair back into the spot light. This made-for-TV movie was th pilot for the successful series *Baa Ba Black Sheep*, based loosely on the expe riences of World War II USMC ace Maj Gregory Boyington. Boyington, com manding officer of VMF-214 Blacl Sheep, was credited with 22 kills whil flying Corsairs.

Pilots for *Flying Misfits* include Frank Tallman, Junior Burchinal, Tom Friedkin, Glenn Riley, John Schaf hausen, Tom Mooney, and Gerald Mar tin. "We flew every day for three or fou weeks on the initial filming [of *Flying Misfits*]," said Tom Friedkin.[188]

The pilot successfully launched th series, which would eventually hav thirty-five episodes. "The Corsairs or set were very reliable," said Friedkin "averaging between 3–5 flight hours fo very hour of maintenance. Avionics nd radio problems were the most freuent maintenance squawks."[189]

Corsair pilots for the series included Steve Hinton, Friedkin, John Schafausen, Tom Mooney, Glenn Riley, and rank Tallman. Later Jim Maloney vould join the flying. "We did all the axi scenes, all the specific flight cenes," Steve Hinton said. "We had cripts. Jim Gavin was the second unit irector. He was the brains of the whole utfit, an amazing guy. Gavin is the ne to get credit for that whole show. Ve just did what we were told. We got irplanes flying, kept them flying, and lew for the scenes. Gavin was the one vho did all the permits with the FAA Federal Aviation Administration], ommunicated with the studios, and ired us to do the job."[190]

Corsairs participating in both *Flyng Misfits* and the *Baa Baa Black Sheep* series included the following:

ype	BuNo	Civil No.	Owner
4U-1A	17799	N83782	Planes of Fame
4U-4B	97359	N97359	Tom Friedkin
4U-7	133714	N33714	John Schafhausen
G-1D	92106	N6897	David Tallichet
G-1D	92132	N3466G	David Tallichet
G-1D	92529	N62290	John Stokes
G-1D	92433	N3440	I. N. Burchinal

Bob Guilford's F4U-7 BuNo 33693, N33693, participated in a halfay of flying with Steve Rosenberg at he controls. During filming, Hinton aid, "We always had four Corsairs on he set, but there were as many as six lying at one time. I think we used ight different ones during the lming."[191]

Other pilots included Gerald Marin, Ted Janczerick, Bill Yoak, Mack terling, Fred Elsberry, Clay Lacy, and rt Scholl. Aircraft types making cameo appearances in the series included a DC-3, B-25, L-5, P-51, Hellcat, Twin Beech, and even a glider in one episode. The "enemy" Vals, Kates, Zeros were ex-*Tora-Tora-Tora* aircraft provided by the Confederate Air Force.

After *Baa Baa Black Sheep*, a made-for-TV special entitled *Space* featured four Corsairs and one F7F Tigercat.

The 1976 Universal film *Midway*, depicting the infamous 1942 battle between the US Pacific Fleet and the Japanese carrier forces of Admiral Yamamoto, has a 6–8-second clip of a Corsair in flight, which is interesting, since the Corsair was not deployed to the Pacific during the Battle of Midway.

Nice formation of Corsairs above a cloud layer during the filming of the TV series Baa Baa Black Sheep. Armand Veronico Collection

Hinton later flew a Corsair in the filming of the 1977 Universal film *MacArthur* and in an episode of TV's *Air Wolf*.

Although only seven Corsairs participated in the filming of *Baa Baa Black Sheep*, the interest generated by the show surely saved a number of airframes from being scrapped. The series was well timed, helping to add wings to the growing warbird movement in the mid- to late 1970s.

Specifications

Specification	F4U-1, FG-1, F4U-1D,	FG-1D and F3A-1
Length	33ft 4in	33ft 4in
Span	41ft	41ft
Height	15ft 3in	15ft 3in
Gross weight	12,000lb	12,000
Engine	R-2800-8	R-2800-8W
Horsepower	2,000 at takeoff	2,000 at takeoff
Top speed	417mph at 19,900ft	425mph at 20,000ft
Guns	6 x .50cal	6 x .50cal
Ammunition	2400 rounds	2400 rounds
Ordnance	1 x 1,000lb bomb or 8 x 5in rockets	2 x 1,000lb bombs or 8 x 5in rockets

Specification	F4U-4	F4U-4B
Length	34ft 6in	34.5ft 6in
Span	41ft 11.7in	41ft 11.7in
Height	14ft 9in	14ft 9in
Gross weight	12,500lb	12,400lb
Engine	R-2800-18W or -42W	R-2800-18W or -42W
Horsepower	2,100 at takeoff	2,100 at takeoff
Top speed	446mph at 26,200ft	446mph at 26,200ft
Guns	6 x .50cal	4 x 20mm
Ammunition	2,400 rounds	984 rounds
Ordnance	8 x 5in rockets, 2 x 1,000lb bombs, or 2 x 11.75in rockets	8 x 5in rockets, 2 x 1,000lb bombs, or 2 x 11.75in rockets

Specification	F4U-5	AU-1
Length	4ft 6in	34ft 1in
Span	41ft	41ft
Height	14ft 9in	14ft 10in
Gross weight	12,900lb	19,398lb
Engine	R-2800-32W	R-2800-83WA
Horsepower	2,300 at takeoff	2,100 at takeoff
Top speed	462mph at 31,400ft	438mph at 9,500ft
Guns	4 x 20mm cannon	4 x20mm cannon
Ammunition	924 rounds	924 rounds
Ordnance	8 x 5in rockets, 1 x 2,000 bomb, or 2 x 1,000 bombs, or 2 x 11.75in rockets	10 x 5in rockets, 4,000lb of bombs, or 2 x 11.75in rockets

Specification	F4U-7
Length	34ft 6in
Span	41ft
Height	14ft 9in
Gross weight	12,900lb
Engine	R-2800-32W
Horsepower	2,100 at takeoff
Top speed	446mph at 26,200ft
Guns	4 x 20mm
Ammunition	984 rounds
Bombs	2 x 1,000lb bombs or 2 x 11.75in rockets

Appendix B

Serial Numbers: US Navy

erial number list provided by Chance 'ought Aircraft from a document comiled by Richard Abrams plus additions y the authors.

'ype	Number Built	BuNos
.F4U-1	1	1443 (1)
'4U-1	734	02153–02705 (553), 02706–02736 (31), 03802–03841 (40), 17392–17456 (65), 18122–18141 (20), 18142–18166 (25)
'4U-1A	2,080	17457–17516 (60), 18167–18191 (25), 17517–18121 (605), 49660–50349 (690), 55784–56483 (700)
'G-1/-1A	2,010	12992–14991 (2,000), 76139–76148 (10)
'3A-1	735	04515–04774 (260), 08550–08797 (248), 11067–11293 (227)
'4U-1C	200	57657–57659 (3), 57777–57791 (15), 57966–57983 (18), 82178–82189 (12), 82260–82289 (30), 82370–82394 (25), 82435–82459 (25), 82540–82582 (43), 82633–82639 (7), 82740–82761 (22)
'4U-1D	1,685	50350–50659 (310), 57084–57566 (483), 57570–57776(207), 57792–57965 (174), 82190–82259 (70), 82290–82369 (80), 82395–82434 (40), 82460–82539 (80), 82583–82632 (50), 82640–82739 (100), 82762–82852 (91)
FG-1D	1,997	67055–67099 (45), 76149–76739 (591), 87788–88453 (666), 92007–92701 (695)
XF4U-2	1	converted F4U-1 02153
F4U-2		34 converted F4U-1s 02243, 02432, 02434, 02436, 02241,02441, 02534, 02617, 02622, 02624, 02627, 02632, 02641, 02672, 02673, 02677, 02681, 02682, 02688, 02692, 02708, 02709, 02710, 02731, 02733, 03811, 03814, 03816, 17412,17418, 17423, 49858, 49914, 18038
XF4U-3		2 converted F4U-1As 17516, 49664
FG-3		26 converted FG-1s 76450, 92252, 92253, 92283, 92284, 92300, 92328, 92232, 92338, 92341, 92344, 92345, 92354, 92359, 92361, 92363, 92364, 92367, 92369, 92382, 92383, 92384, 92385, 92429, 92430, 92440
F4U-4X		2 converted F4U-1As 49763, 50301
XF4U-4		5 built 80759–80763
F4U-4	2,045	80764–82177 (1,414), 96752–96765 (14), 96767–96797 (31), 96799–96810 (12), 96812–96817 (6), 96819–96850 (32), 96852–96855 (4), 96857–96891 (35), 96893–97083 (191), 97085–97390 (306)
F4U-4B	296	62915–62919 (5), 62921–62949 (29), 62951–62961 (11), 62963–62989 (27), 62971–62989 (19), 62991–63009 (19), 63011–63019 (9), 63021–63029 (9), 63031–63049 (19), 63051–63069 (19), 63071, 96826 (1), 96851 (1), 96856 (1), 96892 (1), 97084 (1), 97409–97486 (78), 97488–97506 (19), 97508–97526 (19), 97528–97531 (4)
F4U-4N		1 converted F4U-4 97361
F4U-4P		11 converted F4U-4Bs 62970, 62990, 62962, 63010, 63020, 63030, 63050, 63070, 97507, 97487, 97527
FG-4	2,371 ordered	Canceled before construction
XF4U-5		3 converted F4U-4s 97296, 97364, 97415
F4U-5	223	121793–121803 (11), 121805–121815 (11), 121817–121831 (15), 121834–121851 (18), 121854–121871(18), 121875–121890(16), 121894–121911(18), 121916–121931 (16), 121937–121951(15), 121958–121972 (15), 121979–121994 (16), 122003–122014 (12), 122023–122036 (14), 122041–122044 (4), 122049–122057 (9), 122066 (1), 122153–122166 (14)

Type	Number Built	BuNos
F4U-5N	214	121816 (1), 121832–121833 (2), 121852–121853 (2), 121872–121874 (3), 121891–121893 (3), 121912–121915 (4), 121932–121935 (4), 121952–121955 (4), 121973–121976 (4), 121995–121998(4), 122015–122018 (4), 122037–122040 (4), 122058–122061 (4), 122175–122206 (32), 123144–123203 (60), 124441–124503 (63), 124523 (1), 124710–124724 (15)
F4U-5NL	101	124504–124522 (19), 124524–124560 (37), 124665–124709 (45)
F4U-5P	30	121804 (1), 121936 (1), 121956–121957 (2), 121977–121978 (2), 121999–122002 (4), 122019–122022 (4), 122045–122048 (4), 122062–122065 (4), 122167–122174 (8)
XF4U-6		1 converted F4U-5N 124665
AU-1	111	129318–129417 (100), 133833–133843 (11)
F4U-7	94	133652–133731 (80), 133819–133832 (14)
XF2G-1		7 converted FG-1s 13471, 13472, 14691, 14692, 14693, 14694, 14695
F2G-1	5	88454–88458
F2G-2	5	88459–88468

Appendix C

Aircraft Allocated to the Fleet Air Arm

Type	RN No.	BuNos
F4U-1B/ Corsair I	JT100–JT169	No BuNos (70)
F3A-1/ Corsair II	JS469–JS554	04689–04774 (86)
	JS555–JS802	08550–08797 (248)
F4U-1A	JT170–JT194	17592–17616 (25)
	JT195–JT219	17697–17721 (25)
	JT220–JT244	17552–17776 (25)
	JT245–JT269	17847–17871 (25)
	JT270–JT280	17952–17962 (11)
	JT281–JT305	18082–18016 (25)
	JT306–JT330	55839–55863 (25)
	JT331–JT355	55944–55968 (25)
	JT356–JT380	56049–56073 (25)
	JT381–JT405	56164–56188 (25)
	JT406–JT424	56279–56297 (19)
	JT425–JT494	50080–50149 (70)
	JT495–JT529	50230–50264 (35)
	JT530–JT564	50325–50359 (35)
	JT565–JT599	50460–50494 (35)
	JT600–JT634	50575–50609 (35)
F4U-1D	JT635–JT669	57109–57143 (35)
	JT670–JT704	57215–57249 (35)
F3A-1D/ Corsair III	JS803–JS888	11067–11152 (86)
	JT963–JT972	11153–11162 (10)
FG-1, FG-1D/ Corsair IV	KD161–KD560	14592–14991 (400)
	KD561–KD867	76139–76445 (307)
	KD868–KD917	87949–87998 (50)
	KD918–KD942	88134–88158 (25)
	KD943–KD967	88269–88293 (25)
	KD968–KD992	88404–88428 (25)
	KD893–KD999	92171–92177 (7
	KE100–KE117	92178–92195 (18)
	KE310–KE349	92386–92425 (40)
	KE350–KE389	92546–92585 (40)
	KE390–KE429	unallocated

Aircraft Allocated to the Fleet Air Arm under Lend-Lease (1,972 total)

Aircraft Allocated to New Zealand

'he RNZAF acquired 424 Corsairs dur-
ng the war under the Lend-Lease pro-
ram. Eventually, thirteen squadrons
vould be equipped with Corsairs. At
he end of the war, many Corsairs were
lown to New Zealand to be scrapped or
eturned to the US Navy inventory.

'ype	RNZAF Nos.
'4U-1A	NZ5201–NZ5396 (196)
	NZ5461–NZ5463 (3)
	NZ5465 (1)
	NZ5487 (1)
	NZ5501–NZ5536 (36)
'4U-1D	NZ5397–NZ5460 (64)
	NZ5464 (1)
	NZ5466–NZ5486 (21)
	NZ5537–NZ5577 (41)
'G-1D	NZ5601–NZ5660 (60)
'otal	424

'ype	BuNo	RNZAF No.
'4U-1A	56432	NZ5201
'4U-1A	56472	NZ5202
'4U-1A	56449	NZ5203
'4U-1A	56437	NZ5204
'4U-1A	56434	NZ5205
'4U-1A	56482	NZ5206
'4U-1A	56467	NZ5207
'4U-1A	56426	NZ5208
'4U-1A	56476	NZ5209
'4U-1A	56470	NZ5210
'4U-1A	56435	NZ5211
'4U-1A	49752	NZ5212
'4U-1A	49732	NZ5213
'4U-1A	49754	NZ5214
'4U-1A	56436	NZ5215
'4U-1A	56483	NZ5216
'4U-1A	56452	NZ5217
'4U-1A	49748	NZ5218
'4U-1A	56441	NZ5219
'4U-1A	56475	NZ5220
'4U-1A	56424	NZ5221
'4U-1A	56446	NZ5222
'4U-1A	56430	NZ5223
F4U-1A	56442	NZ5224
F4U-1A	56448	NZ5225
F4U-1A	56459	NZ5226
F4U-1A	56477	NZ5227
F4U-1A	56425	NZ5228
F4U-1A	56428	NZ5229
F4U-1A	56468	NZ5230
F4U-1A	56462	NZ5231
F4U-1A	56469	NZ5232
F4U-1A	56473	NZ5233
F4U-1A	56465	NZ5234
F4U-1A	56460	NZ5235
F4U-1A	56444	NZ5236
F4U-1A	56479	NZ5237
F4U-1A	56433	NZ5238
F4U-1A	56453	NZ5239
F4U-1A	56478	NZ5240
F4U-1A	56445	NZ5241
F4U-1A	56474	NZ5242
F4U-1A	56443	NZ5243
F4U-1A	56447	NZ5244
F4U-1A	56429	NZ5245
F4U-1A	56458	NZ5246
F4U-1A	49747	NZ5247
F4U-1A	56455	NZ5248
F4U-1A	56466	NZ5249
F4U-1A	49730	NZ5250
F4U-1A	56440	NZ5251
F4U-1A	49756	NZ5252
F4U-1A	49737	NZ5253
F4U-1A	56451	NZ5254
F4U-1A	56438	NZ5255
F4U-1A	56463	NZ5256
F4U-1A	56457	NZ5257
F4U-1A	49750	NZ5258
F4U-1A	49877	NZ5259
F4U-1A	49761	NZ5260
F4U-1A	49771	NZ5261
F4U-1A	49714	NZ5262
F4U-1A	49722	NZ5263
F4U-1A	49728	NZ5264
F4U-1A	49740	NZ5265
F4U-1A	49751	NZ5266
F4U-1A	49753	NZ5267
F4U-1A	56427	NZ5268
F4U-1A	56431	NZ5269
F4U-1A	56461	NZ5270
F4U-1A	56471	NZ5271
F4U-1A	56480	NZ5272
F4U-1A	56481	NZ5273
F4U-1A	49738	NZ5274
F4U-1A	49843	NZ5275
F4U-1A	49856	NZ5276
F4U-1A	49866	NZ5277
F4U-1A	49969	NZ5278
F4U-1A	49977	NZ5279
F4U-1A	49980	NZ5280
F4U-1A	49999	NZ5281
F4U-1A	50023	NZ5282
F4U-1A	50069	NZ5283
F4U-1A	50073	NZ5284
F4U-1A	50076	NZ5285
F4U-1A	50078	NZ5286
F4U-1A	49672	NZ5287
F4U-1A	49744	NZ5288
F4U-1A	49745	NZ5289
F4U-1A	49768	NZ5290
F4U-1A	49788	NZ5291
F4U-1A	56450	NZ5292
F4U-1A	56456	NZ5293
F4U-1A	49759	NZ5294
F4U-1A	56464	NZ5295
F4U-1A	56439	NZ5296
F4U-1A	56454	NZ5297
F4U-1A	49968	NZ5298
F4U-1A	49962	NZ5299
F4U-1A	49861	NZ5300
F4U-1A	49808	NZ5301
F4U-1A	49887	NZ5302
F4U-1A	49764	NZ5303
F4U-1A	49773	NZ5304
F4U-1A	49848	NZ5305
F4U-1A	49873	NZ5306
F4U-1A	49867	NZ5307
F4U-1A	50203	NZ5308
F4U-1A	49876	NZ5309
F4U-1A	49855	NZ5310
F4U-1A	49772	NZ5311
F4U-1A	49869	NZ5312
F4U-1A	49853	NZ5313

Type	BuNo	RNZAF No.
F4U-1A	49959	NZ5314
F4U-1A	49909	NZ5315
F4U-1A	49990	NZ5316
F4U-1A	49852	NZ5317
F4U-1A	49859	NZ5318
F4U-1A	49964	NZ5319
F4U-1A	49846	NZ5320
F4U-1A	50199	NZ5321
F4U-1A	50224	NZ5322
F4U-1A	49996	NZ5323
F4U-1A	50053	NZ5324
F4U-1A	49961	NZ5325
F4U-1A	49863	NZ5326
F4U-1A	49781	NZ5327
F4U-1A	49921	NZ5328
F4U-1A	50317	NZ5329
F4U-1A	50307	NZ5330
F4U-1A	49892	NZ5331
F4U-1A	49830	NZ5332
F4U-1A	49937	NZ5333
F4U-1A	49874	NZ5334
F4U-1A	49878	NZ5335
F4U-1A	49871	NZ5336
F4U-1A	49760	NZ5337
F4U-1A	49885	NZ5338
F4U-1A	49944	NZ5339
F4U-1A	49868	NZ5340
F4U-1A	49947	NZ5341
F4U-1A	49865	NZ5342
F4U-1A	49872	NZ5343
F4U-1A	49957	NZ5344
F4U-1A	49958	NZ5345
F4U-1A	49976	NZ5346
F4U-1A	50075	NZ5347
F4U-1A	49965	NZ5348
F4U-1A	50065	NZ5349
F4U-1A	49960	NZ5350
F4U-1A	49954	NZ5351
F4U-1A	49966	NZ5352
F4U-1A	49967	NZ5353
F4U-1A	49749	NZ5354
F4U-1A	50215	NZ5355
F4U-1A	50216	NZ5356
F4U-1A	50290	NZ5357
F4U-1A	50310	NZ5358
F4U-1A	50322	NZ5359
F4U-1A	50211	NZ5360
F4U-1A	50311	NZ5361
F4U-1A	50321	NZ5362
F4U-1A	50152	NZ5363
F4U-1A	50162	NZ5364
F4U-1A	50205	NZ5365
F4U-1A	50218	NZ5366
F4U-1A	50222	NZ5367
F4U-1A	50223	NZ5368
F4U-1A	50225	NZ5369
F4U-1A	50304	NZ5370
F4U-1A	50229	NZ5371
F4U-1A	50181	NZ5372
F4U-1A	50272	NZ5373
F4U-1A	50164	NZ5374
F4U-1A	50267	NZ5375
F4U-1A	50167	NZ5376
F4U-1A	50210	NZ5377
F4U-1A	50206	NZ5378
F4U-1A	50217	NZ5379
F4U-1A	50265	NZ5380
F4U-1A	50067	NZ5381
F4U-1A	50293	NZ5382
F4U-1A	50324	NZ5383
F4U-1A	50320	NZ5384
F4U-1A	50305	NZ5385
F4U-1A	50318	NZ5386
F4U-1A	50314	NZ5387
F4U-1A	50070	NZ5388
F4U-1A	50155	NZ5389
F4U-1A	50303	NZ5390
F4U-1A	50312	NZ5391
F4U-1A	50316	NZ5392
F4U-1A	50182	NZ5393
F4U-1A	50298	NZ5394
F4U-1A	50313	NZ5395
F4U-1A	50319	NZ5396
F4U-1D	50455	NZ5397
F4U-1D	57107	NZ5398
F4U-1D	50638	NZ5399
F4U-1D	50647	NZ5400
F4U-1D	57095	NZ5401
F4U-1D	50568	NZ5402
F4U-1D	57144	NZ5403
F4U-1D	57090	NZ5404
F4U-1D	50566	NZ5405
F4U-1D	50659	NZ5406
F4U-1D	57089	NZ5407
F4U-1D	50550	NZ5408
F4U-1D	50565	NZ5409
F4U-1D	50561	NZ5410
F4U-1D	50658	NZ5411
F4U-1D	57250	NZ5412
F4U-1D	57202	NZ5413
F4U-1D	57211	NZ5414
F4U-1D	57092	NZ5415
F4U-1D	57268	NZ5416
F4U-1D	57213	NZ5417
F4U-1D	57105	NZ5418
F4U-1D	50563	NZ5419
F4U-1D	57098	NZ5420
F4U-1D	57195	NZ5421
F4U-1D	57156	NZ5422
F4U-1D	57205	NZ5423
F4U-1D	57262	NZ5424
F4U-1D	57212	NZ5425
F4U-1D	57145	NZ5426
F4U-1D	57192	NZ5427
F4U-1D	57201	NZ5428
F4U-1D	50560	NZ5429
F4U-1D	57252	NZ5430
F4U-1D	50654	NZ5431
F4U-1D	57197	NZ5432
F4U-1D	50656	NZ5433
F4U-1D	50653	NZ5434
F4U-1D	57257	NZ5435
F4U-1D	57200	NZ5436
F4U-1D	57209	NZ5437
F4U-1D	57269	NZ5438
F4U-1D	50444	NZ5439
F4U-1D	50459	NZ5440
F4U-1D	57208	NZ5441
F4U-1D	50450	NZ5442
F4U-1D	50449	NZ5443
F4U-1D	57191	NZ5444
F4U-1D	57102	NZ5445
F4U-1D	57088	NZ5446
F4U-1D	50458	NZ5447
F4U-1D	50443	NZ5448
F4U-1D	50644	NZ5449
F4U-1D	50646	NZ5450
F4U-1D	50452	NZ5451
F4U-1D	57462	NZ5452
F4U-1D	57500	NZ5453
F4U-1D	57478	NZ5454
F4U-1D	57454	NZ5455
F4U-1D	57472	NZ5456
F4U-1D	57463	NZ5457
F4U-1D	57447	NZ5458
F4U-1D	50414	NZ5459
F4U-1D	50381	NZ5460
F4U-1A	50323	NZ5461
F4U-1A	50315	NZ5462
F4U-1A	50308	NZ5463
F4U-1D	50439	NZ5464
F4U-1A	50158	NZ5465
F4U-1D	50404	NZ5466
F4U-1D	50422	NZ5467
F4U-1D	50411	NZ5468
F4U-1D	57271	NZ5469
F4U-1D	57428	NZ5470
F4U-1D	57493	NZ5471
F4U-1D	57467	NZ5472
F4U-1D	57446	NZ5473
F4U-1D	57445	NZ5474
F4U-1D	57430	NZ5475
F4U-1D	57443	NZ5476
F4U-1D	57469	NZ5477
F4U-1D	57452	NZ5478
F4U-1D	57539	NZ5479
F4U-1D	57549	NZ5480
F4U-1D	57457	NZ5481
F4U-1D	57459	NZ5482
F4U-1D	50549	NZ5483
F4U-1D	57479	NZ5484
F4U-1D	57473	NZ5485
F4U-1D	57470	NZ5486
F4U-1A	50044	NZ5487
F4U-1A	49746	NZ5501
F4U-1A	49984	NZ5502
F4U-1A	50000	NZ5503
F4U-1A	50051	NZ5504
F4U-1A	50060	NZ5505

F4U-1A	50066	NZ5506	F4U-1D	50547	NZ5550	FG-1D	88246	NZ5617
F4U-1A	50071	NZ5507	F4U-1D	50436	NZ5551	FG-1D	88205	NZ5618
F4U-1A	50077	NZ5508	F4U-1D	50445	NZ5552	FG-1D	88197	NZ5619
F4U-1A	50159	NZ5509	F4U-1D	50451	NZ5553	FG-1D	88261	NZ5620
F4U-1A	50188	NZ5510	F4U-1D	57106	NZ5554	FG-1D	88036	NZ5621
F4U-1A	50200	NZ5511	F4U-1D	50533	NZ5555	FG-1D	88228	NZ5622
F4U-1A	50204	NZ5512	F4U-1D	50541	NZ5556	FG-1D	87879	NZ5623
F4U-1A	50209	NZ5513	F4U-1D	50548	NZ5557	FG-1D	88200	NZ5624
F4U-1A	50219	NZ5514	F4U-1D	50553	NZ5558	FG-1D	88204	NZ5625
F4U-1A	50220	NZ5515	F4U-1D	50556	NZ5559	FG-1D	88100	NZ5626
F4U-1A	50221	NZ5516	F4U-1D	50557	NZ5560	FG-1D	88047	NZ5627
F4U-1A	50227	NZ5517	F4U-1D	50558	NZ5561	FG-1D	88031	NZ5628
F4U-1A	50291	NZ5518	F4U-1D	50562	NZ5562	FG-1D	88328	NZ5629
F4U-1A	50294	NZ5519	F4U-1D	50564	NZ5563	FG-1D	88065	NZ5630
F4U-1A	50295	NZ5520	F4U-1D	50567	NZ5564	FG-1D	88330	NZ5631
F4U-1A	50297	NZ5521	F4U-1D	50569	NZ5565	FG-1D	88310	NZ5632
F4U-1A	50302	NZ5522	F4U-1D	50570	NZ5566	FG-1D	88313	NZ5633
F4U-1A	50064	NZ5523	F4U-1D	50572	NZ5567	FG-1D	88335	NZ5634
F4U-1A	49769	NZ5524	F4U-1D	50573	NZ5568	FG-1D	88311	NZ5635
F4U-1A	49875	NZ5525	F4U-1D	50574	NZ5569	FG-1D	88345	NZ5636
F4U-1A	49945	NZ5526	F4U-1D	50610	NZ5570	FG-1D	88226	NZ5637
F4U-1A	49956	NZ5527	F4U-1D	50611	NZ5571	FG-1D	88356	NZ5638
F4U-1A	49963	NZ5528	F4U-1D	50612	NZ5572	FG-1D	88334	NZ5639
F4U-1A	49970	NZ5529	F4U-1D	50618	NZ5573	FG-1D	88248	NZ5640
F4U-1A	49971	NZ5530	F4U-1D	50623	NZ5574	FG-1D	88234	NZ5641
F4U-1A	49979	NZ5531	F4U-1D	50635	NZ5575	FG-1D	88223	NZ5642
F4U-1A	50028	NZ5532	F4U-1D	50640	NZ5576	FG-1D	88005	NZ5643
F4U-1A	50040	NZ5533	F4U-1D	57096	NZ5577	FG-1D	88032	NZ5644
F4U-1A	50054	NZ5534	FG-1D	76466	NZ5601	FG-1D	88237	NZ5645
F4U-1A	50074	NZ5535	FG-1D	76715	NZ5602	FG-1D	92125	NZ5646
F4U-1A	50306	NZ5536	FG-1D	87873	NZ5603	FG-1D	92111	NZ5647
F4U-1D	50424	NZ5537	FG-1D	88184	NZ5604	FG-1D	92044	NZ5648
F4U-1D	50425	NZ5538	FG-1D	88084	NZ5605	FG-1D	92120	NZ5649
F4U-1D	50426	NZ5539	FG-1D	88221	NZ5606	FG-1D	88442	NZ5650
F4U-1D	50432	NZ5540	FG-1D	88236	NZ5607	FG-1D	92199	NZ5651
F4U-1D	50438	NZ5541	FG-1D	88179	NZ5608	FG-1D	92167	NZ5652
F4U-1D	50446	NZ5542	FG-1D	88213	NZ5609	FG-1D	92113	NZ5653
F4U-1D	50447	NZ5543	FG-1D	88208	NZ5610	FG-1D	92149	NZ5654
F4U-1D	50453	NZ5544	FG-1D	88104	NZ5611	FG-1D	92166	NZ5655
F4U-1D	50454	NZ5545	FG-1D	88090	NZ5612	FG-1D	92210	NZ5656
F4U-1D	50456	NZ5546	FG-1D	88209	NZ5613	FG-1D	92083	NZ5657
F4U-1D	50457	NZ5547	FG-1D	88255	NZ5614	FG-1D	92165	NZ5658
F4U-1D	50502	NZ5548	FG-1D	88215	NZ5615	FG-1D	92140	NZ5659
F4U-1D	50540	NZ5549	FG-1D	88233	NZ5616	FG-1D	92196	NZ5660

Appendix E

Corsairs Operated by Foreign Governments

Honduras

The FAH received twenty-two aircraft in a swap with the late Bob Bean. Bean traded the Corsairs to the Hondurans in exchange for five Lockheed P-38 Lightnings and four Bell P-63 Kingcobras. The following aircraft are confirmed FAH aircraft:

Type	FAH No.	BuNo
F4U-5NL	600–602	124724, 124560, 124447
F4U-5N	603–609	123168, 122179, 122184, 124486, 124692, 124493, unknown
F4U-4	610–619	97388, 96885, 97288,unknown, 96995, 97280, 97320, 97059, 96885, unknown

The following aircraft were purchased by Bob Bean and delivered to the FAH, but their FAH serial numbers have not been cross referenced:

97382—Purchased by Bean, registered N5212V, exported to Honduras

97143—Purchased by Bean, registered N5220V, exported to Honduras

El Salvador

The FAS purchased twenty FG-1Ds under the MAP in June 1957. Five more aircraft were purchased as spares ships, delivered unflyable, in an effort to maintain a balance of power in the region, arriving in October 1959. The FAS flew its last Corsair sortie in the summer of 1971.

FAS No.	BuNo
201	92460
202	67070
203	67071
204	67082
205	92349
206	92443
207	92458
208	92489
209	92490
210	92494
211	92095
212	92590
213	92618
214	92623
215	92629
216	92642
217	92650
218	92653
219	92690
220	92697

Argentina

Argentina received twenty-si F4U-5s and F4U-5NLs in 1956 an 1957. The following aircraft have bee confirmed as having served with th Commando Aviacion Naval Argentina:

Type	Bu. No
F4U-5	121881
F4U-5	121928
F4U-5NL	124559
F4U-5N	124705
F4U-5N	124707

The Commando Aviacion Naval Argentina assigned its aircraft the following serial numbers: 0374–0395 (22) and 0432–0435 (4)

France

The French Aeronavale received ninety-four aircraft under the MAP. These special-built F4U-7s incorporated a 2,100hp Pratt & Whitney R-2800-18W turning a four-blade Hamilton Standard propeller. Armament consisted of four 20mm cannons plus 4,000lb of external stores. Aircraft included BuNos 133652–133731 (80) and 133819–133832 (14).

Appendix F

Squadrons that Flew Corsairs: USN, USMC, FAA, RNZAF, French

US Navy
OTU-VF-1
OTU-VF-2
OTU-VF-3
OTU-VF-4
OTU-VF-5

CQTU-4

ATU-VF-1
ATU-1-VF
ATU-4-VA
ATU-5-VA

AES-12

VA-1A
VA-3A
VA-7A
VA-14
VA-74
VA-13A
VA-24
VA-134

VC-3
VC-4
VC-11
VC-61
VC-62
VC-190

VF-1B
VF-1L
VF-2A
VF-2B
VF-3
VF-3B
VF-4A
VF-4B
VF-5
VF-5A
VF-5B
VF-6B
VF-10
VF-10A
VF-11
VF-12
VF-13A
VF-14
VF-14A
VF-17
VF-17A
VF-18
VF-18A
VF-21
VF-22
VF-22A
VF-23
VF-32
VF-33
VF-34
VF-41
VF-42
VF-44
VF-53
VF-54
VF-55
VF-58
VF-61
VF-62
VF-63
VF-64
VF-74
VF-75
VF(N)-75
VF-81
VF-82
VF-83
VF-84
VF-85
VF-89
VF-92
VF-94
VF-95
VF(N)-101
VF-103
VF-104
VF-113
VF-114
VF-122
VF-131
VF-133
VF-152
VF-192
VF-193
VF-653
VF-671
VF-713
VF-783
VF-791
VF-821
VF-871
VF-874
VF-884
VF-916

VBF-1
VBF-3
VBF-4
VBF-5
VBF-6
VBF-10
VBF-14
VBF-15
VBF-17
VBF-19
VBF-20
VBF-74
VBF-74A
VBF-74B
VBF-75
VBF-75A
VBF-75B
VBF-81
VBF-82
VBF-83
VBF-85
VBF-88
VBF-92
VBF-93
VBF-94
VBF-95
VBF-97
VBF-98

VBF-99
VBF-100
VBF-150
VBF-151
VBF-152
VBF-153

VFO-1
VFO-2

VRF-2
VRF-3
VRF-12

VT-4
VT-6

VX-3

US Marine Corps
VMA-312
VMA-323
VMA-324
VMA-332
VMO-154
VMO-155

VMF-112
VMF-113
VMF-114
VMF-115
VMF-121
VMF-122
VMF-123
VMF-124
VMF-211
VMF-212
VMF-213
VMF-214
VMF-215
VMF-216
VMF-217
VMF-218
VMF-221
VMF-222
VMF-223
VMF-224
VMF-225
VMF-235
VMF-236
VMF-251
VMF-311
VMF-312
VMF-313
VMF-314
VMF-321
VMF-322
VMF-323
VMF-331
VMF-332
VMF-351
VMF-422
VMF-451
VMF-452
VMF-461
VMF-462
VMF-471
VMF-481
VMF-482
VMF-511
VMF-512
VMF-513
VMF(N)-513
VMF-521
VMF-522
VMF-523
VMF-524
VMF(N)-532
VMF-542
VMF-911
VMF-912
VMF-913
VMF-914
VMF-922
VMF-923
VMF-924

VMFT-10
VMJ-1
VMP-254
VPM-354
VMT-1
VMBF-931

VMSB-931
VMSB-933
VMSB-934

FASRON-3
FASRON-5
FASRON-6
FASRON-8
FASRON-9
FASRON-11
FASRON-691

British Fleet Air Arm
No. 700 Squadron
No. 703 Squadron
No. 706 Squadron
No. 715 Squadron
No. 716 Squadron
No. 718 Squadron
No. 719 Squadron
No. 721 Squadron
No. 723 Squadron
No. 731 Squadron
No. 732 Squadron
No. 733 Squadron
No. 736 Squadron
No. 738 Squadron
No. 748 Squadron
No. 757 Squadron
No. 759 Squadron
No. 760 Squadron
No. 767 Squadron
No. 768 Squadron
No. 771 Squadron
No. 772 Squadron
No. 778 Squadron
No. 787 Squadron
No. 791 Squadron
No. 794 Squadron
No. 797 Squadron
No. 885 Squadron
No. 1830 Squadron
No. 1831 Squadron
No. 1833 Squadron
No. 1834 Squadron
No. 1835 Squadron
No. 1836 Squadron
No. 1837 Squadron
No. 1838 Squadron
No. 1841 Squadron
No. 1842 Squadron
No. 1843 Squadron
No. 1845 Squadron
No. 1846 Squadron
No. 1848 Squadron
No. 1849 Squadron
No. 1850 Squadron
No. 1851 Squadron
No. 1852 Squadron
No. 1853 Squadron

RNZAF
No. 14 Squadron
No. 15 Squadron
No. 16 Squadron
No. 17 Squadron
No. 18 Squadron
No. 19 Squadron
No. 20 Squadron
No. 21 Squadron
No. 22 Squadron
No. 23 Squadron
No. 24 Squadron
No. 25 Squadron
No. 26 Squadron

French Aeronavale
12 Flotille
14 Flotille
15 Flotille
17 Flotille

Appendix G

Surviving Aircraft

ype	BuNo	N no.	Owner	Status*
4U-1	56198	N83782	Planes of Fame, Chino, CA	F
4U-1A	17995	ZK-FUI	Alpine Fighter Collection, Wanaka, New Zealand	F
4U-1A	13459	—	USMC Museum	PV
4U-1D	50375	—	NASM, Washington, DC	PV
F4U-4	80759	—	New England Air Museum	PV
4U-4	81415	—	Korean War Museum, Seoul, South Korea	PV
4U-4	81698	N53JB	John MacGuire, Santa Teresa, NM	PV
4U-4	81857	—	Tri-State Aviation, Wahpeton, ND	R
4U-4	93877	—	Tri-State Aviation, Wahpeton, ND	R
4U-4	96885	—	Earl Ware, Jacksonville, FL	S
4U-4	96995	OE-EAS	Tyrolean Jet Service, Austria	F
4U-4	97142	—	Pima Air Museum, Tucson, AZ	PV
4U-4	97143	N713JT	Joseph Tobul, Wexford, PA	R
4U-4	97259	N6667	EAA Museum, Oshkosh, WI	R
4U-4	97264	N5218V	Chuck Hall/C. Harp, Ramona, CA	F
4U-4	97280	N712RD	World Jet, Ft. Lauderdale, FL	F
4U-4	97286	N5215V	Weeks Air Museum, Miami, FL	R
4U-4	97288	N4907M	Joseph Bellantoni	R
4U-4	97302	N68HP	Howard Pardue, Breckenridge, TX	R
4U-4	97320	—	John Roxbury, Princeton, MN	R
4U-4	97349	—	US Naval Aviation Museum	PV
4U-4	97353	N240CA	The Old Flying Machine Co.	F
4U-4	97369	N5214V	USMC Air Ground Museum, VA	PV
4U-4	97388	—	Gerald Beck, Wahpeton, ND	R
4U-4	97390	N47991	Yankee Air Corps, Chino, CA	PV
4U-4	96885	FAH611	Ray Adams, Melborne, FL	R
4U-5	121881	N43RW	Lone Star Flight Museum, TX	F
4U-5	122179	N179NP	Warbirds of Great Britain	F
4U-5	122184	N65WF	EXEC Aviation, Cincinnati, OH	F
4U-5P	122189	—	MCAS El Toro, CA	PV
4U-5N	124447	N100CV	USMC Air Ground Museum, VA	PV
4U-5N	124486	N49068	Dick Bertea, Chino, CA	F
4U-5NL	124569	N4901W	David K. Burnap, Dayton, OH	F
4U-5N	124692	—	Collings Foundation, Stow, MA	R
4U-5NL	124724	F-AZEG	Jean Salis Collection, France	F
4U-7	133722	N1337A	Erickson Air Crane, OR	F
4U-7	133704	—	USS Alabama Memorial Museum	PV

Type	BuNo	N no.	Owner	Status*
F4U-7	133710	C-GWFU	Blain Fowler, Alberta, Canada	F
FG-1	13486	—	USMC Air Ground Museum, VA	F
FG-1	A14862	—	Fleet Air Arm Museum, Yeovilton	PV
FG-1D	67087	—	Javier Arrango, Rialto, CA	R
FG-1D	67089	N97GM	Gary Meermans, Chino, CA	F
FG-1D	88026	—	Walter Soplata, Newberry, OH	S
FG-1D	88086	N63382	Weeks Air Museum, Miami, FL	F
FG-1D	88090	—	Museum of Transportation and Technology, Auckland, New Zealand	PV
FG-1D	88297	G-FGID	The Fighter Collection, Duxford	F
FG-1D	88303	N700G	Larry Rose, Peoria, AZ	F
FG-1D	88382	—	Museum of Flight, Seattle, WA	PV
FG-1D	88439	N55JP	Warbirds of Great Britain	F
FG-1D	92013	—	US Navy Yard, Washington, DC	PV
FG-1D	92050	N194G	James Axtell, Denver, CO	
FG-1D	92085	—	Selfridge Military Museum, MI	PV
FG-1D	92095	N67HP	Evergreen Air Venture Museum	F
FG-1D	92106	N6897	MARC, Chino, CA	S
FG-1D	92132	N3466G	MARC, Chino, CA	S
FG-1D	92246	N766JD	US Naval Aviation Museum	PV
FG-1D	92399	N448AG	John Hooper, Harvey, LA	S
FG-1D	92436	C-GCWX	Canadian Warplane Heritage	F
FG-1D	92443	N3440G	Sale Reported	
FG-1D	92460	—	Sikorsky Memorial Airport, CT	PV
FG-1D	92468	N9964Z	Confederate Air Force, TX	F
FG-1D	92489	—	Frank Arrufat, Los Angeles, CA	S
FG-1D	92508	N46RL	Robert Lammerts, Oklahoma City, OK	S
FG-1D	92509	N3PP	Kalamazoo Aviation History Museum, Kalamazoo, MI	F
FG-1D	92629	N62290	Bob Pond, Plymouth, MN	F
FG-1D	88368	—	Patriots Point, Mt. Pleasant, SC	PV
F2G-1	88454	N4324	Champlin Fighter Museum, AZ	PV
F2G-1	88457	N5588N	Lone Star Flight Museum, TX	S
F2G-2	88463	N5577N	Walter Soplata, Newberry, OH	S
F4U-1	—	N31518	Planes of Fame (Super Corsair)	F

** F means that the aircraft is flyable; PV means that the aircraft is displayed on public view; R means that the aircraft is under restoration; S means that the aircraft is stored.*

Bibliography

Allen, Hugh. *Goodyear Aircraft.* Cleveland, Ohio: Corday & Gross, 1947.

Andrade, John M. *US Military Aircraft Designations and Serials Since 1909.* Earl Shilton, Leicester, England: Midland Counties Publications, 1979.

Berliner, Don. *Unlimited Air Racers: The Complete History of Unlimited Class Air Racing, 1946 Thompson Trophy to 1991 Reno Gold.* Osceola, Wisconsin: Motorbooks International, 1992.

Chance Vought Aircraft. *Corsair IV.* Stratford, Connecticut; 1944.

Cox, Bryan. *Too Young To Die.* Glenfield, Auckland, New Zealand: Century Hutchinson Group, 1989.

Dienst, John and Dan Hagedorn: *North American F-51 Mustangs in Latin American Air Force Service.* Arlington, Texas: Aerofax, 1985.

Doll, Thomas E. *USN/USMC Over Korea: US Navy/Marine Corps Air Operations Over Korea 1950 -1953.* Carrollton, Texas: Squadron/Signal Publications, 1988.

Farmer, James H. *Celluloid Wings: The Impact of Movies on Aviation.* Blue Ridge Summit, Pennsylvania: TAB Books, 1984.

Flintham, Victor. *Air Wars and Aircraft: A Detailed Record of Air Combat, 1945 to the Present.* New York, New York: Facts on File, 1990.

Foss, Joe and Mathew Brennan. *Top Guns: America's Fighter Aces Tell Their Stories.* New York: Pocket Books, 1991.

Futrell, Robert F. *The United States Air Force in Korea 1950-1953.* Washington, D.C.: Office of Air Force History, 1983.

Green, William. *US Navy and Marine Corps Fighters.* New York: Arco, 1977.

Guerlac, Henry E. *History of Modern Physics 1800 to 1950.* Vol. 8. Los Angeles, California: Tomash Publishers/American Institute of Physics, 1951.

Guyton, Boone T. *Whistling Death: The Test Pilot's Story of the F4U Corsair.* New York: Orion Books, 1990.

Hallion, Richard. *The Naval Air War in Korea.* Baltimore: The Nautical and Aviation Publishing Company of America, 1986.

Hull, Robert. *September Champions: The Story of America's Air Racing Pioneers.* Harrisburg, Pennsylvania: Stackpole Books, 1979.

Huntington, Roger. *Thompson Trophy Racers: The Pilots and Planes of America's Air Racing Glory Days 1929–1949.* Osceola, Wisconsin: Motorbooks International, 1989.

Johnson, John W. "Corsair Outline." Chance Vought Aircraft. Unpublished manuscript, 1953.

Kinert, Reed. *Racing Planes and Air Races.* Various volumes. Fallbrook, California: Aero Publishers, 1972.

Larkins, William T. *US Navy Aircraft 1921-1941 and US Marine Corps Aircraft 1914-1959.* New York: Orion Books, 1988.

Larsen, Jim. *Directory of Unlimited Class Pylon Air Racers.* Kirkland, Washington: American Air Museum, 1971.

Moran, Gerard P. *The Corsair, and other Aeroplanes Vought, 1917–1977.* Terre Haute, Indiana: SunShine House, 1978.

Morrison, Samuel Eliot. *History of United States Naval Operation in World War II.* Vols. VI, VII, X, XII. Boston: Atlantic, Little, Brown, 1951.

Ogden, R. *The Aircraft Museums and Collections of North America.* West Drayton, Middlessex, England: The Aviation Hobby Shop, 1988.

Orriss, Bruce W. *When Hollywood Ruled the Skies.* Hawthorne, California: Aero Associates, 1984.

Robertson, Bruce. *British Military Aircraft Serials 1887–1987.* Earl Shilton, Leicester, England: Midland Counties Publications, 1987.

Schoeni, Arthur L. *Vought: Six Decades of Aviation History.* Plano, Texas: Aviation Quarterly, 1978.

Sherrod, Robert. *History of Marine Corps Aviation in World War II.* Baltimore: The Nautical and Aviation Publishing Company of America, 1987.

Sturtivant, Ray. *The Squadrons of the Fleet Air Arm.* Kent, England: Air Britain (Historians), 1984.

———. *Fleet Air Arm at War.* Shepperton, Surrey, England: Ian Allan, 1982.

Sullivan, Jim. *F4U Corsair in Action.* Carrollton, Texas: Squadron/Signal Publications, 1977.

Swanborough, Gordon and Bowers, Peter M. *US Navy Aircraft Since 1911.* 3rd ed. Annapolis: Naval Institute Press, 1990.

Tegler, John. *Gentlemen, You Have A Race.* Severna Park, Maryland: Wings Publishing, 1984.

Tillman, Barrett. *Corsair: The F4U in World War II and Korea.* Annapolis: Naval Institute Press, 1979.

Trimble, William F. *Wings for the Navy: A History of the Naval Aircraft Factory, 1917–1956.* Annapolis: Naval Institute Press, 1990.

US Navy. *United States Naval Aviation 1910 to 1980.* NAVAIR 00-80P-1 Washington, D.C.: US Government Printing Office, 1981.

———. *Pilot's Handbook for Navy Model F4U-5 Aircraft*, AN 01-45HD-1, including Appendices III (F4U-5P) and IV (F4U-5NL), 1947.

———. *The Campaigns of the Pacific War.* United States Strategic Bombing Survey (Pacific), Naval Analysis Division. Washington, D.C.: US Government Printing Office, 1946.

Endnotes

1. "Chronology of LTV Airplanes and Missiles, Proposal and Engineering, Report Number 2-51130/3R50155B" (an LTV document).

2. Ibid.

3. Although renamed Vought-Sikorsky, the company continued to use the Chance Vought Aircraft Corporation letterhead and logo when dealing with the BuAer. Because of this and to simplify matters, Chance Vought Aircraft and Vought-Sikorsky will be referred to as Vought throughout the text.

4. Boone T. Guyton, quotes from his speech at the EAA Air Adventure Museum Mini Forum, August 1, 1992. Guyton was discussing his experiences with the Corsair while promoting his book *Whistling Death: The Test Pilot's Story of the F4U Corsair.* (Orion Books, 1990). Guyton's book is a must read for anyone interested in or associated with the Corsair.

5. The Navy renumbered its contracts to streamline purchasing after the war broke out. Vought's Contract Number 82811 was reorganized as Contract Number 198.

6. Guyton, EAA Air Adventure Museum Mini Forum, August 1, 1992.

7. Records of Aircraft History Cards (RAHC), XF4U-1 BuNo 1443, and "Pratt & Whitney Aircraft Engines: Model Designations and Characteristics" (P&W document). The XR-2800-4 installed in the XF4U-1 was serial number 4045.

8. John W. Johnson, "Corsair Outline" (unpublished manuscript, Vought, 1953).

9. RAHC, BuNo 02156.

10. Inspector Naval Aircraft Stratford (INAS), telegram to Vought, April 17, 1943.

11. Master Change Record, Change Number 156.

12. Vought letter E-98404 to the INAS, April 15, 1943.

13. Vought letter E-88949 to the INAS, March 5, 1943.

14. Master Change Record Number 303.

15. Cdr. J. B. Pearson, Jr., USN, memo from the BuAer fighter design section to procurement via head of engineering, March 27, 1943.

16. Change Order CW, Contract Number 198, May 16, 1944.

17. "Daily Report on Airplanes at Contractor's Plant in Flight Status" (Vought document, September 4, 1943).

18. Change Order CW, Contract 198, May 16, 1944.

19. Ibid.

20. "Daily Report on Airplanes at Contractor's Plant in Flight Status" (Vought document, September 4, 1943).

21. "Report of Production Inspection Trials on Model F4U-1 Airplane Held July 1942 to December 1944: Carrier Acceptability Tests" (Navy Department, Board of Inspection and Survey, Washington).

22. *Corsair IV* (an undated Vought pamphlet).

23. "Daily Report on Airplanes at Contractor's Plant in Flight Status" (Vought, August 17, 1943).

24. INAS telegram to the BuAer.

25. "Report of Production Inspection Trials on Model F4U-1 Airplane Held July 1942 to December 1944: Carrier Acceptability Tests" (Navy Department, Board of Inspection and Survey, Washington).

26. Ralph O. Romaine, letter to author Veronico.

27. BuAer telegram to the INAS.

28. INAS telegram to the BuAer, March 25, 1943.

29. Vought letter R-37646 to the BuAer, October 25, 1943, forwarding the quotation on Model F4U-1P aircraft.

30. "Report Number 658, Air Force and Moment for F4U-1 Airplane" (Aerodynamical Laboratory, Department of Aeronautics, US Navy).

31. G. M. Bellanca, letter to Charles H. Chatfield, United Aircraft Corporation, December 17, 1942.

32. C. B. Townsend, letter to G. M. Bellanca, January 18, 1943.

33. Vought letter E-94447 from Acting General Manager Rex B. Beisel to the INAS, March 31, 1943.

34. Johnson, "Corsair Outline."

35. Kenneth A. Walsh, telephone interview with James N. Bardin on behalf of the authors, February 8, 1993.

36. J. T. Blackburn, interview with Veronico.

37. Ibid.

38. Ibid.

39. Leo Horacek, interview with Veronico.

40. Ibid.

41. Many sources report that FG-1Ds, British serials KE390–429, were the last of the British Corsairs, and that the Fleet Air Arm received 2,012 Corsairs of all models. The authors believe these aircraft (KE390–429) were contracted for, but not delivered. All FG-1Ds subsequent to BuNo

92585/KE389 were delivered to the US Navy. Also the BuAer publication *Naval Aircraft: Record of Acceptances 1935–1946* does not show any Fleet Air Arm Corsair deliveries after BuNo 92585/KE389.

42. "F4U-1 Sequence of Fabrication, F4U-1 Bu. 02153 through Bu. 18121" (Vought document).

43. RAHC, F4U-1 BuNos. 02705, 02706; and "F4U-1 Sequence of Fabrication, F4U-1 Bu. 02153 through Bu. 18121" (Vought document).

44. Vought Letter E-83437, "Provision for Stowage Aboard British Carriers," to the INAS, February 9, 1943.

45. H. J. Brow, INAS, memo to the Chief of the BuAer, February 10, 1943.

46. LCdr. R. M. Smeeton, RN, memo "Comments By British Liaison Office On Chance-Vought's Suggestions For Reduction in Folded Height Of Corsair I," February 1943.

47. Ibid.

48. Ibid.

49. Bruce Robertson, *British Military Aircraft Serials 1878–1987* (Midland Counties Publications, 1979).

50. Vought letter E-1572 to BuAer Costs, Changes and Statistics Section, October 31, 1945.

51. Vought memo to the INAS, April 4, 1944.

52. "Report of Production Inspection Trials on Model F4U-1 Airplane Held July 1942 to December 1944: Carrier Acceptability Tests" (Navy Department, Board of Inspection and Survey, Washington).

53. W. K. Munnoch, interview with Veronico.

54. Ibid.

55. C.D.S. Millington, interview with Veronico.

56. Ibid.

57. Munnoch, interview.

58. Ibid.

59. Ray Sturtivant, The *Squadrons of the Fleet Air Arm* (Air Britain [Historians] Ltd., 1984).

60. Munnoch, interview.

61. Ray Sturtivant, *Fleet Air Arm at War* (Ian Allan Ltd., 1982).

62. RAHC, FG-1D BuNo 92585, Fleet Air Arm serial KE389.

63. RAHC, FG-1D BuNo 92181, Fleet Air Arm serial KE104.

64. Cyril White, interview with Veronico.

65. Sturtivant, The *Squadrons of the Fleet Air Arm.*

66. Brian Cox, logbook entries.

67. Ibid.

68. *United States Naval Aviation 1910 to 1980* (NAVAIR 00-80P-1, US Government Printing Office, 1981).

69. Ibid.

70. Ibid.

71. Ibid.

72. Ibid.

73. Ibid.

74. Ibid.

75. Ibid.

76. Ibid.

77. "Chronology of LTV Airplanes and Missiles, Proposal and Engineering, Report No. 2-51130/3R50155B" (LTV document).

78. *United States Naval Aviation 1910 to 1980.*

79. Johnson, "Corsair Outline."

80. Henry E. Guerlac, *History of Modern Physics 1800 to 1950*, Vol. 8 (Tomash Publishers/American Institute of Physics, 1951).

81. Vought letter to INAS, August 9, 1943, requesting permission to discontinue all work on the development of the exhaust flame damper for the F4U-2 in view of the fact that all of the F4U-2 developmental work had been transferred to the NAF.

82. The following aircraft were converted to F4U-2: BuNos. 02153 (XF4U-2), 02243, 02421, 02432, 02434, 02436, 02441, 02672, 02534, 02617, 02622, 02624, 02627, 02632, 02641, 02672, 02708, 02709, 02710, 02673, 02677, 02681, 02682, 02688, 02692, 02731, 02733, 03811, 03814, 03816, 17412, 17418, 17423, plus 49858 and 49914, which were converted in the field by VMF(N)-532.

83. RAHC, BuNo 02153.

84. *United States Naval Aviation 1910 to 1980.*

85. Guerlac, *History of Modern Physics 1800 to 1950*, Vol. 8.

86. *United States Naval Aviation 1910 to 1980.*

87. "VMF(N)-532 War Diary" (squadron document).

88. Robert Sherrod, *History Of Marine Corps Aviation in World War II* (Nautical and Aviation Publishing, 1987).

89. "VMF (N)-532 War Diary" (squadron document).

90. Howard W. Bollmann, interview with Veronico.

91. Frank C. Lang, interview with Veronico.

92. Bollmann, interview.

93. "Pratt & Whitney Aircraft Engines: Model Designations and Characteristics" (P&W document).

94. Bill Horan, logbook entries.

95. Vought letter E-69385 to the BuAer, March 1, 1944.

96. Vought letter E-92245 to the BuAer, May 31, 1944.

97. "Pratt & Whitney Aircraft Engines: Model Designations and Characteristics" (P&W document).

98. Vought letter E-62075 to the BuAer, November 17, 1942.

99. RAHC, BuNo 02157.

100. BuAer change order to Vought, "Cancellation of Change No. O," February 4, 1944.

101. Bill Horan, telephone interview with Veronico, December 29, 1992.

102. Ibid.

103. Horan, telephone interview, January 18, 1993.

104. Horan, logbook entries.

105. RAHC, Goodyear FG-3 BuNos. 76450, 92252, 92253, 92283, 92284, 92300, 92328, 92232, 92338, 92341, 92344, 92345, 92354, 92359, 92361, 92363, 92364, 92367, 92369, 92382, 92383, 92384, 92385, 92429, 92430, 92440.

106. RAHC, BuNo 92983.

107. Horan, telephone interview, January 18, 1993.

108. Vought letter E-94547 to the INAS, April 5, 1943.

109. BuAer Contract Number 198, Amendment Number 58, May 22, 1944.

110. Ibid.

111. Ibid.

112. Aeromatic Aircraft Propellers letter to Vought, October 21, 1943.

113. Johnson, "Corsair Outline."

114. *Corsair IV* (an undated Vought pamphlet).

115. In his book *Goodyear Aircraft: A Story of Man and Industry,* The Corday & Gross Co. Cleveland, Ohio, 1947, author Hugh Allen refers to the FG-4. A number of others have reported that an FG-4 was hung in the rafters at Goodyear's Akron, Ohio, plant and remained there until the mid-1950s.

116. F4U-4s converted to F4U-4P armed-photo-reconnaissance configuration include 62930, 62962, 62970, 62990, 63010, 63030, 63050, 63070, 97084, 97487, 97507, 97527.

117. Pilot Accident History Card for February 20, 1951.

118. Johnson, "Corsair Outline."

119. Sherrod, *History of Marine Corps Aviation In World War II.*

120. *United States Strategic Bombing Surveys. The Campaigns of the Pacific War* (US Government Printing Office, 1946).

121. "Aircraft Accident Report for January 15, 1951" (Naval Aviation Safety Center).

122. *United States Naval Aviation 1910 to 1980.*

123. Harry S. Truman, Medal of Honor citation for Lt. (j.g.) Thomas J. Hudner.

124. Horan, interview.

125. BuAer Engineering Division letter of intent to contract, February 7, 1944.

126. Memo from the BuAer chief to the BuAer Representative Akron (BARA), "Model F2G-1 Airplane Catapulting Strength, Information on," October 21, 1944.

127. RAHC, BuNo 14091.

128. RAHC, BuNo 14092. Also "Weekly Summary Report of Flight Engineering Activity" (Goodyear document, week ending October 30, 1944).

129. RAHC, BuNo 13703.

130. "Weekly Summary Report of Flight Engineering Activity" (Goodyear document, week ending October 30, 1944).

131. "Weekly Summary Report of Flight Engineering Activity" (Goodyear document, week ending November 20, 1944).

132. Ibid.

133. Ibid.

134. "Weekly Summary Report of Flight Engineering Activity" (Goodyear document, week end-

ıg October 30, 1944).

35. RAHC, BuNos. 02312 and 02460. Also elegram from the INAS to the BuAer, March 25, 943.

36. BARA telegram to the BuAer, May 24, 1944.

37. Goodyear letter CD-2904 to the BARA, Octoer 17, 1944.

38. Goodyear letter to the BARA regarding the evelopment program for the first two XF2G-1 irplanes, July 5, 1944.

39. "Daily Flight Reports on Naval Aircraft In light Status at Constructor's Plants," February 5, 1945.

40. Don Armstrong, interview with Veronico.

41. Ibid.

42. Donald Armstrong, statement in a Goodyear ocument concerning hydraulic failure of F2G-2 uNo 14695 and resulting belly landing.

43. Ibid.

44. Tower operator's report of crashes of Decemer 12, 1945, Russell E. Keller, tower operator.

45. "Damage To Number 7 XF2G-1 Airplane uNo 14695" (Goodyear document, January 8, 946).

46. Chief of BuAer, letter to the BARA, May 8, 945.

47. "Service Tests, Report of Service Acceptance rials on Model F2G-1, -2 Airplanes," (Bureau of ıspection and Survey Project Ted, BIS Number 170, November 21, 1947).

48. "Naval Air Test Center Report Serial Numer TT-C-57," January 9, 1942.

49. Armstrong, interview.

50. Horan, interview.

151. *The Bee Hive* (a Vought magazine), January 1951, p.24.

152. *Pilot's Handbook for Navy Model F4U-5 Aircraft, AN 01-45HD-1,* Appendix IV—F4U-5NL Winterization Equipment.

153. *Pilot's Handbook for Navy Model F4U-5 Aircraft, AN 01-45HD-1,* Appendix III—F4U-5P.

154. Fred Blechman, letter to Veronico, February 3, 1993. Also Fred Blechman's address to the Association of Naval Aviation, March 17, 1988.

155. Guy P. Bordelon, Jr., interview with Veronico, February 1993.

156. Blechman, letter.

157. *United States Naval Aviation 1910 to 1980.*

158. Richard P. Hallion, *The Naval Air War in Korea* (The Nautical and Aviation Publishing Company, 1986), pp. 110, 190.

159. Barrett Tillman, *Corsair: The F4U in World War II and Korea* (Naval Institute Press, 1979).

160. Bordelon, interview.

161. Dan Hagedorn, telephone interview with Veronico, February 20, 1993.

162. Ibid.

163. Victor Flintham, *Air Wars and Aircraft* (Facts on File, 1990).

164. Tillman, *Corsair.* Also, John Dienst and Dan Hagedorn, *North American F-51 Mustangs in Latin American Air Force Service*, (Aerofax, 1985).

165. Sales records of Interamericana de Honduras, S.A. de C.V. via Hollywood Wings.

166. Jim Nettle, interview with Veronico.

167. Mike Penketh, telephone interview with Veronico, February 21, 1993.

168. Letter of agreement between Hollywood Wings and Robert L. Ferguson and Howard E. Pardue.

169. Hagedorn, telephone interview, February 20, 1993.

170. Cook Cleland, interview with Veronico.

171. Ibid.

172. Dick Becker, interview with Veronico.

173. Cleland, interview.

174. Becker, interview.

175. Ibid.

176. Cleland, interview.

177. Ibid.

178. Gene Akers, interview with Veronico.

179. Ibid.

180. Ibid.

181. Ibid.

182. Steve Hinton, interview with Veronico.

183. Ibid.

184. Ibid.

185. James H. Farmer's *Celluloid Wings: The Impact of Movies on Aviation* (TAB Books, 1984) lists this squadron as VMF-323.

186. Trailer for *Flying Leathernecks* (RKO Pictures).

187. Bruce Orriss, *When Hollywood Ruled the Skies* (Aero Associates, 1984).

188. Tom Friedkin, interview with Veronico.

189. Ibid.

190. Hinton, interview.

191. Ibid.

Index